Honor in German Literature

UNC | COLLEGE OF ARTS AND SCIENCES
Germanic and Slavic Languages and Literatures

From 1949 to 2004, UNC Press and the UNC Department of Germanic & Slavic Languages and Literatures published the UNC Studies in the Germanic Languages and Literatures series. Monographs, anthologies, and critical editions in the series covered an array of topics including medieval and modern literature, theater, linguistics, philology, onomastics, and the history of ideas. Through the generous support of the National Endowment for the Humanities and the Andrew W. Mellon Foundation, books in the series have been reissued in new paperback and open access digital editions. For a complete list of books visit www.uncpress.org.

Honor in German Literature

GEORGE FENWICK JONES

UNC Studies in the Germanic Languages and Literatures
Number 25

Copyright © 1959

This work is licensed under a Creative Commons CC BY-NC-ND license. To view a copy of the license, visit http://creativecommons.org/licenses.

Suggested citation: Jones, George Fenwick. *Honor in German Literature.* Chapel Hill: University of North Carolina Press, 1959. DOI: https://doi.org/10.5149/9781469657608_Jones

Library of Congress Cataloging-in-Publication Data
Names: Jones, George Fenwick.
Title: Honor in German literature / by George Fenwick Jones.
Other titles: University of North Carolina Studies in the Germanic Languages and Literatures ; no. 25.
Description: Chapel Hill : University of North Carolina Press, [1959] Series: University of North Carolina Studies in the Germanic Languages and Literatures. | Includes bibliographical references.
Identifiers: LCCN 60062591 | ISBN 978-1-4696-5759-2 (pbk: alk. paper) | ISBN 978-1-4696-5760-8 (ebook)
Subjects: Honor in literature. | German literature — History and criticism.
Classification: LCC PD25 .N6 NO. 25 | DCC 830/ .9093

To my wife JOYCE, who has patiently borne my cogitations on the subject of this book for two long years

TABLE OF CONTENTS

Page

Preface

Chapter One	The Problem	1
Chapter Two	Heathen Shame Culture	10
Chapter Three	Christian Guilt Culture	38
Chapter Four	Knightly Honor – The Native Heritage	59
Chapter Five	Knightly Honor – Refining Influences	88
Chapter Six	Courtier, Cleric, and Contradiction	104
Chapter Seven	Origins of Bourgeois Honor	123
Chapter Eight	Honor in Reformation and Baroque Literature	138
Chapter Nine	Inner Honor	149
Chapter Ten	Honor and the Common Man	160
Chapter Eleven	Loss of Honor	167
Chapter Twelve	Ridicule of Traditional Honor	181
Conclusion		190
Bibliography		193
Index		200

Der werlt ist niht mêre wan strît umbe êre.
(Nothing in the world is greater than the struggle for honor)

Freidank's *Bescheidenheit*, 92, 3-4

PREFACE

This is not a history of German literature. It is a study of the concept of honor as expressed in German literature, and it selects and treats literary works only in relation to the light they throw upon this subject. Therefore the discriminating reader must not be offended if many important works are neglected and less important ones are discussed, or if Sudermann is cited more than Goethe. Also, original verse is quoted as prose, although nothing is more prosaic than a literal prose translation of rimed verse. It is hoped that non-Germanists will not be prejudiced against German literature by these matter-of-fact samples.

To make this study accessible to the non-specialist, all quotations from the older literatures are translated into English; the original passages being relegated to the notes. Although this study deals chiefly with German literature and civilization, it aims to be of interest to those concerned with the history of ideas in general. It avoids German terminology except for a few frequently used terms, mostly archaic, which cannot be translated adequately because they have no English equivalents or because their meanings changed too radically during the period in question. All these terms are explained when first introduced and are also listed in the index.

For the benefit of non-Germanists, the following often-used terms and abbreviations are explained in advance:

> Old High German (*OHG*), the language of the southern and middle parts of Germany from ca. 750 to ca. 1100 A.D.
> Middle High German (*MHG*), the language of the southern and middle parts of Germany from ca. 1100 to ca. 1350.
> Early New High German (*ENHG*), the transitional stage between Middle High German and New High German, from ca. 1350 to ca. 1650.
> New High German (*NHG*), the standard literary language of Germany from ca. 1350 to the present.
> Low Germany, the northern part of Germany, the low coastal plain.
> Germanic or Teutonic, pertaining to the Germanic peoples or Teutons, a family of closely related tribes of Northern Europe, from which are descended the English, Scandinavians, Germans, Dutch, and Flemings.
> German, pertaining to the people of Central Europe who speak

Germanic dialects, including the Germans, Austrians, Alsatians, and German Swiss.

High Middle Ages, in Germany the period roughly from 1150 to 1250, known also as the Hohenstaufen period.

It is to be noted that, for convenience, German terms will be spelled in their *MHG* form, even though they may have been spelled or pronounced quite differently during the specific period under discussion. Also, for the benefit of non-Germanists, most proper names and the titles of literary works are anglicized. French scholars see fit to speak of Rodolphe de Neuchatel instead of Ruodolf von Niuwenburg, and German scholars see fit to speak of Wilhelm von Conches instead of Guillaume de Conches. This is particularly justifiable in the case of medieval names, which were often not standardized and were unlike their modern derivatives. American historians speak of the emperors Henry and Frederick instead of Heinrich and Friedrich, and there is no reason why the American Germanists cannot do likewise. If they did so, perhaps old German literature would not be so unfamiliar to most Americans.

I wish to extend my heartfelt thanks to the many friends and colleagues who have so generously aided me with advice, suggestions, and criticism. A list of all their names would make too imposing a dedication for this modest volume. I also wish to thank the Research Committee of Princeton University for financing the typing and publication of this book.

Goucher College
September 1959

CHAPTER ONE

THE PROBLEM

Honour... the spurr of vertue
(ROBERT ASHLEY, *On Honour*, IV).

When we read references to honor, like the one above, we usually agree or disagree with them; but we seldom ask just what the authors meant by the word. To the question: "What is honour?", Falstaff replied, "A word... a mere scutcheon"; and Thomas Hobbes said that honor is "the opinion of Power". George Stanhope said it is "a greatness of mind which scorns to descend to an ill and base thing"; and William Wordsworth said it is "the finest sense of justice which the human mind can frame".[1] All these thinkers would have agreed with Ashley's maxim, which was borrowed from Ovid,[2] but they would not have agreed as to the nature of this spur. The first two would have understood the maxim to mean that virtuous deeds are done in the hope of fame, whereas the second two would have thought them the result of a noble sentiment.

We smile when we read of chivalric knights jousting before the walls of Troy in medieval epics or when we see cannons in early illustrations of Old Testament battlefields; and we laugh when Samson and Delilah appear as prosperously plump Dutch burghers in Rembrandt's paintings. On the other hand, we tend to be less critical of the thoughts and values attributed to historical characters by modern novelists. Being so deeply rooted in our culture, we find it difficult to realize that people can experience life through a completely different set of terms and values, unless by chance we have read recent anthropological studies of primitive civilizations. And when, in their literature, people far from us in time or place express what appear to be sentiments like our own, we seldom ask if the familiar words meant the same to them as to us. Etymological

---

[1] *King Henry IV*, Part I, V, i, vv. 135-143; *Leviathan*, X; George Stanhope, *A Paraphrase and Comment upon the Epistles and Gospels*, London, 1705, II, 94; *The Poetical Works of William Wordsworth*, ed. T. Hutchinson, Oxford, 1923, p. 316.
[1] "inmensum gloria calcar habet" (*Epistulae ex Ponto*, IV, ii, 36). Cf. "Fame is the spur, that the clear spirit doth raise (That last infirmity of noble mind) To scorn delights and live laborious days" (Milton, *Lycidas*, 70).

similarities may cover a multitude of differences. If someone familiar with the customs of the ancient Germanic tribes reads Ruth Benedict's popular *Patterns of Culture,* he can easily see that the ancient Teutons' mode and code of life was more similar to that of the Kwakiutl Indians of Vancouver Island than to that of the Pueblo Indians of the Southwestern United States. On the other hand he may find it difficult to believe that the Teutons were in many ways closer to the Kwakiutl Indians than to their own present-day descendants.[1]

As Claudius von Schwerin once remarked about the study of Germanic legal history, "the task is to enter the spirit of the time and place represented by the source, to adjust one's own thinking to that of the source."[2] It is a difficult task to enter the spirit of a past time, as Goethe's Faust complains to Wagner: bygone days are a book with seven seals, and what we call the spirit of the times is basically our own spirit, in which the times are reflected. This task is particularly difficult in the study of old Germanic civilization, especially for German-speaking people, who are often misled by linguistic habits as well as by national pride. Nearly a century ago Karl Müllenhoff warned thus against the dangers involved: "Our New High German deceives us time and again, and uninterrupted attention is necessary to avoid this deception. It takes much exercise and practice to understand the Middle High German correctly, especially when the distinctions are very fine."[3]

Four score years later Jan de Vries similarly explained a modern German's difficulty in understanding the thoughts of his Germanic forefathers: "One speaks the same language, even if at another stage of its development; but it seems that strangers are talking to each other. Even if we say faith, honor, holiness, gift, or marriage, we mean something essentially different by these words from that which our heathen ancestors meant. In any case, their concept has an

---

[1] This is especially apparent with regard to honor and status. Dr. Benedict states: "The object of all Kwakiutl enterprise was to show oneself superior to one's rivals" (p. 175). "All the motivations they recognized centered around the will to superiority. Their social organization, their economic institutions their religion, birth and death, were all channels for its expression. As they understood triumph, it involved ridicule and scorn heaped publicly upon one's opponent..." (p. 177). "The Kwakiutl stressed equally the fear of ridicule, and the interpretation of experience in terms of insults. They recognized only one gamut of emotions, that which swings between victory and shame" (p. 198). As this study will show, these and many other of Dr. Benedict's statements about the Kwakiutls' sense of honor would hold equally well of the early Teutons. Largess among the Kwakiutls, as among the Teutons, was motivated chiefly by a desire for prestige (p. 180); and grief was associated with shame and insult (p. 222). *Mentor Books,* New York, 1936.
[2] Cited from G. Kisch, *The Jewry-Law of the Medieval German Law-Books,* New York, 1937, p. 86.
[3] Cited from A. Leitzmann, *Der kleine Benecke,* Halle, 1934, p. v.

entirely different nuance. We must even be ready to expect that the similarity of the language will sometimes hinder us more than help us, because we are all too inclined to overlook the gulf between the old and the new meaning of the words." [1]

Vera Vollmer had previously commented on the difficulty caused by the apparent similarity of the old and new languages. "Nothing makes the understanding of Middle High German poets more difficult for the modern reader than the numerous abstract words like *güete, kiusche, êre, riuwe, genâde, zuht, mâze, triuwe, stæte,* and *reine, valsch, sælic.* To be sure, most of these expressions still exist in the language of today; but the difficulty lies precisely therein. Instead of investigating the meaning of the expressions in Middle High German thoroughly in order to find the New High German word corresponding most closely (as one would do if the words no longer existed today), one is tempted merely to use the present linguistic form."[2] Because this study is being written in English, it should avoid some of the pitfalls against which these scholars have warned.

To illustrate this we can take an example from the prologue to Chaucer's *The Canterbury Tales,* in which the Knight in the pilgrimage "loved chivalrie, Trouthe and honour, fredom and curteisie." [3] At first glance we see a Victorian gentleman dedicated to chivalry, truth, honor, freedom, and courtesy; yet Chaucer's own meaning was perhaps more like "he loved mounted warfare and tournaments, fealty, fame, liberality, and courtly behavior." Similarly, generations of schoolboys have thought that the Saxon king Ethelred the Unready, unlike a good Boy Scout, was not prepared. Since Modern English is not Anglo-Saxon, this epithet should now be rendered as "the Ill-advised", or perhaps "of Ill-counsel", since the word *rǣd* could mean advice from without or wisdom from within, or even plan or resolve.[4]

As this study will demonstrate, an understanding of honor in the old German literary works depends upon an understanding of precisely the terms previously mentioned by Vera Vollmer. These terms have subsequently developed into the New High German words *Güte* (goodness), *Keuschheit* (chastity), *Ehre* (honor), *Reue* (repentance), *Gnade* (mercy), *Zucht* (breeding, discipline, or propriety), *Mässigkeit* (moderation), *Treue* (loyalty), *Stetigkeit* (constancy), *rein* (clean or pure), *falsch* (false), and *selig* (blessed or

---

[1] *Die geistige Welt der Germanen,* Halle, 1945, pp. 2-3. Cf. "Es bricht ja überhaupt die Erkenntnis immer mehr Bahn, dass sich der Bedeutungsinhalt vieler Wörter nur bei genauer Kenntnis der Kultur der betreffenden Periode feststellen lässt" (Vera Vollmer, *Die Begriffe der Triuwe...,* p. 1).
[2] Vollmer, p. 1.
[3] *Chaucer,* ed. F. N. Robinson, *C.T.* I, vv. 45-46.
[4] See *NED Unrede* and *Rede.*

blissful); and thus they appear in many allegedly "modernized" versions of old literary works, thereby corrupting their meaning and confusing their motivation.[1] To her list we might add the *MHG* words *prîs, wirde, werdecheit, tugent, biderbe, vrum, tühtic,* and *wacker,* which will be discussed.

Above all, *êre* should not be rendered as *Ehre,* except in certain specific contexts, such as in "show honor to" or "in honor of". Well more than a century ago Adolf Ziemann grasped the true meaning of the word *êre,* which he defined as "splendor, glory, the higher standing, partly that which arises from power and wealth (high position, superior feudal rank), partly that which arises from courage and bravery."[2] A century later Albert Bachmann explained the word similarly but added the additional meaning *edle Gesinnung* (noble sentiment),[3] which would approach our term "sense of honor". As we shall see, there are some passages in courtly and clerical literature during the High Middle Ages where this meaning seems to attach to the word *êre,* but they are relatively few. The modern reader should be on his guard not to intuit this meaning unless the context explicitly demands it.

There is controversy over the origin of the term *êra,* as the word was written in earliest times. Until recently scholars usually agreed with Friedrich Kluge in relating it to the Latin word *aestumâre* (to value or estimate).[4] On the other hand, Professor Elisabeth Karg-Gasterstädt, who is editing the new Old High German lexicon, traces it to a root meaning "awe before the gods".[5] Regardless of its ultimate origin, scholars are fairly well agreed that *êra* was an objective value, a good of fortune without ethical overtones. Karg-Gasterstädt defines it thus: "On the part of the person doing the honoring, it is an action through which an inner attitude finds visual and audible expression. For the one honored it is a passive acceptance, a desirable possession. Êra is external honor, the position, respect, or rating that one receives from the surrounding world and that one enjoys in public life. In so far as it is given, it is the object of to bear, to bring, to give, to show, to offer; in so far as it is received, it is the object of to have, to win, to merit, or to seek."[6] Thus she defines the word *êra* in much the same way as Friedrich

[1] I have indicated the danger of translating the word *êre* in too modern a sense in my review of *Ulrich von Zatzikhoven: Lanzelet,* trans. K. G. T. Webster, in *Modern Language Notes,* 69, 1954, pp. 537-540.
[2] *Mittelhochdeutsches Wörterbuch,* ed. Adolf Ziemann, Quedlinburg and Leipzig, 1838, p. 78.
[3] *Mittelhochdeutsches Lesebuch,* ed. Albert Bachmann, Zurich, 1936, p. 279.
[4] Still explained thus in eleventh edition of Fr. Kluge-Alfred Götze, *Etymologisches Wörterbuch,* Berlin and Leipzig, 1934, p. 122. The fifteenth edition (Berlin, 1951, p. 158) now agrees with Karg-Gasterstädt. See next note.
[5] Karg-Gasterstädt, pp. 308-331.
[6] *op. cit.,* pp. 312-13.

Klose defines the Latin term *honos* or *honor*, which became the usual rendering of the thought *êra* in medieval Latin writings. He says, "*Honos* never denotes an inner (moral) quality, the inner personal worth of a person; but rather, in so far as it is used as a personal possession, it denotes purely externally the esteem, the respected position, etc." [1]

To be sure, the word *êra* was also used later to render the Latin word *honestum*, even with its additional meaning of moral rectitude as found in the writings of the Stoic philosophers; yet, as we shall see, this new meaning never took firm root in the vernacular. In fact, because it seems to appear almost only in translation, it is even conceivable that the translators did not really appreciate the new value implied by the Stoic authors. In any case, I am not ready to believe that the vernacular word *êra* actually began to have a moral connotation at the time of Notker, the eleventh-century monk of St. Gall, as Theodor Frings and Elisabeth Karg-Gasterstädt suggest.[2]

My own findings lead me rather to agree with Friedrich Maurer, who feels that this development was considerably later, even later than the courtly poets of the High Middle Ages. He goes so far as to say, "Painstaking interpretation of all passages in which Hartmann, Walther, Wolfram, and Gottfried use the word *êre* shows that, with ever diminishing and uncertain exceptions, only 'external honor' is designated." [3] But this controversy should be joined only after much material has been sifted. The evidence assembled in this study indicates that the new meanings of the word *Ehre*, particularly

[1] Klose, pp. 133-134.
[2] Frings, pp. 22-23; Karg-Gasterstädt, pp. 308-331. Both scholars seem to base their argument solely on the questionable passages in Notker. When Frings states: "Unter dem Einfluss des ciceronischen *honestum* und *honestas* beschreitet *êra* den Weg zum beherrschenden Wert des ritterlichen Tugend- und Pflichtsystems," we hear echoes of Ehrismann's inspiring but discredited theory (See page 114 below). Of some 77 cases listed in *Notker-Wortschatz*, ed. E. Sehrt and W. Legner, Halle, 1955, nearly all have clearly objective meaning. In almost every case it renders *honor* or *honores*, in expressions such as "in honor of": e.g. *dîr ze êron* (*in honore tuo*); *in gotes êra* (*obsecro*); "wealth and honor", and "glory and honor": *scaz unde êra, ôtuuále unde êra* (*Opes, honores*); *gûollichi unde êra* (*gloriam et honore*). It is also used as the object of verbs of giving: *êra geben, êra wellen, êra guunnen*, or of taking away: *êra geirren* (*honorem repellere*). In a single case *êra* renders *decus* (adornment) where *decus* is used in a transferred sense to mean virtue: *Neque enim aliena improbitas decerpit probis animis proprium decus* (*Nóh ánderro úbeli neinfûoret tién gûotên nîomêr íro êra* (Piper, I, 246, 31). On another occasion it renders *honestum*, which is contrasted with *turpe* (Piper, I, p. 605). In this case the usage is derived directly from Latin, not vernacular, custom. According to J. Knight Bostock, it "may be accepted as a general principle that the written word is always more probably founded on Latin than on a popular oral tradition" (J. Knight Bostock, *A Handbook on Old High German Literature*, Oxford, 1955, p. 1).
[3] Maurer, "Zum ritterlichen Tugendsystem", p. 526.

in the sense of personal integrity or inner voice, did not become widespread before the middle of the eighteenth century. In any case, throughout the Middle Ages the word *êre* usually designated the recognition, respect, reverence, or reputation which a person enjoyed among men, or else physical tokens thereof.

In this way *êre* was often the equivalent of *dôm*, the most prevalent word for fame in early Germanic days. As Hans Kuhn has observed, the word *dôm*, which happens to be related to the English verb *deem*, denoted a judgment; that is to say, it denoted not what a man had in him, but only what other people thought of him.[1] Since *êre*, by definition, was also the approval or respect of other people, it would be incongruous to confuse it with "inner honor"; and honor continued to be a wordly possession. As such, it was usually associated with wealth, the other great incentive to effort, in formulas like *guot und êre, nutz und êre, vrum und êre*, etc.,[2] all of which mean wealth or profit and fame. Friedrich Maurer states that, "*Honos et gloria, ruom und êre, lop unde prîs* are *utilia* and belong to the *bona corporis et fortunae*, like beauty, strength, health, nobility, and possessions."[3] Medieval writers are well aware of this fact too. Chaucer, to name but one, stated: "Goodes of fortune been richesse, hyghe degrees of lordshipes, preisynges of the peple."[4] It will be observed that German poets often used *prîs* as a synonym for *êre*.

Because *êre* was a good of fortune, it was logical for Chaucer's Swiss contemporary, Henry Wittenwiler, to say that in a husband's absence a good wife will guard his "house and *er* and other goods."[5] Luther used the word *êre* only in this external sense; for example, his hymn "A Mighty Fortress" associates "wealth, *er*, child, and wife."[6] Goethe too seems to have used the word *Ehre* only in its external sense: his disillusioned Faust complains that he has neither *Ehr* nor splendor of the world; and, in his tale *The Procurator*, Goethe even distinguishes between a wife's virtue (*Tugend*) an her good name (*Ehre*).[7]

[1] Schneider, p. 216.
[2] These appear so often in *NHG* that it would be useless to illustrate. Many examples will appear in the following footnotes.
[3] Maurer, "Zum ritterlichen Tugendsystem," p. 527.
[4] *Chaucer*, ed. Robinson, X (I), 453 ("The Parson's Tale").
[5] *Ring*, v. 2804.
[6] "Gut, Ehr, Kind und Weib, Lass fahren dahin."
[7] Goethe (or Boccaccio?) distinguishes between a woman's *Ehre* and her *Tugend*. In the *Procurator*, a short story in Goethe's *Unterhaltungen deutscher Ausgewanderter*, a merchant husband warns his young wife against frivolous young men who "der Ehre noch mehr als der Tugend einer Frau gefährlich sind." This contrast need not go back to Boccaccio's original, since Schiller contrasts them likewise. In his *Kabale und Liebe* (II, 3), Ferdinand distinguishes between *Tugend* and *Ehre* and says that the former often survives the latter. Lady Milford compares her own *Ehre* with Luise's *Tugend* (IV, 8). Paul Fischer's *Goethe-Wortschatz* (Leipzig, 1929) lists no example of *Ehre* or its compounds in the moral sense of the word.

The problem of tracing the semantic development of the word *ère* presents many barriers, among which are chronological, geographic, and sociographic factors. Since honor was a progressive concept, one might argue that it is impossible to define honor as such, but only a first-century honor, a second-century honor, etc., which might be further divided into decades if sufficient sources were at hand. Secondly, dates have only relative significance in our study: the concept of honor in South Germany during the eighth century might appear more modern than that during the ninth century in North Germany, which was more remote from Roman and Christian influences. If sufficient material were at hand, it might be possible to distinguish between the concepts of honor found in the Germanic north, the Roman-Celtic south, and even the Slavic east of Germany.

Far more important is the sociographic factor; for the concept of honor is, in the final analysis, a matter of social class, each class having its own peculiar code. For our purpose we are primarily concerned with the honor-code professed by the social element culturally dominant at any given period, the caste that set the style and was envied and emulated by the others. In the earliest centuries it was clearly the military aristocracy that prevailed and later the bourgeoisie; and during most of the interim we find an irreconcilable dichotomy of aristocratic and monastic codes. Each of these terms will be defined when the occasion arises.

Henceforth the term "Germanic" will, by definition, refer to the values of the ruling classes and will generally coincide with "aristocratic". Except in Iceland, where political power lay in a landed peasantry, the Germanic literature that has survived was largely the monopoly of the leisure classes. Nevertheless, even if the upperclass code predominated in literature, it is probable that the lower classes had their own codes for judging their peers. The beauty of Germanic handicrafts suggests that their creators took pride in their work and won praise and esteem by means of it. The famous golden horn of Gallehus bears the runic inscription, "I, Hlewagast... made this horn." Obviously the maker inscribed his name on it in hope of winning acclaim. The same probably held true of the scops and bards, who no doubt created their ballads in hope of winning praise as well as remuneration; for the author of the Anglo-Saxon poem *Widsith* shows definite pride in his work. Even though ancient artisans and singers took pride in their work, it scarcely affected literature until after the bourgeoisie became the bearers of culture.

It is to be noted that the term "Germanic" will refer to all the mores of the Germanic peoples before their conversions, even if some of their concepts and values may have been recent importations from the Celts or Romans. At this late date it is particularly difficult to distinguish between Germanic and Latin thoughts, since nearly all our informants about the ancient Teutons wrote in Latin and therefore perceived the world through a Latin perspective, or *Weltansicht*, to use Wilhelm von Humboldt's brilliant, but sadly neglected, term. When the Roman historian Tacitus says that the Teutons preferred death in battle to a life of shame, he is expressing a Roman commonplace, one which he himself attributed to Agricola, his father-in-law.[1] This sentiment was no doubt indigenous to the Teutons; yet they probably experienced it differently or would at least have expressed it in other terms.

From the founding of the Roman Empire until its fall, Latin language and civilization served as models for the Teutons across the Rhine. Many barbarians visited Rome and spoke Latin, among whom was Arminius, the German chieftain who defeated three Roman legions in the Teutoburg Forest in the year 9 A. D. Just as primitive people today are overwhelmed by what they see in Europe or America, so too the Germanic peoples were ready to absorb whatever they could from the Romans. In view of the great quantity of material skills which the Teutons learned, it is likely that they also learned some intangibles.

Roman thought probably influenced the Teutons' concept of honor, or at least their reflections about it. Word may have traveled back to Germania that the Roman general Marius had erected a temple to the deity Honor in commemoration of his and Catulus's victories of 102 and 101 B. C. over the fierce Teutones and Cimbri, the first Germanic tribes that fought against the Romans. On the other hand, Roman and Germanic codes of honor may have owed some of their similarities to their common Indo-European origin; and it is not surprising that the heroic concept of honor expressed in the *Iliad* is quite similar to that of the early Germanic epics. As we shall see, when the Teutons first became familiar with the words *honos* and *honestus*, these words still had completely amoral connotations.[2] Most of the Teutonic visitors to Rome were mercenary troops, who naturally met more soldiers than philosophers.

In tracing the gradual development of the concept of honor, this study will discuss literary works largely in chronological order. Nevertheless, there will be occasional references to earlier or later works in order to show that the sentiments or attitudes under discussion were of long duration. There will also be occasional references to foreign cultures to show that these sentiments or attitudes were not limited to the Teutons or to the Germans.

Aware of all the problems involved, I shall first define the heathen-

---

[1] "honesta mors turpi vita potior" (*Cornelii Tacitii de Vita Agricolae*, Oxford, 1922, Chap. 33).
[2] Klose, pp. 47, 133-134. See also Maurer, "Zum ritterlichen Tugendsystem", pp. 526-529.

aristocratic-Germanic code of honor, a code that prevailed before the conversions and continued long thereafter in varying degrees. As we shall see, some elements of this code have lasted almost unchanged to this day and others have persisted with only minor alterations. Even after an ideal takes an about-face, popular behavior often tends to follow the older code.

Secondly, I shall formulate the Christian code of honor, or rather code of ethics, since honor as originally understood was incompatible with Christian humility. In this regard it should be recalled that the so-called "Christian code of ethics" includes all new values brought by the missionaries to the heathen Teutons, including some pre-Christian pagan values. Of prime importance were the theories of the Greek and Roman Stoics, who, incidentally, were often thought to have been Christians. According to J. H. Breasted, many of the Hebrews' concepts of justice and righteousness, which eventually became ingredients of honor, had been derived from much older Egyptian sources.[1]

Thirdly, this study will show how heathen-aristocratic and Christian-Stoic values were juxtaposed in the honor-code of the age of chivalry; and then it will explain how they were later adopted, with major changes, by the rising bourgeoisie. Next it will investigate the new ideal of honor which arose in the eighteenth century, partially as a result of the Reformation and the English and French Enlightenment. Lastly, it will show how traces of all these codes appear in the literature of the nineteenth century, by which time the ideal of honor had made a complete about-face.

[1] J. H. Breasted, *The Dawn of Conscience*, New York, 1933

CHAPTER TWO

HEATHEN SHAME CULTURE

For a noble man death is better than a shameful life.
Beowulf, vv. 2890-2891.

Because our earliest informants about the Germanic barbarians were Greeks or Romans or else Hellenized or Latinized barbarians, it is fitting to investigate the meaning of honor as it was understood in the Greco-Roman world. A good definition of honor (*timê*), as understood by the Greeks in their Golden Age, appears in Xenophon's *Hiero*, in which the lyric poet Simonides of Ceos is quoted as saying to Hiero I, tyrant of Syracuse:

"O Hiero, there is a potent force, it would appear, the name of which is honour, so attractive that human beings strain to grasp it, and in the effort they will undergo all pains, endure all perils. It would further seem that even you, you tyrants, in spite of all that sea of trouble which a tyranny involves, rush headlong in pursuit of it. You must be honoured. All the world shall be your ministers; they shall carry out your every injunction with unhesitating zeal. You shall be the cynosure of neighboring eyes; men shall rise from their seats at your approach; they shall step aside to yield you passage in the streets. All present shall at all times magnify you, and shall pay homage to you both with words and deeds. Those, I take it, are ever the kind of things which subjects do to please the monarch, and thus they treat each hero of the moment, whom they strive to honour.

"Yes Hiero, and herein precisely lies the difference between a man and other animals, in this outstretching after honour. Since, it would seem, all living things alike take pleasure in meats and drinks, in sleep and sexual joys. Only love of honour is implanted neither in unreasoning brutes nor universally in man. But they in whose hearts the passion for honour and fair fame has fallen like a seed, these unmistakably are separated most widely from the brutes. These may be called *men*, not human beings merely. So that, in my poor judgment, it is but reasonable you should submit to bear the pains and penalties of royalty, since you are honoured far beyond

[1] *The Works of Xenophon*, trans. D. H. Dakyns, London, 1897, III, 375-376.

all other mortal men. And indeed no pleasure known to man would seem to be nearer that of the gods than the delight which centres in proud attributes."[1]

Although Hiero denies that kings enjoy such pleasures, most of his contemporaries would have agreed with Simonides's definition of honour, which was somewhat like that of Aristotle and not unlike that of Haman, as told in the Old Testament story of Esther.[1] To be sure, philosophers like Plato regretted that honor was shown primarily to rank and wealth instead of to qualities of the soul as it would be in the ideal Republic,[2] but they could not deny that it was. With his absolute or transcendental standards of goodness, Plato disparaged public opinion as a criterion of virtue; but in this he and the Stoics, who followed him in this view, were exceptions and stood somewhat apart from the general stream of Greek thought.

Aristotle, who was more representative of his age, fully endorsed honor as the greatest of external goods, since it is the prize of virtue.[3] "People of superior refinement and of active disposition identify happiness with honour; for this is, roughly speaking, the end of the political life. But it seems too superficial to be what we are looking for, since it is thought to depend on those who bestow honour rather than on him who receives it, but the good we divine to be something proper to a man and not easily taken from him. Further, men seem to pursue honour in order that they may be assured of their goodness; at least it is by men of practical wisdom that they seek to be honoured, and among those who know them, and on the ground of their virtue; clearly, then, according to them, at any rate, virtue is better. And perhaps one might even suppose this to be, rather than honour, the end of the political life."[4]

Because Plato and the Stoics held a negative view toward honor, which accorded with the Christian concept of otherworldliness, their ideas were quickly adopted by the Christian writers; but Aristotle's views on this subject were not fully appreciated until revived in the Renaissance, even though they appear to have influenced the thirteenth-century poets to some degree. The ideas

---

[1] Cf. "The elements of honour are − sacrifices; records in verse or prose; privileges; grants of domain; chief seats; public funerals; statues; maintenance at the public cost; barbaric homage, such as salaams and giving place; and the gifts honourable among each people" (Aristotle, *Rhetoric*, 1161a, 9, trans. R. C. Jebb). *Esther*, 6.
[2] "We declare, then, that a state which is to endure, and to be as happy as it is possible for man to be, must of necessity dispense honours rightly. And the right ways is this: it shall be laid down that the goods of the soul are the highest in honour and come first, provided that the soul possesses temperance; second come the good and fair things of the body; and third the so-called goods of substance and property" (Plato, *Laws*, 697-B-C, trans. R. G. Bury).
[3] Aristotle, *Ethics*, IV, 3 (trans. Ross).
[4] *op. cit.*, I, 5.

of the Greek Stoics reached Rome at least a half century before the Teutones and Cimbri clashed with the Romans.[1] A decade after Caesar had driven the Suebi back across the Rhine, Cicero wrote several works championing the view that honor and fame were of no real value.[2]

In his *De Finibus*, Cicero summarized the views of some of his predecessors as follows: "About good fame (that term being a better translation in this context than 'glory' of the Stoic expression *eudoxiâ*) Chrysippus and Diogenes used to aver that, apart from any practical value it may possess, it is not worth stretching out a finger for; and I strongly agree with them. On the other hand their successors, finding themselves unable to resist the attacks of Carneades, declared that good fame, as I have called it, was preferred and desirable for its own sake, and that a man of good breeding and liberal education would desire to have the good opinion of his parents and relatives and of good men in general, and that for its own sake and not for any practical advantage; and they argue that just as we study the welfare of our children, even of such as may be born after we are dead, for their own sake, so a man ought to study his reputation even after death, for itself, even apart from any advantage."[3]

Although Cicero "strongly agreed" with the Stoic view in this work and, even more so, in passages of his *De Officiis*, his other writings do not indicate that he really questioned the value of fame. As M. L. Clarke says, "The longing for glory, the desire to leave a name to posterity, was a marked feature of the Roman temperament and was present to an abnormal degree in Cicero himself."[4] In his *De Officiis*, Cicero tells of having composed two books *De Gloria*, but these are now lost, after being extant as late as Petrarch's time.[5]

---

[1] Professor P. R. Coleman-Norton of Princeton has kindly advised me that Diogenes the Stoic visited Rome in 156 B.C. as a member of a Greek embassy and lectured to the Romans until forbidden to do so.

[2] Ariovistus was defeated in 58 B.C. Most of Cicero's philosophical writings appeared between 46 and 43 B.C.

[3] "De bona autem fama (quam enim appellant *eudoxiâ* aptius est bonam famam hoc loco appellare quam gloriam), Chrysippus quidem et Diogenes detracta utilitate ne digitum quidem eius causa porrigendum esse dicebant, quibus ego vehementer assentior. Qui autem post eos fuerunt, cum Carneadem sustinere non possent, hanc quam dixi bonam famam ipsam propter se praepositam et sumendam esse dixerunt, esseque hominis ingenui et liberaliter educati velle bene audire a parentibus, a propinquis, a bonis etiam viris, idque propter rem ipsam, non propter usum; dicuntque, ut liberis consultum velimus etiamsi postumi futuri sint propter ipsos, sic futurae post mortem famae tamen esse propter rem etiam detracto usu consulendum" (Cicero, *De Finibus*, III, 17, 57, Loeb).

[4] Clarke, p. 63.

[5] *De Officiis*, II, ix, 31. See P. R. Coleman-Norton, "The Fragmentary Philosophical Treatises of Cicero", (*The Classical Journal*, 34, 1939, p. 223).

Cicero's many speeches suggest that both he and his audience never seriously doubted the importance of reputation; and it is safe to say that, while the Teutons were first under their influence, most Romans judged the pursuit of fame and honor to be a noble virtue. However, during the Middle Ages, when learning was largely a monopoly of the clerics, Cicero was quoted most often as a Stoic, most frequently from his *De Officiis*. Known as "Tullius", he was an important factor in training young clerics not only in style, rhetoric, and composition, but also in evaluating the world. Seneca too was usually quoted as a Stoic philosopher, as he appears in his *Moral Essays*.

Although Roman thinkers like Cicero and Seneca sometimes deprecated external honor, it is safe to say that Roman civilization was predominantly a "shame culture". That is to say, men avoided evil deeds mainly to escape public disgrace or disapproval, or, to express the same idea in reverse, they performed good ones to gain public honor. This was also true of the ancient Teutons, as is so often the case among primitive peoples. Like many books about the Germanic peoples, this investigation of German honor will begin with the *Germania* of the Roman historian Tacitus. This concise little area-study, which was written about 98 A.D., is an admirable work. Although it contains many literary commonplaces, mostly from Greek authors who had been writing about the Egyptians, Thracians, and other exotic peoples, they nevertheless seem to have been chosen with great care and to have been employed only where applicable.[1] Also, even though Tacitus seems to write as a Romantic and to idealize his noble savages, he says enough derogatory things about them to show that this was not his purpose. Many passages from later German literature, some of which are cited in this study, confirm the accuracy of the *Germania*.

Tacitus does not discuss the Germanic code of honor as such; yet he mentions it occasionally and illustrates it often. According to him,[2] the Teutons chose their kings for their noble birth (*nobilitas*, chapter 7); noble birth, as well as military distinction and eloquence, gained attention at the council (c. 11); and distinguished nobility could win the rank of chief for adolescent boys (c. 13). Although the sons of masters and slaves grew up together, the innate spirit of courage eventually separated the free from the unfree (c. 20). Masters usually treated their slaves kindly; yet they were free to kill them at will in a fit of passion (c. 25), and slaves were freely used for human sacrifices (c. 40).

---

[1] For a concise and convincing defense of the *Germania*, see *Cornelii Taciti de Origine et Situ Germanorum*, ed. J. G. C. Anderson, Oxford, 1938, xxvi-xxxvii.
[2] All references to *Germania* from above-mentioned edition.

Wealth resulted from birth and reputation, since the tribe distributed lands among its members according to their relative rank (*dignatio*, c. 26). Wealth was usually measured in numbers of cattle rather than in gold and silver, although these metals were used for trading purposes by the neighbors of the Romans (c. 5).

Whereas the Teutons chose their kings for their noble birth, they chose their military leaders for their courage (*virtus*), and a chief owed his leadership more to the example of courage he set than to his authority (c. 7). Young men took service in the following (*comitatus*) of a renowned chief and vied with other youths for a place beside the chief. Likewise, the chiefs competed for the largest and most courageous following, since their status (*dignitas*) and power depended upon the number and quality of their following, which determined their glory (*decus*) in time of peace and their security (*praesidium*) in time of war (c. 13).

A chief was disgraced if surpassed in valor by his followers, and his followers were disgraced if they did not equal the chief. Leaving the battle field alive after the chief had fallen brought lifelong ignominy and shame, for true allegiance (*sacramentum*) meant defending and protecting the chief and giving him credit for one's own exploits. The chief fought for victory, the followers fought for their chief (c. 14).

If a tribe was at peace, its youths sought out tribes engaged in war; for peace was a distasteful condition. War was necessary for winning renown and plunder and for maintaining a following. The Teutons considered it spiritless to gain by sweat what could be purchased with blood (c. 14). They recovered the bodies of their slain even when the battle was still in doubt. It was the greatest disgrace to throw away one's shield; the guilty party was banned from sacrifice and council, and survivors of battles often ended their disgrace with the noose (c. 6). Deserters and traitors, when convicted, were likewise hanged on trees; and shirkers and cowards were drowned in the bogs (c. 12).

Courage in battle was increased by mustering troops according to family and kinship; for a man looks to his family for the highest praise (c. 7). Women were known to restore broken battle lines by urging the warriors to greater effort with the reminder that defeat would mean the enslavement of the women. Women were also honored for being endowed with an element of holiness or prophecy (c. 8).

Teutonic warriors loved indolence but hated peace. When not fighting they spent their time in sloth and gluttony (c. 15), and drinking bouts lasting a day and a night were not considered disgraceful even when they resulted in bloody quarrels (c. 22). All productive effort was scorned and relegated to the women, old men, and weaklings (c. 15). Although youths performed sword dances to show their skill and to entertain their friends, they did not accept compensation (c. 24). It was accounted wrong (*nefas*) [1] to refuse hospitality to friend or stranger, and the host always conducted his guest to his next quarters (c. 21).

To understand Tacitus's description, we must understand his use of the words *dignitas* and *dignatio*. According to Friedrich Klose, the word *honos* (honor) represented an "objective condition, the means of achieving a certain goal. *Dignitas*, on the other hand, is the final result, a personal possession that is composed of *honos* and *honores*." [2] This meaning is the same as that of the MHG word *wirde* or *werdekeit*, which meant the status or condition of a person who received honors. This thought was sometimes included in the term *êre* itself, which extended its meaning to include not only the signs and tokens of respect, but also the high status resulting from their enjoyment. Thus it had about the same meaning as our word "dignity" in expressions such as "That is beneath my dignity", or in Shakespeare's remark that the Montagues and Capulets were "alike in dignity". The words *dignitas* and *wirde* could also connote elevated rank or else an office or position of honor and trust.
Although it may sometimes have suggested worthy character, this connotation cannot be assumed for the word, since high titles and offices were often held by unworthy incumbents.

Honor is traditionally shown by the weak to the strong, by the subordinate to his superior. In Germanic society that meant from warrior to leader, from vassal to liege. Although there have always been some men of simple birth who succeeded through their own virtues (or vices), Germanic poets conventionally attributed superiority to good birth. As in the fairy tale, if a man of apparently humble origins succeeded in life, his success proved that he was actually of good birth. As Tacitus mentions in his *Germania*, some tribes had hereditary kings and others elected their chiefs; but in either case the leader was supposed to come from the most illustrious and powerful family of the tribe. Rank was thus equated with good birth; and good birth, when fortified by the virtues incumbent upon it, demanded respect or *êre*.

Because he enjoyed a higher degree of honor, a wellborn man did not have to risk his honor by accepting the challenge of a social inferior; and it may be for this reason that the heroes of ancient songs often asked the identity of their opponents. This fact is illustrated in the *Lay of Hildebrand*, the earliest extant German lay,

---

[1] Since the Teutons had a shame culture, perhaps *nefas* here means shameful. Vergil once used the word to refer to the shame felt at losing a boat race (*Aeneid*, V, 197).
[2] Klose, p. 19.

which was written down at the end of the eighth or beginning of the ninth century but may have originated not long after the reign of the East Gothic emperor Theoderic the Great, who is mentioned in it. This song, which has survived only as a fragment, tells of a combat between father and son. The father, Hildebrand, who is returning at the head of an army after thirty years of exile, is confronted by his son Hadubrand, whom he does not at once recognize. Before offering battle, the older man demands to know who his opponent is and who his father was.[1]

The origin of the social classes was explained in the *Lay of Ríg*, a Norse poem included in the *Poetic Edda*. Once the god Ríg came down to earth and spent three nights with a poor couple who could give him only coarse bread and broth. Nine months later the woman bore a son, Thraell, who developed into an ugly laborer. He then visits another couple in better circumstances, who serve him veal. In due time they are blessed with a son, Karl, who has a flashing face and flashing eyes and develops into a skilled craftsman and husbandman. At last Ríg visits a wealthy couple who give him white bread, meat, fowl, and wine. The outcome of this hospitality is Jarl, who has blond hair, bright cheeks, and eyes that glow like those of a snake. Jarl occupies himself only with weapons, horses, hounds, swimming, and runes.[2] Most Germanic and medieval German poems are concerned only with Jarl's leisure-class descendants.

Many peoples are accustomed to name their children for the virtues they are to acquire, and so it was with the Teutons. Like their Indo-European ancestors, they usually chose names composed of two meaningful elements. The elements were often logically related, as in Bernhard (strong as a bear) or Edward (keeper of the treasure); but sometimes they were not, as in the case of Fredegar (peace-spear) or Brunhild (byrnie-battle). It is to be noted, however, that these names give an insight only into the period in which they were formed, since succeeding generations did not always understand the names they transmitted.[3] It is significant that many "Christian" names of Germanic origin referred to noble status. By adding another root to *aethel* or *adel* (noble), we get Adelbert, Adelheit, Adelaide, Adolf, Albert, Alfred, Alice, Alonzo, Alphonse, Aubrey, Audrey, Elmer, Ethel, Ethelbert, Etheldred, Ethelred, and numerous other

---

[1] "hwer sin fater wari... eddo hwelihhes cnuosles du sis" (*Hildebrandslied*, vv. 9-11).

[2] *Edda*, trans. Bellows, pp. 203 ff. Although the name Ríg is of Celtic origin, there is no evidence that this tale is not Norse. In any case, it was acceptable to the Norsemen.

[3] Scholars like Hrabanus Maurus explained Friedrich as "ulciscere pacem", Ratmund as "consilium oris", and Richmunt as "potens bucca" (*Deutsche Namenkunde*, ed. Edward Schröder, Göttingen, 1944, p. 7). On the other hand, Hrotsvitha of Gandersheim explained her name as *clamor validus*.

names in all Western languages. The ancient Teutons were less impressed by the age of a family than by its current power. In periods of decadence men take pride in their remote ancestors and in ancient titles, even if the family has since decayed. That would have helped a Teuton but little. To be respected and honored he needed to be feared, and for that he needed a strong kinship imbued with family solidarity. Even the modern German word for respect (*Ehrfurcht*) includes the words for both honor and fear.

Like the ancient Greeks before them,[1] the Teutons showed honor not only to good birth but also to wealth and power. As we shall see, the early Teutons hardly distinguished between these qualities. The *Germania* explains how land was distributed to the chiefs according to their *dignatio*, which depended upon their strength, which depended upon the size of their following. A chief's following in turn depended upon his largess; and this in turn depended upon his own material resources, be they inherited or acquired. Thus the snake has its tail in its mouth. In other words: rank, wealth, power, and *dignatio* were only different aspects of one's relative importance in society.

For the purpose of this study we shall arbitrarily distinguish among rank, wealth, and power, as later generations have tended to do. Of these, wealth may be considered the most immediate source of *êre*; for the whole system of vassalage was ultimately based upon property. The contract between liege and vassal, like that between husband and wife,[2] was sealed and legally validated only by the giving of gifts. The importance of property in feudal relationships is also suggested by the derivation of the word "feudal" from the Late-Latin word *feudum* (fief), which in turn was derived from the OHG *fehu* (cattle, wages, property). Naturally the war-lord, as the giver of gifts, had to be wealthier than his followers, it being unnatural for rich men to serve poor ones. Wealth was essential for heroes in Germanic literature, except for a few wellborn ones who are momentarily in exile but will surely recover their wealth, and other people's too, before the epic ends. Some scholars seem to doubt the importance of landholding as a requisite for nobility;[3] yet the very words *adel* (nobility) and *edel* (noble) are derived from the Germanic word whence come OHG *uodal* and Late-Latin

---

[1] E. R. Dodds notes that wealth is a sign of virtue in all shame cultures, such as that of Homeric Greece (*The Greeks and the Irrational*, Berkeley, 1951, p. 60, note 95).
[2] Note the relationship between *Heirat* and *Hausrat* and between *wedding* and *gage*.
[3] "Der Adel der alten Deutschen beruht auch nicht auf besonderem Landbesitz, wie überhaupt die Beschaffenheit des Grundbesitzes, den er hat, von keinem Belang für seine Stellung gewesen ist" (Christian Meyer, *Kulturgeschichtliche Studien*, Berlin, 1903, p. 78).

allodium, both of which mean inheritable property. We shall see that it was as dishonorable to lack property as it was to lack kinsmen.

Wealth was requisite for winning respect, as long as lack of wealth indicated lack of virtue. In an age of fist-law, when everyone had a right to take other people's property if only he had the might, lack of property was proof of cowardice, weakness, or shiftlessness; and poverty rightfully merited scorn and shame. As Herbert Buttke states, when a man's possessions diminished, so did his esteem and honor, for the Teuton knew neither pity nor compassion.[1] In the sagas it was considered better for impoverished warriors to go into voluntary exile rather than to bring shame upon their kinsmen. The importance of wealth as a fitting goal for ambition is indicated by the frequency of the word for wealth as a component in personal names. By adding another element to the root *ēad* or *auđa* (wealth, treasure) we get Edgar, Edith, Edmund, Edward, Edwin, Odo, Otto, Odoardo, etc.

Whereas wealth was a definite prerequisite for *êre*, it could also be its enemy if amassed at the cost of largess. In other words, a miser won no *êre*, as poets have attested throughout the ages.[2] This was true not only in theory, but also in practice. As we shall see, failure to dispense lavishly would cause a leader to lack followers, a lack of followers would bring defeat, and defeat would bring a loss of honor and wealth. Thus expenditures were as indispensable as the proverbial horseshoe. This process is illustrated in the *Gesta Danorum* of the Danish poet Saxo Grammaticus, a thirteenth-century cleric who recorded many ancient legends of his country. In one of them a hero named Hjalte tells of an avaricious king named Rorik, who has accumulated wealth instead of friends and then tries, unsuccessfully, to bribe his enemies to spare him. Because he has been unwilling to give arm rings to his friends, his enemies finally take all his treasure and his life too.[3] Elsewhere Saxo tells of an ideal king named Frode who shared all his booty with his soldiers, being free of greed and hungering only for the reward of glory.[4]

Of the rank-wealth-power-*dignitas* complex, power was most manifestly important in an era of fist-law, when it decided all questions of right. The Suebic chieftain Ariovistus expressed this

---

[1] "Mit dem Zurückgehen des Besitzes gingen auch das Ansehen und die Ehre zurück; denn Nachsicht und Mitleid kannte der Germane nicht" (Buttke, p. 9). See story of Thorbjörn (*Thule*, II, 31).
[2] Somewhat later a didactic poet named Spervogel said, "swem daz guot ze herzen gât der gwinnet niemer êre" (*Minnesangs Frühling*, 22, 5).
[3] *Gesta Danorum*, p. 62, vv. 4-24. Thomas Hobbes expressed this truth in Chapter X of his *Leviathan* as, "Riches joined with liberality, is Power; because it procureth friends, and servants: Without liberality, not so: because in this case they defend not; but expose men to Envy, as a Prey."
[4] *Gesta Danorum*, p. 169, vv. 18 ff.

legal concept when Julius Caesar obstructed his invasion of Gaul: "It is the law of war that the victors command the vanquished in whatever way they wish."[1] Needless to say, the property of the conquered, as well as his life, became the rightful possession of the conqueror. According to Hans Kuhn, trials by combat were not originally concerned with moral reward or punishment.[2] Might did not *make* right, it *was* right. This view is suggested in the *Lay of Hildebrand*. Forced by honor to accept his son's challenge, the father bewails the fact that either he must slay his son or his son must slay him and take his armor, "if he has any right to it";[3] and in this case his words mean no more than "if he has the power to take it." Because the Christian Church upheld the belief in reward and punishment, it had to accept, even if reluctantly, the assumption that God would stand by the righteous contestant in a duel; and in Germany a trial by combat was called a *Gottesurteil*, i.e., God's ordeal or judgment.

The symbol of wealth and power in many old stories is the hoard, the uncanny treasure for which heroes fight and die, a sinister and curse-laden force spelling doom to all possessors. In early times the hoard consisted of arm bands, often worn by the chieftain; in the *Lay of Hildebrand* the old warrior tries to placate the younger one by offering him arm bands.[4] Such arm bands were the conventional currency with which leaders rewarded their faithful followers: *Beowulf* calls a treasure a *beaghord* (ringhoard) and calls a lord a *beaggiefa* (ring-giver). Later, in the hyperbolic style of the popular epics, the hoard often reached fabulous size and included all the gold and jewels of Araby.

Germanic chieftains had to maintain a ready supply of treasure to assure themselves of honor in time of peace and of support in time of war; and, lest enemies think them weak, they had to display their treasures at all times. Because wealth and power were so mutually dependent, poets often linked them together as if they were almost synonymous.[5] This fact is indicated in the expression "power of wealth" for "wealth" and in the almost tautological pair "king's hoard and emperor's might".[6] Even today the German word

[1] *Gallic War*, I, 36.
[2] "Er (trial by combat) hat in der germanischen Zeit nichts mit dem sittlichen Lohngedanken zu tun gehabt. Er war ein Mittelding zwischen Fehde und Prozess, eine Austragung des Streites mit Waffengewalt, jedoch in öffentlich geregelten Formen. Erst die Christliche Zeit hat aus ihm ein Gottesurteil gemacht" (Schneider, p. 178).
[3] "ibu du dar enic reht habes" (*Hildebrandslied*, v. 57).
[4] "wuntane bauga" (*Hildebrandslied*, v. 33).
[5] Typical is the pair *gewalde ende richdoem* or *richdoem ende gewalt*, which appears often in Henry of Veldeke's *Eneide* (vv. 2380, 2645, *et passim*). *König Rother*, a minstrel epic, links them by saying, "golt unde schaz, des ein michil mânkraft... da mid stent dîn êre." (v.v. 590-597).
[6] "künges hord und kaisers macht" (*Ring*, v. 6062). Cf. "guotes die kraft" (*Gregorius*, v. 1168).

Vermögen, like the English word *means*, can mean either ability or wealth.

It was not only the right of a powerful ruler to seize a weaker neighbor's lands, but even his duty, since his followers deserved an opportunity for plunder and self-assertion. Without warfare a youth could not prove himself in battle and thereby win renown, the only positive value that made life worth living. Honor was an invidious thing. No one could enjoy honor unless someone else suffered disgrace, the two being judged by a relative rather than an absolute standard. As Goethe explained so many centuries later, "If we give honor to others, we debase ourselves." [1] A successful king reflected honor upon his kinship, and an unsuccessful one brought shame and was in danger of assassination or exile. As Saxo Grammaticus states, fame was an indispensable attribute for a king.[2]

Defeat in battle always brought dishonor, as is illustrated in the *Gesta Danorum*, which, although not written until the turn of the thirteenth century, preserves much of the flavor of the ancient Germanic legends that it records. In one of these stories a youth is about to fight a Slavic champion in single combat in hope of winning a sixfold arm band from his lord. Before beginning the fray he says that the loser must win "bitter death or grave ignominy".[3] It was unthinkable that a loser could win honor, no matter how courageously he fought. The *Chanson de Roland* could use a single word (*hunie*) to mean either scorned or defeated.[4]

Captivity was the greatest disgrace, as the English word *caitiff* and the French word *chetif* suggest. These words, derived from Latin *captivus*, meant not only miserable but also contemptible or bad. The same development can be seen in the word *wretch*, which originally designated an exile. From the Germanic point of view, captives and exiles should be scorned; but, from the Christian point of view, they should be pitied. Thus each of these words acquired two contradictory meanings.

Admiration for power is suggested in the selection of certain names, even in those of women. Matilda or Machthilda, for example, is combined of words meaning might and battle and Mildred means largess and strength. The animals most respected by the Teutons were the bear, wolf, and wild boar, and later the lion, but not the lamb. Therefore we find names like Bernard, Wolfgang, Wolfram, Wolfdietrich, Rudolph, Rolf, Ralph, Adolf, Eberhard, and Leonard,

---

[1] "Wenn wir Andern Ehre geben, Müssen wir uns selbst entadeln" (*West-Östlicher Divan*, Book V, str. 7).
[2] "nihil enim in rege celebrius fama" (*Gesta Danorum*, p. 142, v. 14).
[3] *op. cit.*, p. 84, v. 5.
[4] The *Chanson de Roland*, v. 969, uses *hunie* (related to *gehöhnt*) to mean defeated.

but not Agnes. Likewise, the rapacious eagle was preferred to the gentle dove, as we see in the popularity of names like Arno, Arnold, and Arnolf and the lack of names like Columba. Power in the sense of authority or rule is suggested in the names Gerald, Henry, Harold, Dietrich, Thierry, Walter, Frederick, Goodridge, and a host of others.

Although the Germanic warrior could defy fate and resist heroically as an individual, his place in society, and therefore his *êre* too, depended largely upon the strength of his kinship (*Sippe*); for his kinsmen, bound by ties of blood to aid him, were his final defense against his enemies and the only force that would avenge him in case he were killed. The very existence of the kinship deterred outsiders from molesting him and his property; and woe to him who had lost or left his kinship. According to Claudius von Schwerin, a kinship had a common honor. The kinship was struck by the disrespect suffered by any of its members, and it participated in his fame.[1]

The inviolable bond decreeing harmony and alliance between kinsmen was called *vridu*.[1] This word will appear here in its earlier spelling, since the *MHG vride* had somewhat changed its meaning, even though the older meaning lingered into the thirteenth century.[2] Although *vridu* is the source of the *NHG* word *Frieden* (peace), it should not be rendered as such, as it often is; for its basic meaning was "protection", as in a defensive or even offensive alliance.[3] It is true that *vridu* enforced peace among the members of the kinship, but it also caused most revenge and all feuds, inasmuch as it required those bound by it to help avenge any insult to any other member. An insult was not considered an individual matter, even if only two individuals were directly involved. Rather it was considered an affront of one kinship against the other, even when the remaining members of both kinships had done all in their power to prevent the friction. Regardless of the merits of the case, all members of the *vridu* had to stand by their fellow to the death.

The greatest hardship and disgrace for a Teuton was to be *vriundlôs* (without kinsmen, not a member of a *vridu*), for that meant being without defense, influence, or *êre*. A man driven into

---

[1] "Die Sippe hatte eine gemeinschaftliche Sippenehre. Sie wurde von der Missachtung mitbetroffen, die der einzelne erfuhr, wie sie andererseits an seinem Ruhm teilnahm" (Schwerin, p. 22). Franz Settegast sees the same attitude in France at the time of the *chansons de geste*: "The honor or dishonor of the individual does not remain restricted to him but is imparted at once to the whole kinship. Thus the honor of the kinship forms a common treasure that is zealously guarded by its members, who endeavor diligently to increase it" (Settegast, p. 4).

[2] E.g. in the *Nibelungenlied*, 1992, 2.

[3] For a through discussion of this word, see Wilhelm Grönbech, *Kultur und Religion der Germanen*, Darmstadt, 1954, I, 33-73. There was an English translation in 1931.

exile and torn from his kinship was a *wrekka*, a word which later developed into the word *wretch*. According to the *Lay of Hildebrand*, Hildebrand's liege lord Dietrich was kinless when expelled by Odoacer.¹ However, it seems that he was later able to recover his *êre* by taking service with Attila, who appeared in German epics as a gracious and hospitable ruler called Etzel.

Honor was won not only through the goods of fortune, but also through certain goods of the body and goods of the mind. The goods of the body, such as facial beauty and muscular strength, were believed inseparable from good birth; and many sagas tell how a prince disguised as a beggar is recognized by his physique, his beauty, and especially by the brilliance of his gaze.² Because the Germanic peoples conquered many non-Germanic peoples, they associated non-Germanic features with slavery and scorned them accordingly. Not only in the Norse sagas, but even in the courtly literature of the High Middle Ages, almost all honorable people had blond hair.

Because Germanic chieftains actually led their warriors into combat, the chieftain's physical prowess was a decisive factor in winning the first shock action, which often decided the final outcome by demoralizing the side that first gave ground. Even late in the Middle Ages, when battles were decided mainly by logistic factors such as supply and relative numbers of mercenaries engaged, public fancy as well as literature conventionally attributed the victory to the personal prowess of the victorious prince. Because of the importance assigned to the ruler's physical fitness, Germanic legal codes usually prevented hunchbacks and other handicapped people from inheriting property.³

The goods of the mind meriting the greatest honor were courage, ambition, fealty, largess, vengefulness, and pride or shame, which was the font of all the rest. Courage is naturally a prime virtue in any military society. As Tacitus reported, both leader and followers vied in this quality. Courage being the greatest virtue, cowardice was the greatest vice, as Tacitus also stated. Germanic legal codes recognized the charge of cowardice as the most grievous insult [4], and

---

[1] *friuntlaos* (*Hildebrandslied*, v. 24).

[2] In the *Lay of Ríg*, Jarl excels not only in physical and facial beauty, but in his glance, which is as fierce as that of a snake. In the *Lay of the Nibelungs*, Volker has such a fierce gaze that the Huns dare not attack him (*Nibelungenlied*, 1794,4). In the *Gesta Danorum* (p. 43, vv. 21-37), Swanhard expresses the prevailing view that beauty of countenance proves noble birth, but this may reflect the author's classical heritage.

[3] "Uppe altvile unde uppe dverge ne irstirft weder len noch erve, noch uppe kropelkind" (*Sachsenspiegel*, I, 4). Likewise lepers could not inherit property, although they could keep and transmit what they had (*Sachsenspiegel*, I, 4). This is the case in *Armer Heinrich*.

[4] See *Grimms Rechtsaltertümer*, II, 206-208.

it is fear of such reproach that forces Hildebrand to kill his son. It is to be noted that the Norse term *neiding* designated not only coward but also traitor or treacherous person. As Claudius von Schwerin states, the dishonorable man who could not bear arms was excluded from the community.[1]

Germanic literature seems to have associated power and prowess; in other words, courage was conventionally accompanied by physical strength and skill. Courage was seldom if ever found in a weak man, just as it was seldom found in a poor one. Courage was more often physical than spiritual; it was fortitude in its older rather than its later meaning. Many adjectives were used to describe the bold and skillful warrior, such as *biderbe, tühtic, tugenthaft, vrum,* and *wacker*. Because a bold and skillful warrior was the most excellent man, these words were later used to refer merely to excellence in general. As we shall see, all of these words changed their meanings drastically under clerical and bourgeois influences, sometimes to the diametrically opposed value. The corresponding vice was weakness, and it is logical that *swach* and *boese* could mean either weak or bad. Courage is commemorated in names such as Baldwin, Conrad, Gerard, Goddard, Hartmann, Hartmut, Leopold, Theobald, Roswitha, Kunegunde, and many others.

The goods of fortune and the warlike virtues would have brought little honor to their possessor if he lacked "high spirits". This quality, which was later known as *hôher muot* (exalted disposition) or *freude* (joy), combined self-assurance, optimism, and an affirmation of life. Its possession attested self-confidence and readiness to meet the challenge of life and strife. Since no one could have *hôher muot* without enjoying *êre*, the former served as evidence of the latter and was similarly praised by the poets. *Hôher muot* or *freude* was indispensable for the court of a successful liege; without it no heroes would take service there. To achieve this atmosphere, the liege had to lead his men successfully in battle, share the booty with them lavishly, and regale them with the best food, drink, and entertainment.

The next virtue on our list after courage and high spirits is ambition or the active desire for superiority, leadership, power and fame. This desire must be compounded with a dynamic force or élan that makes men wish to compete, excel, and seek adventure and self-assertion regardless of danger or hardship. In a warlike society, in which all productive work was relegated to women and servants, such ambition and energy could naturally be expressed only in warfare. Enthusiasm for war, and later for tournaments, remained a primary ruling-class virtue throughout the Middle Ages.

[1] "Aber der Ehrlose, der die Waffen nicht führen durfte, schied aus der Gemeinschaft der Staatsbürger aus" (Schwerin, p. 26).

Later, as the knights lost their dominance, equal sources of energy were tapped by the burghers in their pursuit of material gain and by scholars and thinkers in pursuit of knowledge and progress. The unbounded energy and optimism of the Germanic tribes astounded the world-weary Romans during their decline, and even Tacitus had marveled at their vigor. Be it due to custom, chance, or climate, the vitality and dynamism of the North Europeans distinguished them from many peoples of the world and subsequently played an important role in colonial and economic expansion and scientific progress. A major source of this vigor was the desire for fame and honor.

In his *Gallic War* (VI, 23), Julius Caesar described the motives behind the Teutons' continuous strife. "Robbery brings no infamy if committed outside the boundaries of the tribe, and they claim that it is done in order to train their youth and to decrease sloth. If any chief has said in the council that he will be a leader and that those who wish to follow should speak up, those who approve both the cause and the man arise and promise their help and are praised by the assembly. Of these, those who do not follow are counted as deserters and traitors, and afterward confidence (*fides*) is denied them in all things." In actual practice, the Germanic will to war seems to have been motivated by desire for adventure, plunder, and self-assertion; yet the poets preached that it should be motivated solely by a greed for fame, which happens to be the literal translation of *Ehrgeiz*, the present German word for ambition. The last verse of *Beowulf* eulogizes the hero as having been *lofgeornest*, or most desirous of praise. This virtue was approximately that which the ancient Greeks designated as *philotimia*.

The importance of renown as a personal goal is suggested in many names formed from the syllable *mar* (famous): for example, Dietmar, Hincmar, Marbod, Margot, and Reinmar. The same is true of names based on the syllable *hrod*, which meant about the same thing. Among these are Orgier, Orlando, Ralph, Robert, Roderick, Rodriguez, Roger, Roland, Rolf, Roswitha, Rowena, Rudlieb, Rudolf, Rupert, and many more. Warfare is suggested in names based on the syllables *hadu*, *hild* or *wic* (battle), *gund*, *gunth*, or *guth* (war), and *hari* (army). A small sample of these are Hadubrand, Brunhild, Kriemhild, Hilda, Ludwig, Ludovici, Lewis, Louis, Machthilda, Matilda, Herwig, Gudrun, Gunther, Kunigunde, Fredegunde, Walter, Werner, Warner, Harold, Heribrand. Love of weapons is suggested in names derived from *gar* (spear), *helma* (helmet), and *brand* (sword). Samples of these are Gerald, Gerard, Gerbert, Gerbold, Gertrude, Gervais, Edgar, Roger, Rüdeger, William, Wilhelm, Guillaume, Helmbrecht, Hildebrand, Hadubrand, and Heribrand.

Will to victory is indicated in the names Siegfried, Sieglind, Siegmar, Siegmund, Siegward, and a host of others. The name Siegfried does not connote peace in our sense of the word, but rather a *vridu* enforced by a victor. Likewise, the name Frederick means the master of a *vridu*. It is of interest that feminine as well as masculine names could refer to weapons, warfare, and victory. This would corroborate Tacitus's statement in his *Germania* (c. 18), that the wedding gifts exchanged by Germanic bride and groom consisted of a warhorse, shield, spear, and sword, and that the women accompanied their men into battle. Because we are accustomed to give women names suggesting soft, sweet, or gentle attributes, we often misinterpret feminine names of Germanic origin. Rosalind and Rosmund, for example, have nothing to do with roses: the former combines the words *hros* (horse) and *lindi* (serpent), and the latter combines *hros* and *mund* (protector). Roswitha does not mean Rose-white: it combines *hrod* (famous) and *switha* (swift, brave, strong).[1] Mildred does not connote mildness; for *milde* meant largess and *thryth* meant power, the two being in causal relationship. Joyce is not related to joy, but is derived from the name of the Goths.

The virtue most praised by the Germanic poets was *triuwe*, which may be explained as fealty, oath-keeping, or allegiance, and which was perhaps the quality expressed by the word *sacramentum* in the *Germania* (c. 14). Although the term gradually assumed spiritual overtones, it originally meant an oath, promise, or contract. Its Indo-European cognates even indicate an earlier meaning of firm, safe, or strong.[2] The early meaning of agreement or contract lingers in its English derivative *truce* and the French *trève de Dieu*. The word *triuwe* was sometimes used as a synonym of *vridu*, in the sense of protective truce. This occurs, for example, in the account of Cain's fratricide in the *Old Saxon Genesis*, a vernacular paraphrase of the Bible adapted to the understanding of a still primitive Germanic tribe. Because Germanic law declared an outcast to be an outlaw, Cain is afraid he will be killed until God sets his *friđu* on him and marks him in order that he may live in the world *an treuuue* without being slain, even though he is an outcast.[3]

Germanic attitudes are even more vividly expressed in the Anglo-Saxon version of this same story. In the so-called *Genesis A*, Cain is cursed and must live in exile (*wrǣc*) and wander from home without

---

[1] Hrotsvitha of Gandersheim rendered her name as *clamor validus*.
[2] "Es gibt eine Treue der Gesinnung, die sich also in der Festigkeit des Herzens und der Zuverlässigkeit des Characters zeigt; aber es gibt auch eine Treue mit Hinsicht auf einen geschlossenen Vertrag. Hier liegt eben die älteste Bedeutung des Wortes: gegebenes Wort, Gelübde, Versprechen. Die indogermanischen Verwandten weisen sogar auf eine ursprüngliche Bedeutung fest, sicher, stark hin" (Vries, p. 20).
[3] In *Heliand*, p. 237, vv. 60-79.

honor (*ārleas*). As a fugitive (*flêma*) he must wander (*wrecan*) loathed by his kinsmen (*winemâgum lâđ*). He realizes that he cannot hope for honor (*âre*) in this world because he has lost the Heavenly King's favor (*hyldo*), love (*lufan*), and friendship (*freođe*). Nevertheless, even though he must wander far from his kinsmen, he does not lack God's protection; for God puts a mark (*frĕođobeacen*) on him so that no one will kill him. Without such a mark, he could be killed with impunity.[1]

The word *triuwe* was often used for the contract or bond between war-lord and follower. As Caesar vouches in his *Gallic War*, this promise was ethically unbreakable after a campaign had been announced, and woe to him who failed his chief in battle. This concept of dependability lingers in the English cognates *trust* and *troth* and also in the Late-Latin derivative *antrustio*, which designated a member of a military retinue. It is also suggested in the Old Saxon words *gitrost* (a following) and *helm-gitrosteon* (heroes). The English word *loyalty* should not be used to translate *triuwe* in the old epics, as it so often is, because it implies a sentiment not always present in the Germanic term. Perhaps a better rendition is "allegiance", which stresses the objectivity of the obligation; for *triuwe* was a temporary relationship which could be severed by either party at will and which lasted only as long as both parties kept their word. In this way it differed from *vridu*, which was automatic among kinsmen and, in theory, almost insoluble.

It is not at all unusual for exemplary heroes to terminate their allegiance with their lord when they hear of another one who rewards more generously. In the *Heliand*, an old Low German poem which will be discussed, the toll collector Matthew is quite content with his generous employers until he hears that Christ gives even greater rewards, whereupon he returns the gifts received from his past employers and goes into the service of Jesus.[2] The same incident occurs in the *Ruodlieb*, an eleventh-century German adventure story in Latin hexameters. The very model of a young hero serves a distant lord for some time; but he finally leaves his service because he is not receiving his just deserts.[3]

In such changes of allegiance, it is usually made clear that the vassal has served due notice and has returned previously received gifts. *Triuwe*, in the sense of truce, could also be terminated by either party as long as he notified the other before attacking, as Liudeger and Liudegast do in the *Lay of the Nibelungs*.[4] Of course, if no *triuwe* had been declared, no declaration of war was demanded,

[1] *Genesis*, p. 15, v. 393 – p. 16, v. 428.
[2] *Heliand*, vv. 1189-1202.
[3] *Ruodlieb*, I, 11-17.
[4] *Nibelungenlied*, 143-146; 877.

war being the normal condition between strangers. Treacherous ambushes, like Arminius's surprising of the Roman legions in the Teutoburg Forest, were considered praiseworthy if successful. The Fetial Code of the Romans, on the other hand, required that war be declared before being waged;[1] and this novel view spread, in theory at least, throughout the Middle Ages.[2] The custom of declaring war lingers in the Western world, where governments officially declare war before (even if only a few hours before) attacking their neighbors. Whenever a nation outside this cultural society attacks without notice, it is considered a "day of infamy". Even though the ancient Teutons approved of surprise attacks, they nevertheless scrupled against killing sleeping men, for that was the way of a *neiding* or coward. Instead, praiseworthy Norse heroes always wakened their victims before killing them. An echo of the old contempt for those who attack sleeping men is seen in the *Lay of the Nibelungs*, when Volker reviles the Huns as cowards because they tried to kill the Burgundians in their sleep.[3] Although this epic was not written in its present form until the thirteenth century, it preserves many values and motifs from remote antiquity.

The old Germanic ideal of service unto death, but only as long as the payments are prompt, lasted until modern times in the ethics of the Swiss mercenaries. As Racine states in the first scene of his *Les Plaideurs*, "Point d'argent, point de Suisse". Whereas a vassal was permitted to terminate his service at will in peace time, he could not do so once hostilities had begun. What Tacitus said about duty unto death was no exaggeration, and history has furnished many actual examples since the annihilation of the Teutones and Cimbri. This fanatic allegiance should not be confused with a selfless devotion; because, as the poets so often attested, the real deterrent to flight was public reproach. As both Caesar and Tacitus said of the Teutonic volunteers, fear of disgrace was the true disciplinary factor.

This fact is evident in *Beowulf* when Wiglaf reproaches those who

---

[1] "Ac belli quidem aequitas sanctissime fetiali populi Romani iure perscripta est. Ex quo intellegi potest nullum bellum esse iustum, nisi quod aut rebus repetitis geratur aut denuntiatum ante sit et indictum" (*De Officiis*, I, xii).
[2] In Conrad of Wurzburg's *Trojan War*, a hero says that, in order to avoid reproach, he will declare war before attacking (*Trojanerkrieg*, 17,956-60). In Hartmann's *Iwein* (vv. 712-714), Askalon upbraids Kalogreant as *triuwelôs* because he has not defied him (*widerseit*) before disturbing his well. Henry Wittenwiler wrote, about 1400, that it was the law of war (*des streites recht*) that, "man den veinten send ein knecht In einem rosenvarwen tuoch Mit swert und auch mit hantschuoch, Gesprenget ser mit rotem pluot. Daz ist ze einem zaichen guot, Daz man vechten mit in well. Dar zuo widersait der gesell Irem leib und irem guot Daz seu sich dester bas in huot Haben schullen" (*Ring*, vv. 7546-56).
[3] "pfî, ir zagen boese,... wolt ir slâfende uns ermordet hân?" (*Nibelungenlied*, 1847, 2-3).

deserted their leader in his hour of need. "Now all treasure-sharing and sword-giving and all pride of ownership will be lost to your kinships," he says, "Every member of your families will have to wander bereft of the law of the land as soon as noblemen far and wide have heard of your flight, your infamous deed. For a noble man, death is better than a shameful life." [1] It is interesting that he ends with a thought attributed to Agricola in Britain some seven or eight centuries earlier.[2] Most poets do not bother to list the social, economic, and political consequences of such a disgrace. It is enough to warn that troth-breakers will lose their honor, it being inevitable that the other dire penalties will follow such a loss.

Oath-keeping was the basis of the whole feudal system. In justifying William's conquest of England, the monk Odericus Vitalis tells of Harold's many physical virtues, such as stature, elegance, physical strength, courage, and eloquence; then he adds, "But what did so many gifts do for him without faith (*fides*), which is the foundation of all good things? For, to be sure, when he returned to his country, he broke his faith to his lord through his desire to reign." [3] The irony was, if we may believe other accounts, that Harold's oath was made under compulsion and was therefore not binding, even though made over a chest of saints' bones. It is to be noted that Odericus used the word *fides*, just as Caeser had done a millennium earlier. This Germanic concept of oath-keeping took some strange forms. In his *Germania* (c. 24) Tacitus tells how a Germanic man will gamble away his wealth, family, and even his freedom, and then voluntarily allow himself to be bound and taken into slavery. "And that they call *fides*." As we shall see, this was the origin of the "debt of honor".

Like *vridu*, fealty or allegiance could require a man to act against his own inclination; and such compulsion furnished tragic conflicts in many medieval epics. In the *Waltharius*, a ninth-century poem in Latin hexameters, King Gunther commands his vassal Hagen to fight with him against his former friend and fellow hostage,[4] even though it was a shameful thing for two to fight against one, as Saxo Grammaticus attests.[5] At first Hagen disobeys Gunther and refuses to break his *triuwe* to Waltharius; but he is released from his *triuwe*

---

[1] "Nû sceal sincþego ond swyrdgifu, eall êðelwyn êowrum cynne, lufen âlicgean; londrihtes môt þære mægburge monna æghwylc îdel hweorfan, syððan æðelingas feorran gefricgean flêam êowerne, dômlêasan dæd. Dêað bið sêlla eorla gehwylcum þonne edwîtlîf!" (*Beowulf*, vv. 2884-91).
[2] See Introduction, note. 26.
[3] "Sed quid ei tanta dona sine fide, que bonorum omnium fundamentum est, contulerunt? In patriam nempe suam ut regressus est, pro cupiditate regni Domino suo fidem mentitus est" (Oderici Vitalis, *Historiae Ecclesiasticae*, ed. A. LePrévost, Paris, 1838-55, III, p. 11).
[4] *Waltharius*, vv. 1075-1129.
[5] *Gesta Danorum*, p. 112, vv. 1-2.

as soon as Waltharius kills his nephew, because that was a particularly grievous insult to the ancient Germans. Saxo Grammaticus tells about a king who must turn against his own son-in-law in order to avenge a friend with whom he has made a vengeance pact.[1] This son-in-law, Amleth, is better known by the name of Hamlet, as he is called in Shakespeare's play.

For women, *triuwe* consisted mainly in marital fidelity. As Tacitus attested, marriage in Germany was chaste in comparison with that in Rome; yet marital fidelity was not required of men, and unmarried women's sex life was of little concern as long as they did not overstep class barriers. Sex played a minor role in the older literature and women served primarily as objects to be stolen, like cattle and other wealth. As Tacitus mentioned, a man who caught his wife in adultery could clip her hair, beat her naked through the streets in returning her to her family, and thus publicly deprive her of her honor for breaking her troth. Because marital infidelity brought disgrace not only to the offender, but also to her entire kinship, the kinship was particularly strict in punishing its wayward daughters.[2] If such women were not legally punished, they still might be lynched by their more virtuous sisters. In reproving an Anglo-Saxon king for fornication, St. Boniface claimed that in Northern Germany, "if a virgin defiles her father's house by adultery or if a married woman breaks the marriage tie and commits adultery, they sometimes compel her to hang herself by her own hand, and then over the pyre on which she has been burned and cremated they hang the seducer. Sometimes a band of women get together and flog her through the village, beating her with rods, and, stripping her to the waist, they cut and pierce her whole body with knives and send her from house to house bloody and torn. Always new scourgers, zealous for the purity of marriage, are found to join in until they leave her dead, or half dead, that others may fear adultery and wantonness." [3]

The vivid language of the above paragraph suggests that the pious priest endorsed the zealous guardians of the moral law. He seems confused about the cause of their righteous indignation, however, for the punishment seems to have been for infidelity rather than for lechery. The *Mirror of the Saxons*, echoing ancient laws, says that a woman who sullies her womanly honor through the inchastity of her body will lose neither her rights nor her inheritance.[4] Schopen-

---
[1] *op. cit.*, p. 101, vv. 15-34.
[2] Claudius von Schwerin says of the kinship: "Zu ihrem Schutze und zur Abwehr des 'Verwandtenschimpfs' handhabte die Sippe eine Strafgewalt, auf Grund deren sie insbesondere gegen sittliche Vergehen weiblicher Geschlechtsgenossen vorging, in schweren Fällen mit der Todesstrafe" (Schwerin, p. 22).
[3] Talbot, p. 193.
[4] "Wîph mach mit unkûscheit ires lîbis ir wîphlichen êre krenken; ir recht ne virlûsit se dar mede nicht noch ir erve" (*Sachenspiegel*, I, 5, 2b).

hauer, with more insight into human nature than Boniface could command, would have attributed the furies' violence to their fear of sexual competition.[1] Perhaps they were more jealous than zealous. Almost as dishonorable as marital infidelity was marriage with a man of inferior rank, since that made a women lose her honor in the eyes of her peers, who could not tolerate such violation of the social hierarchy. Saxo Grammaticus seems to have been correct in stating that, among the ancient Danes, "If a free woman agreed to marry a slave, she had to take on his rank and lose the benefit of her liberty and accept the standing of a slave." [2] The same held true of extra marital intimacies with socially inferior men.

The fourth on our arbitrary list of virtues is largess or *milte*. The purpose of *milte* was to win friends and influence people, that is, to obligate and impress, as the *Poetic Edda* says.[3] Because the Germanic vassal fought for his liege in return for support in peace time and a share of the spoils in wartime, *milte* was one of the prime virtues of a feudal lord, without which there would have been no *triuwe* and consequently no social structure. Regardless of any emotional, sentimental, or spiritual values we may read into the liege-vassal relationship, the poets of the time never failed to stress its monetary basis. The author of *Beowulf* expresses the function of *milte* by saying, "Thus a young man shall do good works with rich money gifts among his father's friends so that afterward, when war comes in his later years, willing companions may stand by him and people may do him service." Later, after Beowulf's vassals have deserted him, Wiglaf reminds them of the gifts which they have received from their lord.[4] In the *Gesta Danorum* the hero Hjalte says, "It is sweet for us to repay the gifts received from our lord, to grasp our swords and to devote our steel to glory." [5]

The favor shown by a chieftain to his follower was generally known as *huld*. According to the feudal pact, the lord was "beholden" to protect his vassal and show him *milte* in return for his service. If the chieftain failed to make good his *huld*, he was as miscreant as a vassal who failed to perform in battle. Being frankly a means to an end, *milte* should not be confused with the modern virtue of gener-

[1] Schopenhauer, IV, pp. 345-446.
[2] "At si libera consensisset in seruum, eius condicionem equaert, libertatisque beneficio spoliata, seruilis fortunae indueret" (*Gesta Danorum*, p. 152).
[3] See *Hovamol*, 40-48, in *Poetic Edda*, trans Bellows, pp. 36-38.
[4] "Swâ sceal (geong g) uma gôde gewyrcan, fromum feohgiftum on faeder (bea) rme, þat hine on ylde eft gewunigen wilgesîþas, þonne wîg cume, lêode gelæsten" (*Beowulf*, vv. 20-24). "Þaet, lâ, maeg secgan sê ðe wyle sôð specan, þaet se mondryhten, sê êow ðâ mâðmas geaf, êoredgeatwe, þê gê þǣr on standað, – þonne hê on ealubence ofte gesealde healsittendum helm ond byrnan þêoden his þegnum, swylce he þrydlîcost ôwer feor oððe nêah findan meahte –" (*Beowulf*, vv. 2864-70).
[5] *Gesta Danorum*, p. 59, vv. 37-38.

osity, which is now supposed to be disinterested, that is, performed without hope of reward. It is not exactly clear what the old warrior in the *Lay of Hildebrand* means when he offers his son the arm bands *bi huldi*.[1] Although *huld* usually referred to the favor shown by a superior to an inferior, it could also refer to the service performed by the inferior.[2]

Because chieftains could attract followers only through *milte*, they had to publicize their ability to bestow; and wealth had to be flaunted at all times. The hospitality so praised by Tacitus helped serve this purpose. Although a stranger was outside the in-group, a sort of international law allowed him to demand hospitality; and no man concerned with his good name could refuse it. The lavishness of Germanic entertainment seems to have served another purpose. Like the potlaches of the American northwest, such hospitality was given through a will to superiority and a desire to impress and to obligate. The recipient was always "beholden" to the donor and, if properly impressed, would spread word of the donor's largess and of the wealth and power it implied. This fact is abundantly clear in later literature. Today, when we say, "I am much obliged", we scarcely think of the literal meaning of the term.

Just as largess was a prime virtue, miserliness, or *gîticheit* as it was later called, was a primary vice. Whereas the ancient Teutons considered stingyness a vice, they considered lust for other men's wealth a sign of virtue. The only vice connected with it was reluctance to share it lavishly. The noble nature of largess is suggested by the derivation of the word "generous" from *generosus*, meaning wellborn. The taint associated with miserliness can be seen in the fact that the *MHG* word *arc* could mean stingy as well as wicked or cowardly, and that *MHG boese* could mean stingy as well as wicked or weak.[3] Likewise, the Middle English word *wretch* could mean either wretch or miser, perhaps through the influence of the parallel development of Latin *miser* (miserable) into miser.

Along with the virtues of courage, ambition, fealty, and largess was that of shame, which may be listed with them or may be considered the basic motivation behind all the others. As David Riesman says of a tradition-directed society, the "sanction for behavior tends to be the fear of being shamed."[4] It is important to note that it is fear of being shamed, not of being ashamed, as it is in our post-Kantian world. In other words, *scham* was not fear of doing

---

[1] *Hildebrandslied*, v. 35.
[2] Rudolf of Ems uses *huld* to mean favor of lord (*Alexander*, v. 13,594) and also duty to lord (v. 13,307).
[3] The word *boese* will appear in this meaning in many later passages in this study. Cf. "der boesen (Frauen) lôn ist kleine" and "vil swache lônent boesiu wîp" (*Moriz von Craun*, vv. 403, 409).
[4] Riesman, p. 40.

wrong, but fear of being publicly censured. Therefore *scham* must not be confused with its present-day English cognate *shame*, which, according to Webster's *Collegiate Dictionary*, means "a painful emotion excited by a consciousness of guilt, shortcoming, or impropriety." The word *scham*, a millennium ago, could better have been defined as the extreme discomfit or fear of being thought guilty, inadequate, or inferior by one's peers. In other words, *scham* was the discomfit or fear of being shamed, not ashamed.

The worst shame that can befall an "other-directed" man, to use another of Riesman's terms, is to be ridiculed by his peers. This is seen in the *Chanson de Roland* in the vengeance that Ganelon wreaks because Roland has ridiculed him.[1] Aristotle had long since observed that ridicule is one of the chief causes of the desire to avenge.[2]

Laughter has not always connoted joviality: in the Middle Ages it more often expressed scornful superiority or group-solidarity against non-conformity.[3] It is no coincidence that the *MHG* word *schimpf* (jest, game) has developed into the *NHG* word *Schimpf* (affront, insult), since laughter was most often directed *at* people.

The *MHG* word *laster*, which was related to the verb **lahan* (to blame), originally meant "reproach", a meaning still found in its modern verbal derivative *lästern* (to slander or blaspheme). During the course of this study we shall see the semantic development of the word *laster* from its original meaning of reproach or calumny to its present meaning of vice or moral turpitude, a development almost identical with that of the word *turpitude* itself. The Teutons strove to avoid not only *laster*, but also *tadel* and *hôn*. Although the modern word *Tadel* means reproof or reproach, the *MHG* word *tadel* is usually translated as defect. This is quite unnecessary, since medieval man drew very little distinction between defect and censure.[4] The German expression *ohne Furcht und Tadel*, like English *without fear and without reproach*, was based on the French *sans peur et sans reproche*. Today we would rather think of Bayard as irreproachable rather than merely as unreproached, but even in the Renaissance the distinction was not generally felt. Germanic warriors feared not only rebuke for cowardice, but also scorn for defeat. Derivatives of the word *hôn*, especially *honir*, *hontage*, *honte*, and *honteus* played an important role in the *chansons de geste*, which express much Germanic spirit with regard to honor and shame.

[1] *Chanson de Roland*, vv. 302-305.
[2] Aristotle, *Rhetoric*, II, 2 (trans. Cooper, p. 97).
[3] St. Martin of Braga said, "Odibilem quoque hominem facit risus aut superbus et clarus (loud) aut malignus et furtivus aut alienis malis evocatus" Martin, *Formula* 4, 27).
[4] When Wolfram says that a fur-lined coat is free of *tadel* (*Parzival*, 228,7), he can mean either. The word is related to Old English *tǣl*, *tâl*, ridicule, calumny, and *tǣlen*, *têlan*, to declare defective.

As Friedrich Maurer has observed, disgrace or dishonor had to be a public matter.[1] This explains why oaths, to be binding, had to be made ceremoniously before many witnesses. One could almost say that an oath owed its validity to the number and rank of the witnesses, for the oath-giver would hesitate to break his word and thus lose the respect of so many people. A fine example of a well-witnessed treaty was the oath of Strassburg, which was made in 842 by two of the heirs of Louis the Pious and was witnessed by two whole armies.

Like the Greeks and Romans before them, the ancient Teutons believed that their military renown lived after them as a sort of worldly immortality. This sentiment appears often in Germanic poetry. Beowulf comforts the grieving king Hrothgar with the words, "Don't sorrow, wise man. It is better for us to avenge a kinsman than to sorrow greatly for him, each of us will see the end of his life in this world. Let him, who can, win renown before his death. That is the greatest joy for the deceased warrior."[2] Likewise, in the *Heliand*, St. Thomas says to his fellow heroes, "It is a hero's choice to stand steadfast with his lord and to die with him at the day of decision (*an duome*). Let us all do so, let us follow him on his journey nor let us consider our lives of any value, if only we die with our lord in the host. Then at least our fame (*duom*) will live for us afterward as good words before men." When St. Thomas says that it is good to die with one's lord, he is following scripture.[3] When he refers to the fame they will win thereby, he reveals Germanic reasoning.

Medieval statements about honor often show classical influences; yet they still expressed feelings native to medieval man. In most cases, the feeling or attitude was deeply rooted, and only the means of expression was new. As we have seen, when the poet of *Beowulf* says that death with honor is better than a life of shame, he is expressing the same thought already used by Tacitus in quoting Agricola. Still, we know that such sentiments were dear to the Germanic warriors. That they were dear to the Germanic women, too, was shown by the female survivors of the Cimbri, who, when refused permission to become Vestal Virgins, killed their children

[1] Maurer, *Leid*, p. 120.
[2] "Ne sorga, snotor guma! Sêlre bið æghwæm, þæt hê his frêond wrece, þonne hê fela murne. Ûre æghwylc sceal ende gebîdan worolde lîfes; wyrce sê þe môte dômes ær dêaþe; þæt bið drihtguman unlifgendum æfter sêlest" (*Beowulf*, vv. 1384-89).
[3] "that ist thegnes cust, that hie mid is frâhon samad fasto gistande, dôie mid im thar an duom. Duan ûs alla sô, folgon im te thero ferdi: ni lâtan ûse fera uuið thiu uuihtes uuirðig, neba uui an them uuerode mid im, dôian mid ûson drohtine. Than lêbot ûs thoh duom after, guod uuord for gumon" (*Heliand*, vv. 3996-4002). In the biblical source of this passage, John 11 : 16, Thomas had declared his willingness to die with Jesus. It was the Germanic poet who motivated such loyalty by alluding to the fame which would be won.

and themselves rather than suffer the disgrace of captivity. Roman and Christian civilization would not have influenced the northern barbarians as it did if they had lacked the necessary predisposition. When the same civilization, in a somewhat altered form, was presented centuries later to the Aztecs, Pueblo Indians, and Philipinos, the results were very different.

One of the poems of the *Edda* states that "possessions die, kinships die, you yourself will die as they. One thing I know that lives forever: the dead man's renown." [1] Strangely enough, this pagan sentiment was inscribed during World War II as an epitaph on the wall of St. Mary's Church in Lübeck. Hans Kuhn summarizes the Germanic belief by writing, "the greatest possession of the Teuton and the decisive yardstick for everything he did and left undone was his good name (*Ehre*) and the fame (*Ruhm*) which was to survive him." [2] This belief in the immortality of fame was still very much alive during the Renaissance. Shakespeare's Cassio was no exception when he cried out to Iago, "I have lost my reputation! I have lost the immortal part of myself, and what remains is bestial." [3]

A man concerned with his good name would brook no slur upon it; and much medieval fiction relates efforts made to avenge injured honor. Modern man distinguishes between insult and injury; and perfectly respectable people can say, "Sticks and stones may break my bones, but names can never hurt me." The ancient Teutons and their medieval descendants, on the other hand, viewed the two offenses as almost identical.[4] Among primitive peoples a word is usually more than a mere sound or symbol; it is a living spirit or power capable of bringing irreparable harm to the person against whom it is spoken.

In the ancient Teutons' exaggerated attitude toward insults we find all the ingredients of the "point of honor", a curse destined to plague the upper classes of Europe for centuries to come. The "point of honor" is now so foreign to most Americans that the term

---

[1] In his *The Saga of the Jómsvíkings* (Austin, 1955), p. 21, L. M. Hollander renders this as, "Cattle die and kinsmen die, thyself eke soon wilt die: but fair fame will fade never, I ween, for him who wins it." F. Niedner, in his *Havamal-Sprüche der Edda* (*Thule Sammlung*, II, p. 121 ff.) renders it as, "Besitz stirbt, Sippen sterben, Du selbst stirbst wie sie, Doch Nachruhm stirbt nimmermehr, Den der Wackere gewinnet."

[2] "Der höchste Besitz des Germanen und der entscheidende Massstab für alles, was er tat und liess, war seine Ehre und der Ruhm, der ihn überleben sollte" (Schneider, p. 215). Andreas Heusler expresses the idea as, "Der Ruhm, die 'guteNachrede nach dem Tode,' ist dem Heiden, was dem Christen die ewige Seligkeit: das höchste gute" (Heusler, *Germanentum*, p. 103).

[3] *Othello*, II, 3, vv. 263-265.

[4] Friedrich Maurer, in his *Leid* (Bern, 1951), shows that *MHG leid* could mean both insult and injury, both *Beleidigung* and *Leiden*.

has recently taken on a new and moral meaning.[1] According to Schopenhauer,[2] the "point of honor" was unknown to the ancients, who thought a slap from a man less objectionable than a kick from a horse. In this he was right, in so far as the Greeks and Romans did not require their peers to avenge insults in order to be considered men of honor. In fact they thought it more commendable to ignore an insult as if it had not occurred: for the offender, rather than the offended, had compromised his good name. According to Cicero, an insult has a sting that a wise man and good man can bear only with difficulty.[3] Perhaps Tacitus, being no "man of honor", was unable to see that the Teutons' shameful after-dinner brawls were actually "affairs of honor", at least in the eyes of the participants. Like the Northwest Indians, the Teutons enjoyed enhancing their own prestige by reviling their fellows in eloquent "flitings", or competitions in abusive railing. These often ended in violence, insults being erased only by worse insults or by bloodshed.

Schopenhauer was wrong in claiming that the "point of honor" is an unnatural drive, a custom based on tradition rather than on human nature. Such an attitude appears in any lawless society and is still evident today in the intercourse between sovereign nations. Concern for one's relative status and fear of aggression are inborn, as can be seen in the similar mores of the henyard and the schoolyard, where each new arrival must assert himself against all aggressions, either actual or potential. The apparently irrational behavior of "men of honor" must be based on some definite, even though inscrutable, logic; for striking similarities appear in family feuds in such remote areas as Montenegro, Corsica, Iceland, and the Tennessee mountains.

An insult to one's honor could be wiped out only if the offender or some other member of his *vridu* was killed by the offended or by one of his clan, and such vengeance furnished the motivation for many Norse sagas. Insults were also used as challenges. When hostile forces met in the field, they called their opponents cowards and thus compelled them to start the fray. This custom is illustrated in the *Lay of Hildebrand,* in which the father must fight his own son rather than have his army think him a coward, since reputation was even more important than ties of blood. Such vituperative challenges, which are now called *Hohnreden,* served to enhance the morale and confidence of the offender as well as to precipitate the struggle,

---

[1] *Brewer's Dictionary of Phrase and Fable* (Harpers, New York, n.d., p. 466) explains the term to mean, "An obligation which is binding because its violation would offend some conscientious scruple or notion of self-respect".
[2] Schopenhauer, IV, pp. 417-419.
[3] "Habet quendam aculeum contumelia, quam pati prudentes ac viri boni difficillime possunt" (cited from Eckstein, p. 99).

for the offended party forfeited all his honor until he cleared himself of the ignominy. A good example of a *Hohnrede*, recorded at a somewhat later date, is found in the *Lay of the Nibelungs* when Hagen reproaches Hildebrand for fleeing from the hall and Hildebrand retaliates by asking why Hagen stood by and let Waltharius kill so many of his friends.[1]

A man of honor was obliged to avenge every insult, and anyone who failed to gain satisfaction was branded as a shirker as well as a coward. In an age of club-law the only deterrent to insult or injury from outside the clan was threat of reprisal: if one turned his other cheek, his kith lost not only their good name but also their only safeguard against further aggressions. Consequently, as Tacitus mentions in his *Germania* (c. 21), a man was obliged to take up the enmities as well as the friendships of his father or kinsmen. Failure to avenge an insult naturally diminished a man's status, that is to say, his *dignitas* or *dignatio*. Consequently an insult was an "indignity" and caused great "indignation". Saxo tells of two Danish youths who are moved with indignation (*indignacione permoti*) because King Athisl of Sweden has killed their father.[2] Until they have avenged their father, they cannot enjoy the *dignatio* due to Germanic chieftains. They are moved not so much by anger, or even by righteous indignation in its present sense, as by a desire to regain their public esteem.

When a member of a kinship was killed, his kinsmen had to avenge him (unless first compensated by a wergild or bloodmoney), even if he had merited his death. In matters of revenge and honor the Teutons drew no distinction between manslaughter and murder. In the *Lay of Waltharius*, Scaramundus must either die or kill Waltharius in order to avenge the death of his uncle Camalo, even though he knows that Waltharius killed him reluctantly and purely in selfdefense.[3] As late as the fourteenth century the word *indignatio* was commonly used to mean "desire for vengeance."[4]

Today revenge is somewhat pardoned, or at least the punishment and censure are somewhat mitigated, when it is perpetrated in heat of passion and immediately after the offense. The ancient Teutons

---

[1] "'Jâ naeme ich ê die suone', sprach aber Hagene, 'ê ich sô lasterlîche ûz einem gademe flühe, meister Hildebrant, als ir hie habt getân. ich wânde daz ir kundet baz gein vianden stân'. Des antwurte Hildebrant: 'zwiu verwîzet ir mir daz? nu wer was der ûf einem schilde vor dem Waskensteine saz, dô im von Spânje Walther sô vil der friunde sluoc? ouch habt ir noch ze zeigen an iu selben genuoc'" (*Nibelungenlied*, 2343-2344).

[2] *Gesta Danorum*, p. 110, v. 23. In the *Gesta Romanorum* (cap. 141) Haman is *indignatus* when Mordecai refuses to worship him.

[3] *Waltharius*, vv. 700-707.

[4] Hans Schulz (p. 191) defines *indignatio*, as used by Peter of Dusburg in the early fourteenth century, as "ein Gefühl, das den Wünsch nach Rache auslöst".

believed that, to be truly praiseworthy, the desire for revenge should be cool, calculated, and protracted. Like the samurai of Japan, the Nordic heroes often spent years planning their revenge, which they would finally wreak perhaps not on the offender himself, but on some other and more important member of his kindred, or *vridu*. Vicarious revenge was necessary if the offender could not give satisfaction, or, as later Germans would have said, was not *satisfaktionsfähig*. As we shall see, revenge remained socially obligatory until almost modern times, particularly in military circles; and many societies used the word *honor* most often in connection with the vengeance of insults. Perhaps the best expression of offended honor is found in Shakespeare's *Richard II* (I,1), when Norfolk implores the king to let him defend his honor from Bolingbroke's accusations by meeting him in a trial by combat: "The purest treasure mortal times afford Is spotless reputation. That away, Men are but guilded loam or painted clay. A jewel in a ten times barr'd-up chest Is a bold spirit in a loyal breast. Mine honour is my life. Both grow in one; Take honour from me, and my life is done. Then, dear my liege, mine honour let me try; In that I live, and for that will I die."

When Germanic heroes kill to avenge their kinsmen, we must not believe their acts motivated primarily by love or loyalty. The poets of the day usually made it clear that they killed to restore their own injured honor, concern for honor being more admirable than concern for friends and kinsmen. When Waltharius kills all Gunther's vassals, the king suffers more from shame than from the death of his friends. Therefore, letting his own sorrow at fighting his friend give way to the king's honor, Hagen joins the fight,[1] since vassals were duty bound to maintain their lieges' honor. When his nephew Roland is killed, Charlemagne's chief regret is that he will have no one to maintain his honor.[2] The precedence of personal honor over ties of blood or friendship appears in both the *Lay of Hildebrand* and the previously mentioned tale of Hamlet's father-in-law. As we shall see, it explains why Rüdeger, a hero in the *Lay of the Nibelungs*, must fight his friends. On the other hand, because an individual's honor reflected upon the honor of his liege, his vassals, his family, and his descendants, his concern for honor was partly altruistic and was considered an ethical value. When Roland is about to blow his horn to summon assistance, Olivier tells him not to do it because it will be a disgrace and reproach to all his kinsmen which will last all their life.[3]

[1] "propriusque honor succumbit honori regis" (*Waltharius*, vv. 1109-1110).
[2] "N'en avrai ja ki sustienget m'onur" (*Chanson de Roland*, v. 2903).
[3] "Vergoigne sereit grant E repruver a trestuz voz parents; Iceste hunte dureit al lur vivant" (*Chanson de Roland*, vv. 1705-1707).

CHAPTER THREE

CHRISTIAN GUILT CULTURE

Soli Deo honor et gloria in saecula
I *Timothy* 1, 17

As we have seen, the shame culture of the ancient Teutons was largely anthropocentric: man was the ultimate purpose of his own existence and the measure of all things. Consequently, a man's success depended more upon his own worth than upon fate or divine grace. Wealth or poverty, power or weakness, honor or shame, these were his to win, provided of course that he was of fitting birth and kinship. Fate played some part to be sure; yet the individual relied upon his own efforts and fought defiantly to a heroic death even against insuperable odds. The rewards for his courage and effort were of this world: wealth, power, and prestige during his life and lasting renown after his death. The penalty for cowardice and other faults was shame, scorn, and oblivion.

As a substitute for this anthropocentric shame culture, the Christian missionaries introduced a theocentric view of life, the belief that man was created for God's own ends and that he could avail nothing without divine grace. This theocentric view is superimposed, rather superficially, to be sure, upon the heroic action of *Beowulf*, in which the author occasionally attributes the hero's virtues and successes to divine aid.[1] Man being but a sinful exile in this vale of tears, most clerical writers declared the rewards of this world not true rewards, but merely distractions or obstacles on the road to salvation. Fame, wealth, and power in this world were not proper incentives: eternal reward in heaven was the only worthwhile goal.

In contrast to the pagans' shame culture, the Christian way of life can be considered a "guilt culture". Society was still based on a system of service and reward, but man was rewarded with glory in heaven rather than with acclaim on earth. Likewise, he was punished by the torments of hell rather than by the scorn of his peers. To understand the term "guilt culture" as applied to the early converts, we must free ourselves of modern concepts of guilt in the

---

[1] *Beowulf*, vv. 1658, 1725, 2184.

sense of an inner feeling of remorse or self-reproach for what we have done, a remorse independent of any fear of punishment. Having no such sense of guilt, the early converts could understand the term only in its basic meaning of liability to punishment. When we scold a naughty dog and reach for a switch, his face usually registers extreme guilt; yet it is clear that he is more concerned with the whipping he will get than with any infringement of divine or human law. And thus it was with the new converts.

As we have seen, if one Teuton killed another, he was in danger of retaliation until he paid a blood-money. Until he paid this debt, or *schult*, he was guilty, or *schuldic*; but once he had paid his indemnity, or *buoze* (related to English *booty*), he was no longer guilty. Although *Busse*, the modern German derivative of this latter word, now means both penance and penitence, this was not originally the case. When a pagan killed another man, he gloated in his triumph. When an early convert killed another man, he sometimes felt regret (*riuwe*), provided he really believed the missionaries' stories about hell's fire. Whereas *Reue*, the modern German word derived from *riuwe*, connotes remorse, its ancestor may have meant no more than regret; for there is no evidence that the Teutons were burdened with guilty consciences.

The origin and development of Western man's guilty conscience is somewhat reflected in the etymology of the word *conscience*, which literally meant common or shared knowledge (*cum*, with; *scientia*, knowledge). The early missionaries may have had some inkling of this etymology; for they rendered *conscientia* literally as *giwizzanî* (from *ge*, a collective prefix related to *cum*, and *wizzan*, to know).[1] In other words, *gewizzanî* was the individual's awareness that someone else (i.e., God) knew what he was thinking. God's omniscience was stressed by all missionaries and preachers. He was a *speculator cordis*, a spy of men's hearts, an all-seeing and all-knowing deity from whom no deed or thought could be hidden,[2] a deity who punished not only the wrong-doer but also his children and children's children to the third and fourth generation. His punishment was a very real thing too: eternal fire and brimstone, more painful than any agony known on earth and many times longer

---

[1] Perhaps the early converts understood the prefix of *giwizzanî* to be a perfective prefix, which would make the word mean "that which is known, consciousness, recognition (of sin)". This is suggested by its frequent use in the meaning of *sapientia*, for example in the *Heliand*, where it appears often in the Old Saxon form *gewit*. Wulfila based his word *miþwissei* on the Greek word *suneidesis*, which also meant "common knowledge".

[2] A typical expression of such a belief appears in the story of Pope Gregory, as told in the *Gesta Romanorum* (cap. 170). When the king makes improper advances to his sister, she says; "Absit a me tale peccatum in conspectu dei perpetrare!"

than life itself. Guilt was not just a pang of remorse felt after disappointing a loving Father, but rather the immediate fear of very real punishment. And yet, despite all clerical admonitions, most laymen continued for centuries to obey God's commandments only in so far as they did not conflict with the demands of their traditional shame culture.

Each Teutonic tribe had its own law; and a vassal obeyed the law of his own lord. After conversion, the Germanic peoples were supposed to obey God's law, which was a single law for all believers.[1] To understand their difficulty in comprehending the new law, we might recall a story told about an African youth who left his native village and went down to the coast to learn the white men's magic. When he asked the missionaries if he could learn their magic, they were delighted at the chance to save his heathen soul and assured him that he could learn their "magic" if only he would study for several years. With great diligence he memorized their prayers, creed, catechism, beatitudes, good works, and other Christian teachings. Finally he was released with the assurance that he had now mastered the Christians' magic and could return to his native village and share his knowledge with his people. The next night he returned to the mission and cut the throats of all the missionaries. That day he had assembled his clan, announced his new power, and publicly put a fatal curse on them. When it failed, he felt humiliated and realized that the missionaries had deceived him. There is no evidence that anything such as this happened among the Germanic converts; but there is evidence that they remained ignorant of the inner meaning of Christianity long after they had accepted its external paraphernalia. This was certainly true of Thranbrand, the first Christian missionary to Iceland, who proved the value of Christianity by winning trials by combat.[2]

Being fighters rather than philosophers, the Teutons never formulated a definite moral dogma; yet their literature and actions made it clear that they had a universally accepted value system. If we permit ourselves the medieval license of parody, we could codify their values as follows:

> Blessed are the rich, for they possess the earth and its glory.
> Blessed are the strong, for they can conquer kingdoms.
> Blessed are they with strong kinsmen, for they shall find help.
> Blessed are the warlike, for they shall win wealth and renown.
> Blessed are they who keep their faith, for they shall be honored.
> Blessed are they who are open handed, for they shall have friends and fame.

[1] "Eadem lex erit indiginae et colono qui peregrinatur apud vos" (*Exodus*, 12, 49); "Aequum iudicium sit inter vos, sive peregrinus sive civis peccaverit" (*Leviticus*, 24, 22).
[2] See Brennu-Njálssaga, C-CV.

> Blessed are they who wreak vengeance, for they shall be offended no more, and they shall have honor and glory all the days of their life and eternal fame in ages to come.

Thus there was not much to which the missionaries could appeal. As we shall see, they could accept the values of courage, *triuwe*, and *milte* by ging them new significance.

The missionaries accepted the heathens' respect for courage; but, except in the case of holy wars, they usually stressed the virtue of passive or moral courage, such as that praised by the Stoics and shown by martyrs and ascetics. This new meaning gradually replaced the older meaning of *fortitudo*, which had formerly meant bravery combined with strength.[1] The clergy traditionally looked upon themselves as soldiers of the cross.

We have seen that *triuwe* was owed to the immediate kinship automatically and without oath or contract. The resulting bond, called a *vridu*, was ethically binding for all kinsmen or *vriunde*; and an offense against one's kinsman was judged a blow against the very pillars of society and brought lifelong reproach. Germanic indignation appears in the exceptionally strong language used in relating Cain's fratricide in the previously mentioned Old Saxon and Anglo-Saxon versions of the *Book of Genesis*. The most insidious thing about slaying a kinsman was that it could not be properly avenged: revenge was a family affair which could not be properly invoked against a member of the family. After the Teutons had accepted Christianity, or God's law, a crime against a kinsman was an affront against God. One of the most serious sins mentioned in the *Muspilli*, which will be discussed later, was boundary disputes between kinsmen.

It is interesting to note that the word *vriunde* meant both friend and relative, thus showing that kith and kin or *Bekanntschaft* and *Verwandschaft* were once almost synonymous. In fact, the *Heliand* uses the words *friund* and *mag* (kinsman) as synonyms.[2] It is also of interest that the words *king*, *koning* and *König* are related to the words *kith* and *kin* and thus show that the largest political unit was once the kinship.

The ancient Hebrews had also stressed the family as the foundation of right and justice and had required children to honor their parents. The New Testament, on the other hand, minimized this bond and tried to extend the in-group to include all the faithful. Jesus seldom mentioned ties of blood, except, for example, when he

---

[1] In 1400 Henry Wittenwiler distinguished between the two kinds of courage as "Die sterkeu nimpt man zwifaltkleich: Die erste macht den leibe reich; Die schol man schätzen für kain tugend, Wan oft ein schalk hat die vermugend" (*Ring*, vv. 4744-47).
[2] *Heliand*, vv. 1493-1502.

said that a man should not call his brother a fool and should become reconciled with his brother before making his offering.[1] On the other hand, he told James and John to leave their father Zebedee in his boat and told another of his disciples to leave his father unburied and follow him.[2] He also denied his family when he heard that Mary and his brothers were waiting outside. "Who is my mother?", he asked, "and who are my brothers?... For whoever does the will of my Father in heaven, is my brother, and sister, and mother." [3]

Although most missionaries had abandoned kith and kin in the Lord's service, they nevertheless recognized the family as the basic social and moral unit, just as the heathens did. This fact is revealed in the prominence they placed upon Cain's fratricide in their treatment of the Old Testament story. Nevertheless, they were gradually able, at least in theory, to extend the loyalty owed to the kinship to include a larger segment of humanity: namely, that of all true believers. As vassals of a single celestial liege lord, Christians had to include all fellow believers in God's *vridu*. The *Heliand* states that we should hate no one, since all men are brothers joined in one kinship.[4]

As subsequent history proved, the Church was never able to enforce this view in practice, even after it resigned itself to certain closed seasons, or *trèves de Dieu*, when it was unlawful to wage war against fellow Christians. None the less, the seeds of a Christian fellowship were sown and a crop eventually began to grow. During campaigns against the infidels this brotherhood was actually of some significance; yet it naturally bound only true believers, as long as heathens, heretics, and dissidents remained beyong the pale. Religious bigotry is beautifully expressed in the *Chanson de Roland* in the words, "Pagans are wrong, and Christians are right." [5] In

---

[1] "Ego autem dico vobis, quia omnis, qui irascitur fratri suo, reus erit iudicio; qui autem dixerit fratri suo: Raca, reus erit concilio; qui autem dixerit: Fatue, reus erit gehennae ignis. Si ergo offers munus tuum ad altare et ibi recordatus fueris quia frater tuus habet aliquid adversum te, relinque ibi munus tuum ante altare et vade prius reconciliari fratri tue et tunc veniens offeres munus tuum" (*Matthew*, 5, 22-24).

[2] "Et procedens inde vidit alios duos fratres, Iacobum Zebedaei et Ioannem fratrem eius, in navi cum Zebedaeo patre eorum reficientes retia sua et vocavit eos" (*Matthew*, 4, 21). See *Luke*, 9, 59-60; 9, 61-62.

[3] "Adhuc eo loquente ad turbas, ecce mater eius et fratres stabant foris quaerentes loqui ei. Dixit autem ei quidam: Ecce mater tua et fratres tui foris stant quaerentes te. At ipse respondens dicenti sibi ait: Quae est mater mea et qui sunt fratres mei? Et extendens manum in discipulos suos, dixit: Ecce mater mea et fratres mei. Quicumque enim fecerit voluntatem Patris mei qui in caelis est, ipse meus frater et soror et mater est" (Matthew, 12, 46-50).

[4] "huuand sie alle gebrôðar sint, sâlig folc godes, sibbeon bitengea, man mid mâgskepi" (*Heliand*, vv. 1439-1441).

[5] "Peien unt tort et chrestiens unt dreit" (*Chanson de Roland*, v. 1015).

Crusade literature, no justice or mercy is owed to the unbeliever; and, as late as John Huss's betrayal, oaths did not have to be kept to heretics. Exceptions to this rule appeared in some thirteenth-century court epics, which presented noble Saracens. However, these benighted heathens usually saw the error of their ways and accepted Christianity.

The gradual disintegration of the clan can also be seen in the new attitude toward oaths. In compurgations, or trials by oath, people had naturally sworn by their kinsmen, regardless of the merits of the case. The Christians, on the other hand, brought the novel idea that absolute truth was more important than friendship. St. Martin of Braga, a bishop of the Suebi in Spain, expressed the idea with the words, "Bear witness of truth, not of friendship." [1] Nevertheless, men were still shamed if they did not stand up for their kinsmen. In the *Chanson de Roland* Pinabel volunteers to give oath and to fight for his kinsman Ganelon, who is clearly guilty of treason. When Thierry, the champion against him, tries to persuade him not to fight, Pinabel answers that he wishes to support his kinsman, for he would rather die than be reproached.[2]

The *Heliand* says you should not follow your kinsman when he beckons you into sin, even if he is closely related, but reject him and show him no love so that you can ascend to heaven alone.[3] This is the exact opposite of the view expressed in the sagas. Here the honor of the *vridu* is being sacrificed for the salvation of the individual.

Whereas Germanic society demanded respect for birth and wealth, the Christians taught that God was no respecter of persons and that one should respect all men, not only the rich and strong. As it is commanded in Leviticus, "Thou shalt not respect the person of the poor, nor honor the person of the mighty." The Benedictine Rule, which was the guide for all monastic life, followed the *First Epistle General of St. Peter* in saying that you should honor all men, and the *Heliand* said you should honor poor men.[4]

The *General Epistle of St. James* states, "For if a man with gold rings and in fine clothing comes into your assembly, and a poor man in shabby clothing also comes in, and you pay attention to the one who wears the fine clothing and say, 'Have a seat here, please,' while

---

[1] "Testimonimum veritati, non amicitiae reddas" (Martin, *Formula*, 2,35).
[2] "Ne placet Damnedeu! Sustenir voeill trestut mun parentet; N'en recrerrai pur nul hume mortel; Mielz voeill murir qu'il me seit reprovet" (*Chanson de Roland*, vv. 3906-3909).
[3] *Heliand*, vv. 1492-1502.
[4] "Non consideres personam pauperis nec honores vultum potentis"(*Leviticus*, 19, 15). "eeren alle man – honorare omnes homines" (*Benediktinerregel*, cited from Karg-Gasterstädt, p. 312). "Omnes honorate, fraternitatem diligite, Deum timete, regem honorificate" (*I Peter*, 2, 17). "Êrod gi arme man" (*Heliand*, v. 1540).

you say to the poor man, 'Stand there,' or, 'Sit at my feet,' have you not made distinctions among yourselves, and become judges with evil thoughts?" [1] As we shall see, this view ran counter to Germanic values, which ruled supreme until almost modern times. As long as it was the right of gay clothing to receive êre, it would have been disrespectful to refuse it its due.

Just as the missionaries tried to give a new meaning to *triuwe*, they also sought to give a new meaning to *milte*. Instead of an ostentatious dispensing of wealth in return for service and renown, it should be a sacrifice to God in return for his future rewards. Instead of giving to the strong and wealthy, who can repay in this world with service or goods, one should give to the poor and needy and receive far greater rewards in heaven. In other words, gift-giving was still strictly a matter of *do ut des*, the difference being only in the time, place, and value of the returns.

Whereas Jesus had said that one should give in secret, such a policy would have brought meager revenues from the new converts; and therefore the Church also appealed to those who gave "that they may have glory of men." St. Augustine had already prepared the way in his *City of God* by reconciling the statements, "Take heed that ye do not your alms before men, to be seen of them" with "Let your light so shine before men that they may see your good works, and glorify your Father which is in heaven." Naturally he stressed the fact that you should do your alms to win glory, not for yourself, but for God.[2] Men were admired if they did good works in return for both salvation and worldly fame simultaneously, nor was it necessary to distinguish between the relative weight of the two incentives. The Venerable Bede claimed that Edwin of Northumbria's conversion to Christianity had given him the possibility of winning the kingdom of heaven and also of increasing his kingdom on earth.[3] Even as late as the twelfth century a satire against the clergy could rebuke clergymen for not giving hospitality "for the sake of God or the sake of êre," [4] Both of these incentives were still approved at that late date, even for clergymen.

Instead of a laudable virtue, the desire for fame was a dangerous

---

[1] "Etenim, si introierit in conventum vestrum vir, aureum anulum habens, in veste candida, introierit autem et pauper in sordido habitu, et intendatis in eum qui indutus est veste praeclara et dixeritis ei: Tu sede hic bene: pauperi autem dictatis: Tu sta illic aut sede sub scabello pedum meorum; nonne iudicatis apud vosmetipsos et facti estis iudices cogitationum iniquarum?" (*James*, 2, 2-4).
[2] "Non ergo ut uideamini ab eis, id est hac intentione, ut eos ad uos conuerti uelitis, quia non per uos aliquid estis, sed ut glorificent patrem uestrum, qui in caelis est, ad quem conuersi fiant quod estis" (*City of God*, V, 14).
[3] Bede, XII, p. 281.
[4] "durch got noch durch êre" (*Priesterleben*, v. 88).

fault in the eyes of the monks, who called it *gloriae cupiditas* and considered it the root of much evil. St. John had long since asked, "How can you believe, who receive glory from one another and do not seek the glory that comes from the only God?" [1] While acknowledging that the Romans had suppressed covetousness and other vices through their love of praise, St. Augustine nevertheless considered love of praise to be a vice.[2] Boethius had expressed the nothingness of fame in his *Consolation of Philosophy* by saying of other men's praises: "And if they are justly won by merits, what can they add to the pleasure of a wise man's conscience? For he measures his happiness not by popular talk, but by the truth of his conscience." [3] St. Martin of Braga expressed this view by saying that, if you wish to practice temperance as a means to an honorable life, you should be contemptuous of vain glory.[4] He also wrote a treatise on how to repel vainglory, or *iactantia* as he called it, since glory can be rightly shown to God alone.[5] As we shall see, this idea appeared often in monastic writings. In view of the Germanic values that survive in the *Waltharius*, it comes as a surprise during the gruesome battle when Hagen suddenly begins to declaim against fame and wealth.[6]

Whereas most clergymen viewed the desire for honor as a worldly and distracting evil, some saw in it a tool for Christian purpose, just as *triuwe* and *milte* were. Like Aristotle before him, St. Paul had believed the desire for glory to be a virtue; for his *Epistle to the Romans* claims that God will render eternal life to "them who by patient continuance in well doing seek for glory and honour and immortality." [7] The desire for a good reputation could be justified by Scripture; the *Book of Proverbs* says that "a good name is rather to be chosen than great riches"; *Ecclesiastes* says that "a good name is better than precious ointment", and *Sirach* says that you "should

---

[1] "Quomodo vos potestis credere, qui gloriam ab invicem accipitis et gloriam quae a solo Deo est, non queritis?" (*John*, 5, 44).

[2] "Nam sanius uidet, qui et amorem laudis vitium esse cognoscit" (*City of God* V, 13).

[3] "Quae si etiam meritis conquisita sit, quid tandem sapientis adiecerit conscientiae qui bonum suum non populari rumore, sed conscientiae veritate metitur?" (*De Consolatione*, III, Prose, VI).

[4] "vanae gloriae contemptor" (Martin, *Formula*, 4, 66).

[5] "Id autem est inane laudis studium, quod Graeci *cenodoxiam*, Latini *vanam gloriam* vel *iactantiam* vocant" (Martin, *Pro Repellenda Iactantia*, 1, 16). "Atque ita dum singuli se plus volunt videri quam sunt, gloriam laudis quae soli Deo veraciter debetur hostiliter depraedantur" (*op. cit.*, 2, 37-38). Cf. I *Timothy*, 1, 17.

[6] "vili pro laude cupit descendere ad umbras" (*Waltharius*, v. 871).

[7] "iis quidem, qui secundum patientiam boni operis gloriam et honorem et incorruptionem quaerunt" (*Romans*, 2, 7).

bring no stain upon your honor."¹ Some medieval clerics followed writers like Cicero and Seneca in using the word *honestum* to mean that which should be honored, in other words, moral rectitude. This may be the way in which Einhard, Charlemagne's biographer, understood the word when he said that the Saxons did not consider it *inhonestum* to besmirch or transgress divine or human laws.² On the other hand, he may have meant that they did not think that it brought ill-repute to do so. The Stoic meaning seems more probable when Godfrey of Winchester said that Lady Edith, Edward the Confessor's widow, had as companions *Cultus honestatis* and *sobrietas*.³ The *Moralium Dogma*, a popular twelfth-century compilation of ancient wisdom, even follows the Stoics in believing *honestum* to be a virtue, in contrast to *gloria*, which is a good of fortune.⁴ As we shall see, the word *êre* served for centuries to come as the usual translation of *gloria*, but not for *honestum*.⁵

Perhaps the best presentation of the Stoic definition of *honestum* was in St. Martin's *Formula Vitae Honestae*. This was probably copied directly from Seneca; its style is so like that of Seneca that it was usually attributed to him, for example by Chaucer in his *Tale of Melibee*.⁶ It is noteworthy that St. Martin's work teaches a purely pagan-Stoic moral with no reference to Christian dogma. For him the way to achieve an honorable life is to practice the four cardinal virtues of prudence, magnanimity, continence, and justice, while observing moderation.⁷ Such values may have brought acclaim to a monk, but they would not have brought it to a layman. The Stoic ideal of moderation was foreign to the Teutons, whose early literature usually extolled extremes of deed and passion.

Even though some scholars followed the Stoics in using the word *honestum* in an ethical sense, there is no positive evidence that most medieval laymen or even clergymen clearly understood by the word anything more than that which would bring respect or admiration. The word was most frequently used in its original meaning of

---

¹ "Melius est nomen bonum quam divitiae multae" (*Proverbs*, 22, 1); "Melius est nomen bonum quam unguenta pretiosa" (*Ecclesiastes*, 7, 2); "ne dederis maculam in gloria tua" (*Ecclesiasticus*, 33, 22).
² "neque divina neque humana iura vel polluere vel transgredi inhonestum arbitrantur" (*Vita Caroli Magni*, VII, cited from *Mittellateinisches Lesebuch*, ed. P. Alpers, Gotha, 1929, p. 1).
³ Cited from *British Latin Selections*, ed. R. A. Browne, Oxford, 1954, p. 40.
⁴ "Virtus et honestum nomina diuersa sunt, res autem subiecta prorsus eadem" (*Moralium Dogma*, p. 7, line 12). Cf. "de honesto, id est de virtute cardinali" (p. 79, line 23).
⁵ See Maurer, "Das ritterliche Tugendsystem" and "Zum ritterlichen Tugendsystem".
⁶ Chaucer, ed. Robinson, *The Tale of Melibee*, v. 1067.
⁷ Martin, p. 204. If by *continentia* St. Martin implied sexual continence, this was a Christian substitute for the Stoic ideal of *temperantia*.

respect, or else a token of respect, such as a salutation or benefice or political office. Even those who copied the word in Stoic writings may have understood it merely as the kind of behavior that earns admiration or respect. In Scripture, in which they most often confronted it, the word *honestus* has only objective meaning; and on one occasion the word *honestas* means riches.[1] Whereas Cicero took the liberty of using the word *honestum* to mean the morally good, equivalent to Greek *tò kalón*, he too realized that it really meant that which is popularly esteemed.[2]

The difficulty of interpreting *honestus* is well illustrated in the previously mentioned passage from Saxo Grammaticus, in which Ket and Wig avenge their father by killing the Swedish king Athisl.[3] By a ruse they succeed in accosting Athisl while he is walking alone fully armed. When the youths announce their purpose and Ket challenges the king, the latter warns them against their greed for fame (*laudis cupido*) and advises them to accept an indemnity and to consider it a great honor (*ingens gloria*) to have forced it from so great a king. Ket refuses compensation and insists upon fighting alone, lest it appear that an inglorious battle was fought unequally (*ne manu impari pugna conseri videretur infamis*), for the ancients considered it unequal or unfair (*iniquum*) and without honor (*probrosum*) for two to fight against one. A victory in such a battle was not considered laudable (*laudibilior*) because more infamy (*dedecus*) than glory (*gloria*) seemed attached to it. In fact, for two to beat one was no great accomplishment, but the greatest shame (*maximus rubor*).

When Athisl, noting their youth, offers to fight both brothers at the same time, Ket fears that this would win him reproach (*vicium*). After fighting gently for some time, the king loses patience, fights in earnest, and forces Ket to his knees. Thereupon Wig, ignoring public usage (*publica consuetudo*) lets his shame give way to brotherly love (*pietas*) and aids his brother; and thus they kill the king. By this act Wig wins more opprobrium than praise (*laus*), because he has broken the established laws of dueling; and his assistance seems more useful (*utilius*) than honorable (*honestius*). On the one hand, he favors shame (*indecus*) and, on the other hand, brotherly love (*pietas*); and they both know that Athisl's death has been more swift (*prompcius*) than glorious (*speciosius*).

When they return home, they receive high honors (*primi honores*) from their king, who thinks that they have performed a most useful (*utilissimus*) task and prefers to see the glory (*gloria*) in the death

---

[1] "Bona et mala, vita et mors, paupertas et honestas" (*Ecclesiasticus*, 11, 14)
[2] "Ut enim consuetudo loquitur, id solum dicitur honestum quod est popular fama gloriosum" (*De Finibus*, II, xv, 48).
[3] *Gesta Danorum*, pp. 110-113.

of a rival than the ill-repute (*fama*) of the inglorious deed (*admissum obprobrium*). However, the Danes' bad reputation lasted for years until finally a king's son named Uffe killed two Saxons in a duel. He chose to fight against two simultaneously so that a fresh example of courage might end the Danes' disgrace (*opprobrium*); for fresh fame (*recens fama litura*) would wipe out the accusation (*crimen*) of ancient infamy (*infamia*).

The difficulty of this passage clearly lies in the present ambiguity of the Latin words, for many of its key terms can be interpreted either amorally or morally. Among these are *infamis*, bringing ill-repute – infamous; *iniquus*, unequal – unfair; *probrosus*, bringing ill repute – vicious; *dedecus*, disgrace – shameful deed; *vitium*, reproach – vice; *honestus*, bringing acclaim – honorable; and *crimen*, accusation – crime. If we read the story with only the amoral meanings of these terms, the action is logically motivated and accords with what other Germanic sagas say about honor and revenge. On the other hand, it could be argued that Saxo tried to write modern motivation into the old story. Writing as he did at the turn of the thirteenth century, he could well have been influenced by the School of Chartres; a center of learning which will be discussed. In view of his extensive knowledge of the classics, it is likely that he himself studied in France; yet, except for numerous pious and rhetorical outbursts against sloth, gluttony, and lechery, he generally retains the old Germanic value system intact and praises revenge as a means to wordly approval. The older values are especially well expressed in the eloquent song by Starkad, an old time hero.[1] Our passage obviously concerns reputation rather than moral rectitude, since Uffe can remove all reproach.

This contrast of *honestum* and *utile*, which was derived from Cicero's *De Officiis*, was popular throughout the Middle Ages; yet there is no proof that people understood precisely what Cicero had meant. Most writers seem to have believed an action profitable only if it brought public approval as well as immediate material advantages. This interpretation is suggested by the way that a Swiss poet named Henry Wittenwiler expressed the commonplace at the beginning of the fifteenth century. When one of the peasants in his *Ring* suggests a certain strategy for defeating a hostile village, another spokesman reminds his colleagues that nothing is useful unless it has the *appearance* of honor.[2] Wittenwiler is here following a passage from the

---

[1] *op. cit.*, pp. 204-212.
[2] "Was nicht enhat der eren schein, Daz mag auch nimer nütz gesein" (*Ring*, vv. 6800-6802). Cf. "Itaque Athenienses, quod honestum non esset, id ne utile quidem putaverunt" (*De Officiis*, III, 11). By the time of Aristides the Just, the Greeks had progressed from a shame culture to a guilt culture, yet this topos could still be interpreted on either level. When MHG authors distinguish between *frum und êre* or *nutz und êre*, they are not distinguishing

Moralium Dogma, which borrowed it from the *De Officiis*. It is most significant that, for the purpose of the rime, he can render *honestum* as "the appearance of honor" (*der eren schein*).

In monastic society all offenses against God naturally brought disgrace upon their perpetrators. Therefore disgrace (*schande*) could easily be equated with sin (*sünde*). In fact the two words, which were etymologically related, were often associated in later clerical writings. At first this made little sense to laymen in view of the fact that God approved of numerous causes of *schande*, such as poverty, humility, and failure to take revenge. In *Barlaam and Josaphat*, a somewhat later religious epic, a king loses his *êre* by showing respect to two beggars;[1] and thus we see that humility was a Christian virtue but a secular vice. Although the missionaries disapproved of the Teutons' belligerence, they agreed with them that activity was better than idleness, activity being understood in terms of prayer, church service, and study for the greater glory of God. Realizing that idleness is an invitation to the devil, they joined native tradition in deprecating sloth, which, as *desidia*, became one of the deadly sins. Like many others, St. Martin thought it imprudent to indulge in leisure.[2]

Because their value system opposed that of the heathens, the Christian missionaries often had to compromise. St. Gregory the Great had advised them to adopt as many heathen customs as possible, and consequently they adapted many items of Yuletide and spring fertility rites to Christian use. Far more important, from a cultural standpoint, were the many heathen values absorbed at the same time. This accommodation was not always intentional, for many of the missionaries were of Germanic descent and came from areas only recently converted and were still imbued with older heathen values. St. Boniface, the "Apostle to the Germans", came from a part of England that had been converted scarcely a half century before his birth. It should be remembered that even the Gallo-Romans, by whom most of the Germans were converted, had only a hazy notion of Christian ethics. Many of their bishops, who were almost invariably of the higher nobility, had little understanding of Christian love or fellowship.[3]

between the expedient and the moral, but rather between two worldly values. This is illustrated in the thirteenth-century tale *Meier Helbrecht*: "swer volget guoter lêre, der gewinnet frum und êre; swelch kint sînes vater rât ze allen zîten übergât, daz stât ze jüngest an der scham und an dem schaden recht alsam" (*Helmbrecht*, vv. 331-336).
[1] His vassals say, "ez missezimt, daz unser herre alsus benimt der krône sô grôz êre: daz swachet in vil sêre!" (*Barlaam*, 44, 19-20). The king may have been mindful of St. Paul's advice to the Philippians (2, 3), "In humilitate superiores sibi invicem arbitrantes".
[2] "Nam prudens numquam otio marcet" (Martin, *Formula*, 2, 43).
[3] According to Nora Chadwick (p. 275), the Gallo-Roman Churchmen of the

In the Mediterranean world Christianity first reached the lowly and downtrodden, who found solace in its egalitarian teaching. Thus the early Church Fathers could stress the ethics of humility (or *Sklavenmoral*, to use Nietzsche's term). Because of the feudal society of Northern Europe, the missionaries there first had to win the allegiance of the rulers, who set the policies for their people. Consequently, the missionaries could not come as apostles of an egalitarian religion, which would have had little appeal to those in power. Instead they had to appeal to the tastes of the ruling class and to omit what would offend them, at least until they had established themselves and won ascendancy. As a result of their accommodation, they produced a hybrid ethos that tried to reconcile two diametrically opposed value codes, a code based on honor and shame before men, and a code based on humility before God.

Because the Teutons admired power and success, the missionaries tried to impress them with the power of their God, whom they explained as a mighty and generous liege lord, a rich rewarder of those in his service. The Teutons believed in a magic quality found in certain trees, springs, and other objects of nature that brought health, wealth, or fertility. This quality, which was of divine origin, was also found in people, especially in certain successful dynasties, whose reigning members could heal by their touch or by their mere presence. This belief lasted until modern times in the "king's touch", the royal ability to cure scrofula. Because this power could heal people and animals or make them hale or whole and thus bring *health*, *Heil*, or *prosperity*, people or objects imbued with it were holy or *heilig*, that is to say, health- or prosperity-bringing. In order to make the Christian God palatable to the practical and this-worldly Teutons, the missionaries had to convince them that he was useful, prosperity-bringing, or holy; and thus "holy" became their way of translating *sanctus*. Consequently, the *Spiritus Sanctus* became the Holy Ghost or "prosperity-bringing spirit." The Germans on the Continent had at first translated *Spiritus Sanctus* as "Holy Breath" (*uuiho atum*) but later switched to *heiliger Geist*, probably under the influence of Anglo-Saxon missionaries.

fifth century still belonged at heart to the classical world. "Christianity was a new and important spiritual concern; but one feels that for these men it was almost more a profession than a vocation, certainly not an all-pervading spiritual revolution. There is no sign of spiritual clash or conflict, or readjustment. The new religion was blended and harmonized with the standards already set by a classical training, and a balance was maintained." C. E. Stevens (p. 133) says of the most prominent prelate of that century: "When we find Sidonius supporting such a savagely retributive theory of punishment as leads him to say that the death of a murderer at least affords the satisfaction of revenge to the survivors of the murdered, one begins to wonder whether he understood the lessons of the New Testament at all; such language becomes an old Roman rather than a Christian bishop."

Because of the higher civilization of the Christian missionaries, the heathens were ready to believe that the Christians' one God must be superior to their own many gods. Besides that, he could give everlasting life, a goal which their own gods could not achieve even for themselves, being doomed, as they were, to perish in the *Götterdämmerung*. It is a moot question whether or not the Teutons could immediately grasp the meaning of everlasting life. A missionary who tried to translate the Bible into an African dialect once found that he could come no closer than "long health".

A series of political events helped prove the superiority of the Christian god; for instance, the conversion of the Franks was followed by great military and political success. The Venerable Bede tells how a pagan high priest in Northumbria advised his king to accept Christianity, when he saw how much better the Christians were favored at court than he; for, if the old gods had stood by their champion so poorly, they could not be considered very dependable.[1] In his life of St. Boniface, Willibald tells how, after the pagans killed the saint, the Christians attacked them and despoiled them of their wives and children and servants, with the result that the pagans were convinced of God's strength and embraced Christianity.[2] Some Germanic tribes accepted Christianity upon seeing the successes of their converted neighbors, others accepted it upon being defeated in battle and forced to give allegiance to a Christian ruler and thereby indirectly to his heavenly liege lord too. According to the feudal system, a vassal continued his allegiance to his lord even if his lord changed allegiance from one ruler to another. Thus, when a chieftain acknowledged fealty to the God of the Christians, all his retainers were *ipso facto* Christians, whether or not they had been personally convinced or even informed of the merits of the new order. It is not hard to believe Jan de Vries when he says. "During the first centuries after the conversions, customs were not essentially changed, and the new Christian faith had scarcely exerted any influence on the Germanic soul".[3]

Because of the limited experiences of the Teutons, the missionaries could explain the relation between God and man only through recourse to feudal terminology. God was the powerful and generous troop leader (*druhtin*) who granted his favor (*huld*) to his faithful

---

[1] Bede, pp. 102-103. Cf. "Et cum ipsi, id est christiani, fertiles terras vinique et olei feraces ceterisque opidus abundantes possident provincias, ipsis autem, id est paganis, frigore semper rigentes terras cum eorum diis relinquerunt", *Die Briefe des heiligen Bonifatius und Lullius*, ed. M. Tangl, 1916, p. 40.

[2] Talbot, p. 58.

[3] "...die Sitten haben sich in den ersten Jahrhunderten nach der Bekehrung nicht wesentlich geändert, und der neue christliche Glaube hatte auf die germanische Seele noch kaum Einfluss ausgeübt" (Vries, p. 5).

followers on earth. The new convert acknowledged his homage (*triuwe*) by the act of baptism and was thereafter God's man. The thought of a feudal pact or *triuwe* appears already in the works of St. Martin of Braga. About the year 572, St. Martin, who came from Pannonia and may have been of Germanic origin, referred to conversion as a *pactum* with God, *pactum* being a word often used for the act of homage.[1] The idea of homage is also implied in various baptismal oaths written in the vernacular for new converts, in which the converts had to forswear all service to other gods or demons (*unholden*), as they were called.[2] This concept of God was actually very close to that of the Old Testament, in which Jehovah was a lord of hosts who had made a covenant with his chosen people.

Clovis himself had struck a profitable bargain with God in promising service in return for victory; and he and his descendants remained God's chosen vassals forever after the resulting victory over the Alemanni. Clovis felt this allegiance strongly. Seeing the rich fields of Aquitaine in the possession of the Goths, he was grieved that they belonged to Arian heretics who did not serve the true God of Rome. As God's faithful vassal, he waged a holy war and annexed the province to his own lands, which he held in fief from heaven.

We should not look upon such motivation as hypocritical. Clovis was acting as honestly as was possible with the beliefs and values available to him (or perhaps we should say "correctly", since "honest" is still a controversial word). Centuries after his death the Church still extolled his war as godly and righteous, and nearly four centuries later a poet explained the victory of another Frankish king of the same name in similar terms: God first sends the Northmen against the Franks to punish them for their sins. Then, after the Franks have suffered sufficiently, he calls upon young King Louis to come to his assistance and expel the invaders. God is still pictured as the warlike Jehovah of the Old Testament, who talks directly with his earthly champion. With God's help, Louis saves his people.[3] Five centuries later God again led the Franks, or at least their French namesakes, to victory, this time with the assistance of a mere peasant maid.

Although they professed Christianity, the early missionaries and monks seem to have admired the worldly values they denounced so eloquently. A good example of this contradiction can be found in the preface to the *Gospel Book* of the ninth-century Alsatian monk Otfried, who claimed in a letter to Archbishop Liutbert of Mainz

---

[1] "considerate quale in ipso baptismo pactum cum deo fecistis" (Martin, *De Correctione*, 15, 2-3).
[2] "Farsakis thu unholden? Forsaku. Forsakis thu unholdon uuerkon endi uuillion? Forsaku..." (*Braune*, XLVI, vv, 1-4).
[3] *Braune*, XXXVI.

that he had written this long religious work in order to displace worldly lay songs.[1] In spite of his religious purpose, he shows himself quite worldly in his preface, in which he explains why he has written his book in his Frankish vernacular.... The Greeks and Romans have written in their tongue, he states, so why should the Franks not do so? Are they not just as brave as the Romans and the Greeks? They are intelligent and are bold in field and forest. They are wealthy, very brave, and swift with their weapons; nor are they disgraced by their good land, which is rich in gold and silver and other metals. They are quite able to defend themselves from their enemies. If their enemies dare begin anything, the Franks quickly defeat them. No one who borders on their land can escape having to serve them, and everyone fears them. There is no nation that will fight with them, they have discouraged it and proved it with weapons. They taught them that with swords, not at all with words, with very sharp spears, and that is why they still fear them so. No nation might consider fighting with them, even though it be the Medes or Persians, without it being all the worse for them. I have read somewhere in a book that, by blood and kinship, they are of the dynasty of Alexander, who so threatened all the world and scattered it all with the sword and subjected it to his control with very hard bonds. Like the Macedonians, the Franks will accept no king unless they have reared him at home [2]... And thus this pious, yet patriotic, monk expresses his surviving pagan values.

For vivid descriptions of violence and savagery the converts did not have to delve into the Germanic past, since the Old Testament brought examples enough. Even the fourth-century Christian poet Prudentius supplied an extreme example of violence in his *Psychomachia* or "Soul Battle", which depicts the struggle between the Virtues and Vices. Although the warring ladies are only abstractions, their battle is presented as blood-thirstily as any conflicts in Homer. Moreover, as each Virtue overcomes her corresponding Vice, she exults maliciously over her victim's fate. Thus it appears that Prudentius himself must have had a latent love for brutality and revenge.

The Old Testament also brought much justification for social and economic inequality, especially in the stories of Abram's begetting of Ishmael by the bondswoman Hagar, Esau's selling his birthright, and Noah's cursing Canaan. The guilt of these people naturally passed on to their descendants, the medieval serfs and bondsmen.

---

[1] *Braune*, XXXII, 21, vv. 7–14.
[2] *Braune*, XXXII, 4, I, 1, vv. 57-94. Similar praise appears in Hartmann von Aue's *Gregorius:* "Sîn lant und sîne marke die bevridete er alsô starke, swer si mit arge ruorte daz er den zevuorte der êren und des guotes" (vv. 2263-2267).

Even the New Testament justified inequality. In his epistle to the Romans, St. Paul, says, "Render therefore to all men their dues: tribute to whom tribute is due; custom to whom custom; fear to whom fear; honour to whom honour." [1] In other words, a good Christian has to show honor, as well as submission, to those in power.

Although the Christian missionaries extolled poverty, peace, and meekness, deep in their hearts they still admired the goods of fortune and the warlike virtues cherished by the heathens; and they attributed precisely these qualities to their newly imported God. This may have been in part a concession to public taste; yet these newly converted missionaries seemed to revel in their warlike descriptions. In any case, they presented their God as a rich and powerful king, who delighted in glory and who practiced the virtues of courage, fealty, largess, and revenge.

God's thirst for glory or êre is expressed in St. Martin's account of the fallen angels: "One of these, who had been made chief archangel of all in heaven, seeing himself shining in such great glory, did not give glory to God his creator, but claimed to be his equal; and for this pride he, along with many other angels who had agreed with him, was cast out of that seat in heaven into this air which is under the heavens." [2] The Biblical story is understood somewhat similarly in an episode added to the Anglo-Saxon Genesis, which may have been translated from an Old Saxon source.[3] It did not dismay the Suebi or Saxons that God was so jealous of his glory, since glory, or êre, was a proper goal for a king. Centuries after the conversions, a *MHG* version of the *Chanson de Roland* has Charlemagne invoke God's help with the words, "Gracious Lord, now think of Thy glory (êre) and show Thy strength." [4] The Hebrews had also appealed to Jehovah's pride in their many exhortations to him to do things "for his name's sake". This was logical, since Jehovah had created man for his own glory.[5]

God's courage did not have to be greatly stressed, since he, like many famous wordly rulers, was conceived as an older person who let his vassals fight for him. After defeating Lucifer he really had

---

[1] "Reddite ergo omnibus debita, cui tributum tributum, cui vectigal vectigal, cui timorem timorem, cui honorem honorem" (*Romans*, 13, 7).
[2] "Ex quibus unus, qui primus omnium archangelus fuerat factus, videns se in tanta gloria praefulgentum, non dedidt honorem deo creatori suo, sed similem se illi dixit; et pro hac superbia cum aliis plurimus angelis qui illi consenserunt de illa caelesti sede in aere isto qui est sub caelo deiectus est...." (Martin, *De Correctione*, 3, 3).
[3] In *Heliand*, pp. 211-219.
[4] "Gnaedeclicher herre, nu gedencke an dîn êre. erzaige dîne tugende" (*Rolandslied*, vv. 8417-8419).
[5] "And every one that calleth on My name, I have created him for My glory" (Et omnem, qui invocat nomen meum, in gloriam meam creavi eum, formavi eum et feci eum), *Isaiah*, 43, 7.

little opposition, except when heathens on earth attacked his honor and forced him to call upon his earthly champions, usually the Franks, to defend it. As a generous liege lord, God repaid the service of his earthly vassals with his favor, or *huld*, as it was expressed in feudal terminology. Since God was a dependable oath-keeper, possession of his *huld* was assurance of salvation, that is, of patronage and protection from the devil on the Day of Judgment.

This fact is delightfully explained in an *OHG* alliterative poem called the *Muspilli*,[1] which was scribbled into a theological work in Bavaria toward the end of the tenth century. The poem, which is really a sermon in disguise, warns of the coming Day of Judgment. First it tells how the fate of the individual soul is decided, as soon as it leaves the body, by a struggle between the armies of heaven and hell. Then it tells how God, like a tribal chieftain, convenes his council and summons all souls to judgment. Again there is a trial by combat this time between Elijah and the Antichrist. At last all the dead are resurrected and forced to stand judgment for their sins on earth. Although the poem appears to recall the spirit and substance of Germanic legal customs, it actually follows scripture and theological tradition very closely.

In order to appeal to the this-worldly heathens, the earliest missionaries had taught that God rewarded his worthy vassals in this world. However, since such recompense was not always forthcoming, they gradually shifted the emphasis to the rewards in the world to come. The word *heil* was used not only to designate one's ability to give help, health, or prosperity, but also to designate one's own welfare, luck, or success. In this way it meant about the same as our word *luck* in expressions such as "he was born lucky" or "he just naturally has luck"; for it was an innate quality of the person, not just a momentary smile from Dame Fortune. If a man succeeded, he had *heil*; if he failed, he lacked *heil*; and thus his *heil* exactly equaled his success and also his honor. Because the missionaries taught that the only true prosperity was that of the soul after death, the word *heil* acquired the added meaning of salvation. With man as a reference, *heil* meant welfare or future bliss; with God as reference it meant the ability to bestow, or the bestowal of, welfare or future bliss. Thus, in both cases, it amounted to salvation.

God not only rewarded his friends with *heil* in this and the next world, but also punished his enemies with *unheil* both here and there. The unnecessary cruelty in the later Crusade epics exceeds the usual violence expressed in old Germanic verse, even when heroes ran berserk; for the *furor Teutonicus* tended to be only as intense as military necessity demanded. The almost malicious joy in the

---

[1] *Braune*, XXX.

suffering of the pagans in the Crusade epics may be influenced by the Old Testament, which reveled in the pain inflicted upon the enemy. If this is so, it would be a case where conversion represented a cultural relapse. During the sack of Jerusalem in 1099, God's champions acted just as brutally as their pagan ancestors had ever done a millennium earlier; and nearly three centuries later the Teutonic Knights, as the Virgin Mary's champions, were just as cruel to the Lithuanians.[1]

God was not only warlike, but also rich; and the word *rich* remained his most frequent epithet down until the Reformation. Because we no longer think of God as being rich, many translators render God's attribute *rich* as "powerful" or "almighty". But, this is not necessary, inasmuch as wealth and power were merely two aspects of a single condition. Later, when it was better known that Christ had selected voluntary poverty on earth, his wealth and good birth were borne vicariously by the Virgin Mary, who was always depicted in the finery befitting a regal origin. As a rich ruler, God was generous, and his *milte* surpassed that of any worldly monarch. According to the *Wessobrunn Prayer*, an early Bavarian alliterative poem, God was the "most generous of men", just like Beowulf.[2] More valuable than any stores on earth or even worldly fame was God's favor or *huld*, which brought *heil* or everlasting rewards and glory in heaven.

Perhaps the most pleasing picture of Christ in Germanic literature is in the *Heliand* (i.e., "*Heil*-bringer"), the previously mentioned Low Saxon epic about Christ. Charlemagne, as one of God's many Frankish champions, had done his best to spread Christ's message with fire and sword, even to the extent of baptizing an entire captive army by marching it through the Weser. Total immersion is not total conversion, and there were many backsliders. Charlemagne's successor, Louis the Pious, tried less violent means, such as encouraging the missionaries to explain Christ to the heathens in their own language. A result of this effort was the *Heliand*, a biography of Christ based upon Tatian's harmony of the Gospels. But Christ has suffered more than a sea change, he emerges as a Germanic war lord, surrounded by his twelve trusted thanes, who journeys to and from Nazarethburg in a style fitting his social station. Even though Christ and his heroes are described in literary clichés taken directly from aristocratic-Germanic literary tradition, the message that he teaches follows very closely the word of the Gospels as harmonized by Tatian.

In reading the various references to Christ in medieval epics, one

---

[1] See *Chronicon Terrae Prussiae* for examples of Christian depredations.
[2] "manno miltisto" (*Wessobrunner Gebet*, v. 8, in *Braune*, XXIX); "manna mildust" (*Beowulf*, v. 3181). Cf. "mildi god" (*Heliand*, v. 3239).

will note that Christ and God are one person and that the Holy Ghost is scarcely mentioned. This is surprising in view of the fervor with which the Franks had championed the Trinity in extirpating the Unitarian heresy of the Goths, Burgundians, Lombards, and other Arian landowners. To be sure, catechisms, prayers, and liturgy stressed the three persons of the Deity;[1] yet this dogma made little impression upon the laymen of the West, who were not deeply concerned with the theological niceties that so disastrously plagued the more speculative minds of Byzantium. In any case, down through the *chansons de geste* and the later German Crusade epics, Christ and God are generally one person, who resembles a jealous Jehovah more than a meek Jesus. This is mentioned only to explain why, in the discussion of such epics, the words Christ and God are used interchangeably.

Although Christian dogma denied the value of worldly honor, the entire Church was organized in a complicated hierarchy of honors and dignities; and God's vicars on earth were rightly called dignitaries or *Würdenträger*. The costly garments of the higher clergy were a far cry from sackcloth and hair shirt; yet they could be justified as fitting tokens of respect to a God so jealous of his own glory.

During the late eleventh and early twelfth centuries, after it had become more firmly rooted, the Church made more effort to enforce some of its other-worldly values. This puritanical movement, which centered in the monastery of Cluny in France and is known as the Cluny Reform, affected German literature greatly by damning all worldly values as the works of the Devil. This attitude is well illustrated, for example, in an ascetic work ascribed to a monk named Hartmann, which attributed all wealth and wordly fame to the Devil.[2] The other-worldly values of the Cluny Reform were nothing new, for nearly all the arguments of the *memento mori* tradition can be found, along with Scriptural documentation, in a letter by Boniface, the Anglo-Saxon missionary to the Germans.[3] Christians had always had before them Isaiah's admonition: "Fear not the reproach of men, and be not dismayed at their revilings."[4] Thus the clerics were trying to undermine the very foundations upon which feudal society was based.[5] Needless to say, such works were read mostly by other clerics.

[1] For catechisms, see *Braune*, XLVI. For vivid explanation of Trinity, see *Ring*, vv. 3943-3977.
[2] *Rede vom Glouven*, vv. 1926-1941.
[3] Talbot, pp. 65-66.
[4] "nolite timere opprobrium hominum et blasphemias eorum ne metuatis" (*Isaiah*, 51, 7).
[5] "Targîs vacht umbe êre, Anseîs umbe di sêle, Targîs umbe ertrîche, Anseîs umbe daz himilrîche" (*Rolandslied*, vv. 4719-4722). The author of the *Makkabäer* (I, 5, vv. 57 ff) says that the ancient kings who sought honor for their own sake rather than for God and Israel were sinful.

The extreme asceticism preached by the Cluny movement is expressed in numerous saints' legends, a good example of these being that of St. Alexius, a saint cultivated in many countries. This saint, as a young man, was heir to a throne and was endowed with all the gifts and virtues befitting his rank. Soon after his engagement to a beautiful princess, he began to fear for his immortal soul; and, leaving home and crown and bride, he wandered to the Holy Land, where he suffered untold hardships. Finally, returning as a beggar to his father's house, he lived there under the stairs in voluntary poverty for thirty years without ever revealing himself to his grieving bride or parents.[1] This selfish concern for his own soul was considered most admirable.

Such an austere idea of poverty and renunciation was extolled as an ideal by the Church, which made little effort to evolve a reasonable compromise that people could actually practice. Thus the whole medieval world was a period of dualism, and man was expected to conform to two contradictory ideals. Some poets resolved this dilemma by telling of wealthy and powerful rulers who fought successful wars, amassed great wealth, married beautiful women, and then, just before it was too late, renounced all worldly honor and entered a cloister.

[1] A life of St. Alexius, written in the eleventh century, is the oldest extant piece of French literature. The best German version was written some two centuries later by Conrad of Würzburg.

CHAPTER IV

KNIGHTLY HONOR - THE NATIVE HERITAGE

A worthy man does good things so that people will praise him. TEICHNER, 1, vv. 10-11.

Historians of German literature usually divide the older literature into heroic, ecclesiastic, courtly, and didactic periods. Although convenient, this chronological division is not entirely justifiable, since these were not really periods but rather concurrent movements or traditions. The German courts of the High Middle Ages, being the successors of the ancient tribal courts, inherited an ancient, even if somewhat altered, tradition. Likewise the didactic poets of the waning Middle Ages were continuing an unbroken tradition introduced by the earliest missionaries. The two traditions, heathen-heroic and Christian-ascetic existed concurrently during the entire period.

The fact that the secular code found little written expression during the Cluny Reform is no proof that it had ceased to dominate the thoughts and actions of the secular courts during that period. Both the *Waltharius* and the *Ruodlieb*, for example, reveal an acceptance of worldly values. Even though the clerics preferred to devote their parchments to the Lord's service, there was no shortage of scops and minstrels to entertain the courts with oral tales of worldly courage, success, and honor. This is proved by the emergence of the ancient Germanic themes and values almost unadulterated in the written literature of the thirteenth and fourteenth centuries. As we shall see, the *Lay of the Nibelungs*, which was written down at the beginning of the thirteenth century, expresses the ancient heathen-heroic values almost intact.

To be truly representative of an age, literature must be social. That is to say, it must be sung, recited, or acted before a group of representative people. Such literature must concur with the values of the group, or at least not run counter to them, if the author is not be rejected or ridiculed. Thus the public is a decisive factor in the poet's choice of subject matter and in his manner of treatment. Samuel Johnson once said of playwrights in the eighteenth century: "Ah! Let not Censure term our Fate our Choice, The Stage but echoes back the publick Voice. The Drama's Laws the Drama's Patrons give, For we that live to please, must please to live." [1]

What Johnson said of the dramatists of his day held equally of the court poets of the twelfth and thirteenth centuries, who, as the Swabian poet Hartmann of Aue frankly admitted,[2] wrote what their patrons wanted to hear. Sometimes the poets expressed their own views on the professional honor of poets, for example when Walther von der Vogelweide, medieval Germany's greatest lyric poet, praised the art of Reinmar of Hagenau or when Gottfried praised that of Henry of Veldeke, Hartmann of Aue, Reinmar, Walther, and others.[3] Gottfried of Strassburg, the author of *Tristan*, even paraphrased Cicero in saying that honor and praise create art, since art is created for praise.[4] Despite these few references to their own professional honor, the court poets stressed almost only the aristocratic honor code. It is not unusual for court poets like Hartmann and Wolfram to address their public personally and consult them in various matters; and we may be sure that they seldom deviated far from the values professed by the courts.

The court epics, being a social literary form, were the most important expressions of current concepts of honor. The court lyrics, on the other hand, have very little to contribute to an understanding of that ideal. This is surprising, since the courtly lyric, or *minnesang*, as it was called in Germany, was an outgrowth of feudal custom. As we have seen, it was the duty of a warrior or knight to enhance his liege's honor by fighting for him in battle and serving him at court. By analogy, it was the duty of a court poet to enhance his liege's honor by singing his praise. In other words, he too performed liege-service (*Herrendienst*) by singing vassal-songs, or *sirventes*, as they were known in Old Provencal.

Good birth was particularly stressed in courtly poems, which were written for wellborn people jealous of the privileges due their rank. The old Germanic distinction between free and unfree status played little part in most courtly verse, which distinguished more between courtly and boorish manners and between aristocratic and common birth. In the *Lay of the Nibelungs*, on the other hand, the tragedy begins when Brunhild scorns Kriemhild as a bondswoman (*eigen diu*) because she believes Siegfried a vassal. Hartmann's *Poor Henry*, which will be discussed at some length, is an exception among

---

[1] *The Poems of Samuel Johnson*, ed. D. N. Smith and E. L. McAdam, Oxford, 1941, p. 53.
[2] "daz man gerne hoeren mac, dâ kêrt er sînen vlîz an" (*Iwein*, vv. 26-27).
[3] Walther, 83, 1-13; *Tristan*, vv. 4619-4818.
[4] Êre und lob diu schepfent list, dâ list ze lobe geschaffen ist" (*Tristan*, vv. 21-22). "Honor alit artes, omnesque incenduntur ad studia gloria" (Cicero, *Ad Tusculanum*, 1,4). In the *Inferno* (I, v. 87), Dante says that Vergil's beautiful style has brought him honor (lo bello stile che m'ha fatto honore).

courtly epics in having its hero marry a peasant girl. However, it is clear that she is of free birth;[1] and it is to be remembered that the work, although courtly in style, is religious in intent.

Despite all Church teachings to the contrary, the upper classes continued to assume that only nobly born people are capable of virtue.[2] As the hero of Conrad of Würzburg's epic *Engelhart* says to Dietrich, "I should have detected without any doubt from your virtue that you were of noble and distinguished birth."[3] As in the earlier Germanic sagas, a man's honor could be smirched only by his social equal, and he did not have to accept the challenge of a man of inferior birth. Also, the shame of defeat was all the greater if the victor had no high rank. This fact is illustrated in *Erec*, an Arthurian romance by Hartmann of Aue, at the turn of the thirteenth century. When the hero of this tale defeats Guivreiz and Mabonagrin, they are relieved to learn that he is well born.[4] Rudolf of Ems also claimed that the disgrace of defeat is greater if the victor has no "high name".[5]

The Church taught the equality of all men before God; yet it never convinced the upper classes that God did not prefer the wealthy and wellborn. This fact is indicated by Rudolf of Ems in his *Good Gerhard*, when he boasts that the church endowed by Gerhard accepted only princes as canons.[6] Hildegard of Bingen explained that she had only noblewomen in her convent because it would be a crime against God to mix the classes, like mixing cattle, asses, sheep, and goats.[7] This may be an echo of Leviticus, which says, "You shall not let your cattle breed with a different kind."[8] God himself continued to be described as wealthy, and *rîch* was his standard epithet. Wolfram expresses this sentiment when he tells God that he is his kinsman, "I poor, and Thou very rich."[9]

Throughout the High Middle Ages wealth continued to be a major source of honor, provided that it was not hoarded but shared

---

[1] Her father was a "vrîer bûman" (*Armer Heinrich*, v. 269).
[2] See Bopp, p. 36.
[3] "ich möchte ân allen zwîfel gar an dîner tugent hân gespurt daz dû waere von geburt edel gar und ûz erkorn" (*Engelhart*, vv. 1480-1483). Cf. "ir tragt geschickede unde schîn, ir mugt wol volkes herre sîn" (*Parzival*, 170, 22-23).
[4] *Erec*, vv. 4514-4534, 9339-9365.
[5] "hohen namen" (*Willehalm von Orlens*, v. 11,1417).
[6] "er nam ze kôrherren dar niht wan der fürsten süne gar" (*Gerhard*, vv. 191-192).
[7] "Et quis homo congreget omnem gregem suum in unum stabulum, scilicet asinos, oves, haedos, ita quod non dissipet se?" (*Migne, Ser. Lat.* Vol. 197, Column 338). She then goes on to prove that God is really a respecter of persons.
[8] "Iumentum tuum non facies coire cum alterius generis animantibus" (*Leviticus*, 19, 19).
[9] "ich arm und dû vil rîche" (*Willehalm*, I, v. 18).

generously. Not only the heroic ethos, but also Christian dogma taught that the value of money lay in its expenditure, as Thomas Aquinas avowed.[1] Words referring to wealth remained among the most frequent in descriptions of worthy knights. Even the most ideal of the courtly poets stressed the ignominy of poverty. Wolfram lets Gurnemanz, Parzival's teacher in courtly matters, tell him to succor those in want, particularly men of gentle birth, who have lost their wealth and therefore contend with shame.[2] Christian charity has progressed enough here, at least towards one's social equals, to change scorn into pity; yet poverty is still considered a disgrace.[3]

In Hartmann's *Gregorius* the abbot advises his poor young friend not to aspire to knighthood, for "if you have won the rank of knight, then you will needs be ashamed of your poverty. Now what will your knighthood avail you, if you do not have the power of wealth?"[4] His contemporary, Gottfried of Strassburg, lets Tristan say that, if he had great wealth, he "would not be ashamed to be called a knight";[5] and on another occasion he uses the word *scham* almost as a synonym for poverty.[6] Elsewhere he describes the ideal knight as handsome, faithful, courageous, generous, and rich,[7] and he says that two things make a man, his person and his wealth.[8] Hartmann expressed the prevailing view, in saying that the beautiful, but impoverished, Enite "lacked nothing but wealth to be a praiseworthy woman".[9] Conrad claimed that a nobleman can not be *wert* if he is poor and that he loses his *wirde* if he has no money.[10] On the other hand Rudolf of Ems, another bourgeois poet, maintained that a sufficiently wise and brave man can achieve praise in spite of

---

[1] "usus pecuniae est in emissione ipsius" (cited from Sombart, p. 13).
[2] "der kumberhafte werde man wol mit schame ringen kan (daz ist ein unsüez arbeit): dem sult ir helfe sîn bereit" (*Parzival*, 170, 29-171, 2).
[3] Three centuries later the Middle Scots poet Weddirburne could still write: "Thairfoir thow sowld richt prudently perpend The danger The dishonor and defame Off povertie or ane mischevous end" (*Bannatyne MS*, IV, 100, vv. 71-73).
[4] "dû hâst gewunnen ritters namen: nû muostû dîner armut schamen. nû waz touc dîn ritterschaft, dû enhetest guotes die kraft?" (*Gregorius* vv. 1665-1668).
[5] "daz ich mich ritterlîches namen noch er sich mîn niht dörfte schamen" (*Tristan*, vv. 4407-4408).
[6] "in fremdem lande êre unde gemach unde schame in vater rîche" (*Tristan*, vv. 11,600-11,601).
[7] "des lîbes schoene und wunneclîch, getriuwe, küene, milte, rîch" (*Tristan*, vv. 249-251).
[8] "zwô sache enmachen einen man: ich meine lîp, ich meine guot, von disen zwein kumt edeler muot und werltlîcher êren vil" (*Tristan*, vv. 5700-5703).
[9] "und waere sî gewesen rîch, so gebraeste niht ir lîbe ze lobelichem wîbe" (*Erec*, vv. 333-335).
[10] "sô mac vil kûme ein edelman wert gesîn in kranker habe. an hôher wirde gêt im abe, swenn er des geldes niht enhât" (*Engelhart*, vv. 270-272).

poverty,[1] but it is to be noted that Rudolf was not a true court poet. Dietrich of Bern, or Theoderic the Great as he was known in German popular epics,[2] continued to receive honor when he was expelled and impoverished by a rival king, and somehow he retained his epithet of "the rich".[3] Nevertheless, when he confesses to Rüdeger that he has lost his wealth, Rüedeger exclaims, "Alas for the great shame." [4]

Worthy and shamefaced heroes were always embarassed by their poverty. Because he has less money, Parzival does not think it fitting to use the familiar form of address in speaking to his own wealthy brother.[5] In the story *Peter of Staufenberg* the hero refuses the king's daughter because "she is free by birth. It would be unfitting for her to marry a poor man like me." [6] Here poverty is contrasted with freedom, which was essential for enjoying honor. Even though wealth could come and go, it was usually felt to be an integral part of the person, just as health, beauty, and intelligence are still felt to be. Today we compliment a person by saying, "You are very beautiful" or "You are very clever"; but we do not say, "You are very wealthy". In the Middle Ages, on the other hand, "rich Sir" and "rich Lady" were perfectly proper modes of address. Despite much clerical moralizing, which will be discussed, poverty continued to merit shame, as Thomas Hobbes observed in the seventeenth century.[7] Otherwise no one would have bothered to say that poverty is no disgrace (*Armut ist keine Schande*). Perhaps the older attitude toward poverty lingered longest in the contempt felt by propertied people in the South of the United States toward the "po' whites".

Stricker, a thirteenth-century aphorist, expressed the prevailing view, in complaining that lords were going with poor women;[8] and clerics defended the inequitable distribution of wealth as an

---

[1] "Wie menic ander notic man Ritters pris alda gewan Der siner armut niht engalt, Er wäre also wis und also balt Das man im hohes prises jach" (*Willehalm von Orlens*, vv. 7741-45).
[2] The term "popular epic" (*Volksepos*) is commonly used to designate less polished epics usually dealing with native themes. Because they deal with native rather than classical or Arthurian matter, they are also called "national epics". The *Lay of the Nibelungs* is a "popular epic" with regard to matter, but a "courtly epic" with regard to style.
[3] "der rîche" (*Dietrichs Flucht*, v. 4774).
[4] "owê der grôzen scham" (*ibid.*, v. 4776).
[5] "bruoder, iuwer rîcheit glîchet wol dem baruc sich: sô sît ir elter ouch dan ich. mîn jugent unt mîn armuot sol sölcher lôsheit sîn behuot, daz ich iu duzen biete, swenn ich mich zühte niete" (*Parzival*, 749, 24-30).
[6] "wan sü ist von gebürte fri: ez were ir ungezeme daz sü mich armen neme" (*Rittermaeren*, vv. 890-892).
[7] "Riches, are Honourable; for they are Power. Poverty, Dishonourable" (*Leviathan*, X).
[8] "armiu wîp" (Stricker, p. 61, v. 263).

inviolable part of the divine scheme. Throughout *MHG* literature the admirable knight is almost invariably wealthy, and in many epics the word *rîch* is the most frequent complimentary adjective. Just as *guot* (wealth) is usually associated with *êre*, *rîch* is often associated with *êrlîch* (honorable).[1] Whereas poverty normally indicated failure and was therefore shameful, voluntary poverty was honorable, provided the public knew that the beggar had formerly been rich but had renounced worldly wealth for heavenly rewards. Naturally it was no great performance for a poor man to renounce the world. Consequently, most European saints, like Buddah and Josaphat before them, were recruited from the wealthier classes of society, regardless of what Scripture says about the difficulty encountered by rich men and camels.

As we have seen, the *Epistle of St. James* says not to show respect to someone because he is rich; yet thirteenth-century society considered it poor taste not to do so. In the *Lay of the Nibelungs*, when Etzel's messengers come to Worms, the people of the city see that they are rich and therefore open their gates to them.[2] Whereas St. James had preached against showing deference to fine clothing, men of the High Middle Ages thought otherwise. Riding through a forest, the hero of the popular epic *Wolfdietrich* finds a well-dressed corpse and exclaims: "Alas, hero! Your fate troubles me. You may well be noble. Silken are your clothes." [3] Although the logical connection is not expressed explicitly, it is easy to see the causal relationship. Because he wears silk he is noble and deserves more sympathy. And hence the great emphasis upon clothes throughout the Middle Ages.

Today, when we say that clothes make the man, we do so with a note of irony and disapproval. But not so with medieval poets. Just as a man's wealth was an integral part of his person, his clothes were an outward and visible sign of his inner worth. The *Poetic Edda* had stated the view bluntly by saying, "The naked man is naught," [4] and most later medieval poets concurred. Gottfried was perfectly sincere in saying that Tristan's person and his clothing made a chivalrous man, and this explains why honor-seeking Tristan

---

[1] "reich und erber" (*Erzählungen aus altdeutschen Handschriften*, ed. A. v. Keller, Stuttgart, 1855, p. 334, v. 5).
[2] "daz si vil rîche waren, daz wart da wol bekant. man schuof in herberge in der wîten stat zehant" (*Nibelungenlied*, 1176, 3-4). While preparing to confront Brunhild and demand precedence, Kriemhild tells her ladies that, to free her of shame, they must show their good clothes and thus prove that her husband is not a bondsman: "Nu kleidet iuch, mîne meide... ez muoz âne schande belîben hie mîn lîp. ir sult wol lazen schowen, und habt ir rîche wat. si mac sîn gerne lougen, des Prünhilt verjehen hât" (*Nibelungenlied*, 831, 1-4).
[3] "dîn kumber ist mir leit; du macht wol edele wesen: sîdîn sint dîniu kleit, (*Wolfdietrich*, A, 563, 3-4).
[4] *Hovamol* 49, in *Poetic Edda*, p. 38.

wore unusual clothes.[1] When a poet occasionally praises a women in spite of her rags, as Hartmann does in the case of Enite, this does not diminish the importance of elegance. Quite to the contrary; being attractive in poor apparel is convincing proof of beauty. Whereas expensive clothes won honor from people in general, they won honor from the ladies in particular. After describing the gorgeous trappings worn by Feirefiz, Wolfram explains, "The unbaptized hero strove for women's reward. That is why he bedecked himself so beautifully. His lofty heart compelled him to strive for worthy love."[2]

Today we are bored by the interminable descriptions of wealth in the *MHG* epics; yet the public of the time must have liked them, or else the poets would not have produced them. This is particularly true in the case of clothing, and we can only feel sympathy for the doughty heroes of the courtly epics who had to wear so many costly garments at one time just to win the approval of their peers or of their authors' public. Clothes had to be costly and they had to be changed often and be discarded after one wearing. For the trip to Brunhild's land, Gunther and his friends in the *Lay of the Nibelungs* have to change their clothes three times a day in order to avoid *schande*; and for their return Kriemhild must attire her ladies so that they will receive *lob* and *êre*.[3]

The descriptions of expensive clothing not only enhanced the status of the heroes in their public's eye, but also brought vicarious pleasure to the public, of whom few had ever worn, or even seen, such finery. The detailed descriptions of extravagant festivals were not merely settings for the action; they were an intrinsic part of the narrative material. This is indicated in the opening verses of the *Lay of the Nibelungs*, in which the poet promises his public that they will hear marvels not only of heroes and battles, but also of joys and festivals (*fröuden, hôchgezîten*).

The poets of the High Middle Ages continued to praise power just as their heathen predecessors had done.[4] Even after the Church had preached for centuries against violence, poets still acclaimed aggressive rulers; and the epithet "the Great" has been bestowed on more conquerors than pacifists. Most medieval, writers, even clerical

---

[1] "der êregire Tristan truoc sunderlîchiu kleider an" (*Tristan*, vv. 4999-5001); "sîn geschepfede und sîn wat die gehullen wunneclîche enein: si bildeten under in zwein einen ritterlîchen man" (*Tristan*, vv. 11,102-11,105).
[2] "Der ungetoufte gehiure ranc nâch wîbe lône: des zimierte er sich sus schône. sin hôhez herze in des betwanc, daz er nâch werder minne ranc" (*Parzival*, 736, 20-24).
[3] "daz ich selbe vierde ze vier tagen trage ie drîier hande kleider und alsô guot gewant, daz wir âne scande rûmen Prünhilde lant" (*Nibelunbenlied*, 360, 2-4). "die suochen ûz den kisten diu aller besten kleit, sô wirt uns von den gesten lob und êre geseit" (*Nibelungenlied*, 568, 3-4).
[1] Cf. "Er het den wunsch der êren... man vorhte sîne sterke" (*Nibelungenlied*, 723, 1-4).

ones, praised aggressive rulers and even delighted in their violence. It is not surprising that a popular epic, like the *Lay of the Nibelungs*, praises Siegfried's resolve to pillage the castles and lands of the Saxons, even though that naturally inflicted untold sufferings on the innocent peasantry.[1] On the other hand, it does seem strange when a clerical writer, like Suger, praises Louis VI of France in the twelfth century for punishing his enemies by depopulating their lands, ruining them with fire, and exposing them to plunder.[2]

Notwithstanding centuries of clerical questioning, might was still right; and victory in battle or duel counted as God's will. The strongest man was still the most valuable, and *vrum* could still mean brave as well as useful. Likewise, *tiur* could mean either strong or worthy, as is evident in Hartmann's most courtly epic, *Iwein*. After the hero of this work has killed a knight named Askalon, the latter's widow, Laudine, needs a husband to preserve her land and her honor from King Arthur, who is reported to be approaching. Lunete, her lady-in-waiting, finally persuades her to marry her husband's slayer by convincing her that he must be more *vrum* and *tiur* than the man he has slain.[3] Similarly, in Rudolf of Ems's *Alexander*, after Alexander has conquered Darius, the latter's mother says that Alexander might well be their lord, since God has let him conquer a man whose honor no one has yet taken.[4] In general, those are *tiur* who have *wirde* or *werdekeit*, as Rudolf states elsewhere.[5] In other words, those who enjoy honor are *tiur*. If a poet sings a woman's praises, she becomes more *tiur*. That is, she becomes *getiuret*, as we can see in a plaint by Walther.[6] The *MHG* verb *swachen*, which literally meant "to weaken" also meant "to diminish one's honor". Even the modern German verb *kränken*, which originally meant "to make sick or weak", now means to insult or offend. As Thomas Hobbes observed, "reputation of power is power." [7]

Although some romances had their knights-errant set out to kill

---

[1] "mit roube und ouch mit brande wuosten si daz lant" (*Nibelungenlied*, 176, 3); "ich gelege in wüeste ir bürge und ouch ir lant" (*Nibelungenlied*, 885, 3).
[2] *The Portable Medieval Reader*, ed. J. B. Ross, The Viking Press, 1956, p. 268.
[3] *Iwein*, vv. 1819-1970.
[4] "dû maht wol unser herre sîn, wan dir die gote hânt gegebn ein alsô saelderîchez lebn daz dû betwungen hâst den man dem êre nieman an gewan" (*Alexander*, vv. 7774-7778).
[5] The "tursten" are those who "in der hoehesten wirdi swebent" (*Willehalm von Orlens*, v. 2132).
[6] "Ich hân ir sô wol gesprochen, daz si maneger in der welte lobet: hât si daz an mir gerochen, owê danne, sô hân ich getobet, daz ich die getiuret hân und mit lobe gekroenet, diu mich wider hoenet" (Walther, 40, 19-25). Henry of Morungen uses the same argument: "dîne redegesellen die sîn swie si wellen, guoter worte unde guoter site, dâ bist du getiuret mite" (*Minnesangs Frühling*, 146, 23-26).
[7] *Leviathan*, X.

dragons and to succor damsels in distress, others let theirs ride out frankly in order to find a fight. In the *Lay of the Nibelungs*, Siegfried journeys to Worms and challenges Gunther to fight for their two kingdoms. Later he leads the Burgundians against the Saxons, partly as service to Kriemhild, partly through sheer love of fighting. In the courtly epics, too, the hero is praised for his love of fighting, which is not necessarily justified by any ideal higher than the desire for renown. In Hartmann's *Iwein*, the hero explains that he has journeyed forth to find a fight in order to win praise and glory. Then, after he has defeated and severely wounded Askalon, he must pursue and kill him so as to have some trophy with which to parry Sir Kay's mockery at court.[1] Even religiously tinged works of the High Middle Ages made no apology for military expansion: Wolfram does not make Feirefiz justify himself, when he boasts that he conquered with his hand whatever land was good. [2]

As in pagan days, victory always indicated right and was decided by God. When Erec defeats Yders, by whose dwarf he was slapped, he taunts his victim with the fact that God has willed his victory.[3]

Honor was still shown to the victor, regardless of the nature of the conflict; and defeat brought shame, no matter how courageously the loser had fought or against what odds. As Rudolf expressed the idea, "No one ever lost honor when he won the victory." [4] In *Moritz of Craun* the Trojans begin to lose their *êre* as soon as Hector falls, even though they continue to fight bravely.[5] In Ulrich of Zatzikhoven's *Lanzelet*, after Iweret has made a noble resistance, Lanzelet defeats and kills him and thereby deprives him of his life and *êre*.[6] Because *êre* was so often associated with victory and *schande* with defeat, they could often be used as replacements for those words.[7] Since defeat brought dishonor, a man who risked his

---

[1] *Iwein*, vv. 1062-1074.
[2] "swelch lant was werlîch unde guot, daz twang ich mîner hende" (*Parzival*, 771, 12).
[3] *Erec*, vv. 965-985. Cf. "Good fortune (if lasting,) Honourable; as a signe of the favor of God" (*Leviathan*, X).
[4] "vil wênec iemen êre vlôs, dô er aldort den sic erkôs" (*Alexander*, vv. 2565-2566). Cf. "unde wirt er denne sigelôs, sô ist er imer êrenlôs" (*Lamprechts Alexander*, vv. 6501-6502).
[5] "Dô aber Ector gelac, dô swachete ir êre tegelîchen sêre" (*Moriz von Craun*, vv. 46-48). Cf. "die dâ heten maht und êre wurden ze Troje gieniedert sêre. dâ Trojâ gewunnen wart, si wurden dô gelastert hart" (*Welscher Gast*, vv. 3395-3398).
[6] "ê er im haete benomen beidiu lîp und êre" (*Lanzelet*, vv. 4554-4555). In a poem by Stricker one king says of another: "der râche erwinde ih nimmer, unz ich im sîn êre benim" (Stricker, p. 3, vv. 30-32).
[7] E.g., *êre* equals victory in a joust, *Parzival*, 460, 13; *schande* equals defeat, *Parzival*, 359, 26. Goethe attributes the same values to the Italian Renaissance when Tasso, in speaking of tournaments, says: "Des Siegers Ehre, des Besiegten Schmach" (*Tasso*, II, 1).

life in battle also hazarded his honor. In the *Chanson de Roland*, although the pagan emir has fought nobly, the queen tells the king that he has died in great dishonor.[1] Four and a half centuries later Edmund Spenser expressed the same view in his *Fairy Queen*. When the Saracen chief Sans Foy fights nobly but loses, the poet adds, "There lies he now with foule dishonor dead."[2] Spenser's contemporary, Montaigne, was most advanced in believing that it can be just as honorable to fight (*combattre*) as to win (*battre*).[3]

Today's literature and popular fancy usually contrast life and honor in battle: the hero who dies nobly preserves his good name, even in defeat. The general who makes a wrong decision and needlessly sacrifices his men can vindicate himself by dying bravely, and the admiral who has blundered can save his honor by going down with his ship. This was not so in the Middle Ages, when defeat brought shame. It will be noticed that the ancient Teutons who sought death in unsuccessful battle did not win glory but merely escaped a life of shame. Likewise, in courtly poetry it was assumed that defeat brought dishonor. When Iwein offers to fight in a trial by combat for a young princess who has been wronged by her older sister, the young princess says she would rather be burned than have such an honored man lose his life and honor for her.[4] Wolfram is afraid Gawan will lose his *êre* if he fights Parzival; and Hartmann's Erec is afraid he will suffer disgrace as well as death if defeated by Guivreiz.[5] In the *Lay of the Nibelungs* Brunhild warns Gunther that he will lose honor and life if she beats him in their contests; and Hagen later warns the Burgundians that they will lose honor and life if they accept Kriemhild's invitation.[6]

Poets of the High Middle Ages still endorsed the ancient view that death with honor is better than a life of shame. In Hartmann's *Erec*, Mabonagrin would rather die than let his honor perish;[7] and in Hartmann's *Gregorius* the young hero thinks it better to die defending his mother than to live in shame.[8] Nearly two centuries

---

[1] "a si grant hunte" (*Chanson de Roland*, v. 3643).
[2] *Fairy Queen*, II, 24, 4.
[3] "Le vrai veincre ha pur son rolle l'estour, non pas le salut; et consiste l'honur de la vertu a combattre, non a battre" (*Montaigne*, II, p. 260). In the *Ackermann aus Böhmen* (xxxiii), God says: "Darumb, klager, habe ere! Tot, habe sige!
[4] "ê ein sus gêret man den tôt in mînem namen kür oder sîn êre verlür, mîn lîp und unser beider lant waeren bezzer verbrant" (*Iwein*, vv. 7304-08).
[5] "laster und den tôt" (*Erec*, v. 4408).
[6] "ir muget wol hie verliesen die êre und ouch den lîp" (*Nibelungenlied*, 425, 3); "ir muget dâ wol verliesen die êre und ouch den lîp" (1461, 3). See also 1774, 2148, 2150.
[7] "ob ich mit êren sterbe dan an den êren verderbe" (*Erec*, vv. 9364-65).
[8] "mir ist lieber daz mîn lîp bescheidenlîche ein ende gebe dan daz ich lasterlîchen lebe" (*Gregorius*, vv. 2064-2066).

later the Swiss poet Henry Wittenwiler still maintained that it is better to die frightfully for honor than to live in shame.[1] This mode of expression probably went back directly to the previously mentioned statement attributed by Tacitus to his father-in-law Agricola: *honesta mors turpi vita potior*.[2]

All captives of war lost their *êre*, which then passed to the victor; for only free men could enjoy *êre*. This fact explains why, when the hero of Rudolf's *Good Gerhard* ransoms some prisoners, they thank him for giving them "honor, wealth, and life".[3] Captivity brought contempt and shame, regardless of its cause. In *Lanzelet* the Queen fears that Walwein and Erec will lose their *êre* if they surrender themselves to Malduc, even though they are doing so voluntarily and out of loyalty to their king.[4] It was amazingly modern of Francis I, after being captured at Pavia in 1525, to say, "All is lost save honor." (Tout est perdu, fors l'honneur).

We have seen that the ancient Teutons could win complete honor only if they had a strong kinship; and this view seems to have lingered for centuries. After living for thirteen years as Etzel's wife and brooding over her injured honor, Kriemhild wishes to invite the Burgundians to visit her in hope of getting revenge. As a pretext, she tells her husband that she is afraid his subjects may think she is in exile and has no kinsmen.[5] The Burgundians are naturally of high-born condition.[6] This does not necessarily mean that they are of ancient lineage, as later poets might have said, but rather that they are a powerful dynasty and therefore innately endowed with its might and virtue. Walther, who often wrote from a more modern perspective than his colleagues, argued that friends are more important than kinsmen. It is a greater honor to win friends than to inherit relatives, and they help more when needed.[7] However, the older attitude toward kinship continued to prevail in literature.

When Parzival's widowed mother takes him to the forest and lets

---

[1] "Won besser ist nach weiser ler Fraisleich sterben um die er Dann mit schanden leben" (*Ring*, vv. 6831-32).
[2] *Agricola*, 33. In the *Chanson de Roland* (v. 1091), Roland says, "Melz voeill murir que huntage me venget".
[3] "wan dû uns wider hâst gegeben êre guot lîp unde leben" (*Gerhard*, vv. 2783-2784).
[4] *Lanzelet*, vv. 4013-4014.
[5] "ich hoere mîn di liute niwan für ellende jehen" (*Nibelungenlied*, 1403, 4); "die Hiunen wellent waenen daz ich âne vriunde sî" (1416, 3).
[6] "von arde hôhe erborn" (*Nibelungenlied*, 5, 1).
[7] "Man hôhgemâc, an friunden kranc, daz ist ein swacher habedanc: baz gehilfet friuntschaft âne sippe. lâ einen sîn geborn von küneges rippe: er enhabe friunt, waz hilfet daz? mâgschaft ist ein selbwahsen êre: so muoz man friunde verdienen sere. mac hilfet wol, friunt verre baz" (*Walther*, 79, 17-24). Cf. "ezn habe deheiniu groezer kraft danne unsippiu geselleschaft" (*Iwein*, vv. 2703-2704).

him grow up apart from his kinship, she is doing him a grave injustice. Only after he has finally been reunited with his kinsmen is he truly a man. It is symbolic that all his worldly and otherworldly knowledge is gained from kinsmen. When Parzival kills the Red Knight with his javelin, his moral guilt is not so much that he has killed a fellow human being, or even a fellow Christian, but rather that he has killed a kinsmen, even though he is unaware of the relation. His confessor, Trevrizent, makes it clear that his sin was parricide, not just homicide.[1] Throughout the Middle Ages and down to modern times a foundling suffered dishonor because of his lack of kinsmen. Gregorious leaves home after his foster mother has reviled him for having no relatives, and one of his reasons is the disgrace he has suffered from her reproach.[2] Since honor depended largely upon kinship, it was inadvisable to marry a women without relatives, as Henry Wittenwiler could attest as late as the beginning of the fifteenth century.[3]

Primitive Germanic society recognized only two distinct classes: the free and the unfree. Among the free, those with the greatest wealth, power, and influence had the greatest *êre*; and the leader of the most powerful dynasty was called king. By the High Middle Ages, on the other hand, free men had been divided into a complicated gradation of ranks, such as emperor, king, prince, duke, count, marquis, and baron, each of which enjoyed a particular degree of honor. Although honor emanated directly from the rank, it lasted, in theory, only as long as merited. When Cundrie comes to King Arthur's court to denounce Parzival for failing to ask the vital question at the Grail Castle, she says: "King Arthur, you used to stand high above your peers in praise. Now your rising fame is sinking, your great dignity is limping. Your high praise is declining, your fame has proved itself false. The great fame of the Round Table has been crippled by the company given it by Sir Parzival, who also bears the mark of knight there."[4] A similar situation obtains in Hartmann's *Iwein* when Lunete denounces the wayward husband. "I shall inform these gentlemen," she says, "that they are to consider you from now on a perfidious (*triuwelôs*) man... and the king can disgrace himself if he keeps you any longer in the rank

---

[1] "dû hâst dîn eigen verch erslagen. wiltu vür got die schulde tragen, sît daz ir bêde wart ein bluot, ob got dâ reht gerihte tuot, sô giltet im dîn eigen leben" (*Parzival*, 475, 21-25).
[2] "daz ein ist diu schande die ich von itewîze han" (*Gregorius*, vv. 1490-91).
[3] "Ist sei ungefreund und arm, So hast du wirser nie gevarn" (*Ring*, vv. 2961-2962).
[4] "Künc Artûs, du stünde ze lobe hôhe dînen gnôzen obe: dîn stîgender prîs nû sinket, dîn snelliu wirde hinket, dîn hôhez lop sich neiget, dîn prîs hât vâlsch erzeiget. tavelrunder prîses craft hat erlemt ein geselleschaft die drüber gap hêr Parzival, der ouch dort treit diu ritters mâl" (*Parzival*, 315, 1-10).

of knight, since *triuwe* and *êre* are dear to him."[1] Nevertheless, the Church taught that a Christian must show honor to his superiors without exception, be they good or bad, as St. Paul preached in his *Epistle to the Romans*.[2] Realizing that many rulers did not merit honor, St. Thomas Aquinas said one should honor them because of the dignity they enjoy as God's ministers, for by honoring them one honors the community they represent.[3]

In theory every free man, including a free peasant, had more honor than any unfree man, regardless of his wealth or function. As the didactic poet Hugo of Trimberg expressed the view, a "free peasant is the equal of lords except that he has no wealth."[4] However, during the High Middle Ages an unfree class of warriors and administrators, the *ministeriales*, reached prominence and began to enjoy more honor than the free peasantry, who were gradually lumped together with the unfree peasantry and serfs. Much, if not most, courtly literature was written by this new class of *ministeriales*, and consequently it places great stress on noble rank and the respect due to it.

Only the nobility was tolerated at court, and the words courtly (*höfisch*) and noble (*edel*) were practically synonymous. For the nobility, honor could be won only at court or in the service of the court; and therefore the Latin word *honestus* could be used to render the word *höfisch*. The love manual of Andreas Capellanus, *Liber de Arte Honeste Amandi*, is rightfully called *The Art of Courtly Love*, since the kind of love he advocated was certainly neither honest nor honorable, in the modern sense of the words. The older order, in which landed peasants were socially equal or superior to the landless *ministeriales*, is portrayed in Schiller's *William Tell*, in which the pesasants Melchtal and Stauffacher seem to enjoy more dignity than Gessler, the envious Austrian governor.

As we have seen, in ancient Germanic days courage was the greatest virtue and cowardice was the greatest vice and the most seriously punished crime against the kinship. The custom of hanging cowards and shirkers or drowning them in the bogs seems to have lasted for a millennium; in Wolfram's *Willehalm* all the French

---

[1] "nû tuon ich disen herren kunt daz sî iuch haben vür dise stunt vür einen triuwelôsen man... ouch mac der künec sich iemer schamen, hât er iuch mêre in rîters namen, sô liep im triuwe und êre ist" (*Iwein*, vv. 3181-3189).

[2] "Reddite ergo omnibus debita, cui tributum tributum, cui vectigal vectigal, cui timorem timorem, cui honorem honorem" (*Romans* 13, 7).

[3] "Dicendum quod si praelati sint mali, non honorantur propter excellentiam propriae virtutis, sed propter excellentiam dignitatis, secundum quam sunt Dei ministri. Et etiam in eis honoratur tota communitas, cui praesunt" (*Summa Theologicae*, II, II, 103, 1, ad. 2).

[4] "Ein frî gebûr ist herren genôz: Alein er sî des guotes blôz, Doch ist er von gebürte frî" (*Renner*, vv. 1407-1409).

knights who refused to take part in the campaign are declared without rights (*rehtelôs*) and are disgraced by having a sack and rope tied on them.[1] The charge of cowardice continued to be the most serious reproach.[2]

Like their heathen ancestors, the courtly knights had to express "high spirits" (*hôher muot*) in order to enjoy honor, high spirits being the surest indication of one's success or prosperity. Naturally the churchmen still damned high spirits, which they considered *superbia*, since only the poor in spirit were truly blessed. This was incongruous to the laymen, who could not distinguish between blissful and blessed, both of which were expressed by the word *sælec*, a word which most often meant fortunate. Despite the teachings of the church, laymen continued to envy and admire their more joyful fellows and scorn those who sorrowed.[3] The word *êre* contrasted with the word *leid* not only in its sense of insult but also in its sense of suffering.

As feminine influence increased at court, the term *hôher muot* expanded to include the joy of the court at large rather than merely the pride, arrogance, and self-reliance of successful individuals. As we shall see, *hôher muot*, or *fröude* as it was often called, prevailed at the courts where the fairest ladies presided. It was precisely this quality that endeared King Arthur's court to the poets.[4] Despite the new meaning acquired by the term in courtly language, the original meaning continued, one might say predominated, even in the works of the most courtly poets. In Eilhart of Oberge's *Tristrant*, Tinas intercedes for the guilty hero by telling King Marke to consider his *hôher muot* and let him live;[5] and in this case the term designates magnanimity born of superiority. Walther advises the German princes to be soft toward their friends but to show *hôhgemüete* to their enemies,[6] in which case the term means haughtiness or arrogance. In Gottfried's *Tristan* King Marke advises his nephew to be *hôchgemuot* toward rich and powerful people.[7] Parzival is not alone when he rides through the forest: he is accompanied by his *hôher muot*, which is so courageous that it should be praised by women. Perhaps courtly poets used the term *hôher muot* most fre-

---

[1] *Willehalm*, 185, 7-19.
[2] *Rechtsalterthümer*, II, 206-208.
[3] See *Willehalm von Orlens*, vv. 4117-4120. Cf. "Sît daz nieman âne fröide touc" (Walther, 99, 13). Perhaps sorrow was confused with the sin of *tristitia*.
[4] See *Iwein*, vv. 31-58.
[5] "Dorch iuwern hôhen muot lâzit den wîgant genesin!" (*Tristrant*, v. 4014).
[6] "sît gegen friunden senfte, tragt gein vînden hôhgemüete" (Walter, 36, 12).
[7] den armen den wis iemer guot, den rîchen iemer hôchgemuot (*Tristan*, v.v. 5029-5030).

quently to designate the vital joy experienced when enjoying honor, especially honor won by success in war or love.[1]

Whereas the Church urged all Christians to devote their energies to prayer and good works, knighthood demanded that, to win honor, a knight must ever exert himself in warfare or else in hunting and tournaments as practice therefor. In theory a knight could win worldly glory and God's grace by righting wrongs, but there was more opportunity to engage in ordinary local war and plundering expeditions. Nevertheless, inactivity brought infamy. Sir Kay, the comical contrast-figure to the ideal knight of the Round Table, prefers *gemach* (indolence) to *êre*,[2] even though that brings him shame.[3] Freidank says only a sluggard would wish a soft life without *êre*,[4] and Gottfried states that *gemach* is the death of *êre*.[5] When Gregorius wishes to ride out in search of adventure instead of remaining in the cloister as the abbot wishes, he says he could not obey the abbot unless he preferred indolence to honor.[6] The contrast of *êre* and *gemach* was a favorite topos in courtly literature.[7]

Triuwe, which remained an important factor in the literature of the High Middle Ages, was still motivated chiefly by desire for approval, as was the case in Tacitus's day. A thousand years after Tacitus, the German version of the *Song of Roland* stated that Roland's heroes "were of such a disposition that they sought death rather than leave their lord through any peril of battle and not bring him from the fray with *êre*." [8] The same is true of the popular

---

[1] "diu guoten(women)gebent hôhen muot: ir lôn ist êre umbe guot"(*Moriz von Craun*, vv. 413-414). The word *guot*, which appears to belong to the world of minstrelsy, seems to be here only for the sake of the rime. When Kriemhild sees Etzel's wealth and power, her anticipation of power raises her spirits: "des wart dô vroun Kriemhilde vil wol gehoehet der muot" (*Nibelungenlied*, 1347,4).
[2] "ze gemache ân êre stuont sîn sin" (*Iwein*, v. 76).
[3] *Helbling* (I, vv. 43-47) says a wealthy man wins *schem* rather than *êre* if he looks for *gemach*.
[4] "Der fûle gert niht mêrè wan senfte leben ân êre" (*Freidank*, 92, 9-10).
[5] "gemach daz ist der êren tôt" (*Tristan*, v. 4430).
[6] "wolde ich gemach vür êre, sô volgete ich iuwer lêre" (*Gregorius*, vv. 1677-1678).
[7] "verlegeniu müezekeit ist gote und der werlte leit" (*Iwein*, vv. 7171-72). *MHG* often denoted erotic indolence as "sich mit wîp verligen". An important motif of Hartmann's *Büchlein* is the conflict between sloth and honorable activity. "swer nâch êren wil streben, er muoz gemaches sich begeben" (*Moriz von Craun*, vv. 443-444). "Sô sprichet lîchte ein boeser man, der mannes herze nie gewan, 'wir sun hie heime vil sanfte belîben, die zît wol vertrîben vil schône mit wîben" (Heinrich von Rugge in *Minnesangs Frühling*, 98, 27-31). "si (*êre*) kumt den êregernden man mit gemache selten an" (*Alexander*, vv. 14,979-14,980). Thomasin repeats all commonplaces about sloth in knights (*Welscher Gast*, vv. 7706-7820).
[8] "die helde wâren sô gemuote daz si ê suhten den tôt denne si durch dehainer slachte nôt chômen von ir herren, sine brêchten in mit êren von dem volcwîge" (*Rolandslied*, vv. 7874-7889).

epic *Laurin*, in which Dietrich must save his vassal Witege, who has been downed by the dwarf, or he will suffer *schande*.¹ As Tacitus mentioned, a Germanic warrior had to bring back the slain even when the battle hung in the balance, or else he would lose his honor. The *Jómsvíkings Saga* tells how a hero named Bjorn retrieved the corpse of a friend to keep it from being desecrated by the enemy. "Then Bjorn got hold of the dead man and put him on his back and returned with him to his men. He did that mostly for glory's sake."² Not only the Norse poets, but even idealistic poets of the High Middle Ages frankly admitted that such brave deeds were done to win praise. In Wolfram's *Willehalm* the hero must save his nephew's corpse from the enemy. "If I leave you here behind me through fear," he says, "no greater reproach (*unprîs*) ever happened to me."³

In the *MHG* tale *St. Oswald*, the pagan king casts Oswald's raven into prison after having promised him safe conduct. His daughter thereupon rebukes him for having broken his word, "You will always suffer disgrace for that. If he loses his life during your truce (*vride*), it will be bad for your reputation and you will ever suffer infamy (*laster*) because of it wherever people sing or tell of it. People will say you have become faithless (*triuwelôs*) and that you will never be the fellow of worthy men."⁴ A century later Rudolf of Ems let Alexander tell his vassals that they would suffer reproach and disgrace if they broke their faith,⁵ and he also let his hero William warn that any man who breaks his word will be *triuwelôs* and without honor.⁶ This would imply that *triuwelôs* did not mean "faithless" so much as "convicted of faithlessness". It is the condition one suffers when a superior "speaks against his loyalty" or "speaks against his honor".⁷

In the *MHG* version of the *Secreta Secretorum*, Aristotle says to Alexander, "If you wish to have *êre*, take care not to break your

---

¹ "neinâ, du vil kleiner man,... lâ den helt geniezen mîn: jâ ist er mîn geselle, daz wizze, swer dâ welle, und ist mit mir ûz komen, würden im solhiu pfant (his hand and foot) genomen, des hête ich iemer schande, swâ man ez in dem lande seite von dem Bernaere. daz waeren mir hertiu maere" (*Laurin*, vv. 383-394).
² *Jómsvíkings*, p. 61.
³ "ob ich dich lâze hinder mir durch vorhte hie, sus grôz unprîs geschach mir nie" (*Willehalm*, 71, 14-16).
⁴ "des muost du iemêre schande haben! verluset er in deme vride daz leben sîn, daz stât übele an den êren dîn unde muost sîn ouch iemêre laster haben, wâ man ez sol singen oder sagen: man sprichet, du sîest worden triuwelôs, unde wirst niemêre deheines biderben mans genôz" (*Oswald*, vv. 1008-1014).
⁵ "brechent die ir triuwe an mir, daz laster und die schande ist ir" (*Alexander*, vv. 14,553-14,554).
⁶ "Brichet er danne die warhait, So muos er iemermere Truwelos sin und ane ere" (*Willehalm von Orlens*, vv. 9494-9496).
⁷ "an sîne triuwe sprichet" (*Tristan*, v. 6365). "und sprach im an sîn êre" (*Iwein*, v. 112). "ir sprechet alze sêre den ritern an ir êre" (*Iwein*, vv. 167-168).

triuwe. Let your oath always be steadfast."¹ Hartmann of Aue says that no man can be completely worthy (*vrum*) without *triuwe*; and Rudolf of Ems maintains that all who are *getriuwe* are called children of honor.² Eberhard Cersne says, "Whoever maintains *triuwe* can grow old with *êren. Triuwe* wins great praise and gives manifold pleasure (*freude*)".³ Both Rudolf and Boppe, a thirteenth-century didactic poet, say that *triuwe* is a garment of *êre*.⁴ Conrad of Würzburg says it is its foundation, and Henry Wittenwiler says it is its key.⁵ Both Boppe and Conrad, using allegorical language, associated Lady *Triuwe* with Lady *Ere*; but it is to be noted that Lady *Ere* represents objective honor, since she can take high praise away from people.⁶

Consequently, the worst fate that could befall an *êre*-seeking hero was to be accused of breaking his *triuwe*, regardless of his guilt or innocence. It is a blow against Iwein's honor to be accused thus, and he even goes mad as a result.⁷ Perhaps it is symbolic that Iwein, while without honor, lives like a wild beast; for it had been a commonplace that honor was the quality that distinguished a man from an animal, as Simonides had told Hiero so many centuries earlier.⁸ Likewise, Parzival refuses to appear at King Arthur's court after being accused of breaking his word.

Triuwe, in the sense of feudal obligation, could force people to act against their personal wishes and thus furnished the tragic motive in many medieval epics. Scholars of German literature often see in this dilemma a typically German motive, which they explain as a

---

¹ "hute dich ouch vil sere, wiltu haben ere, daz du icht brechst die truwe din. din gelubde laz stete sin" (*Secreta Secretorum*, vv. 1143-1146).
² "daz niemer ein wol vrum man âne triuwe werden kan" (*Iwein*, vv. 3179-3180); "Aelle die getruwe sint Nemmet man der eren kint" (*Willehalm von Orlens*, vv. 11-12).
³ "wer an sich haldit truwe vil, der mac eren werden alt. truwe irwerbit hoen prys, sye gebit liebe menigfalt" (*Minne Regel*, vv. 689-692). Cf. "daz (getriuwe sein) ist zen êren uns gewant" (*Nibelungenlied*, 1211, 4).
⁴ "Truwe, zuht, beschaidenhait sind der eren beste klait" (*Willehalm von Orlens*, vv. 3404-3405). "Diu triuwe ist ein kleit der êren" (Boppe, cited from Vollmer, p. 18).
⁵ "es ist der êren fundament unde ein hort der saelikeit, daz man triuwe in herzen treit und swaz der man versprichet, daz er daz niht enbrichet" (*Partonopier*, vv. 6442-6446). "Die treuw ein schlüssel ist der er" (*Ring*, v. 4714).
⁶ Lady *Ere* is with Ladies Erbarmeherzekeit, Triuwe, Staete, Bescheidenheit, Güete, Milte, Schame, Mâze, Zuht, Kiusche, Wârheit, Minne, and Kunst (*Klage*, 9,1-12,7). "Frou Êre im hôhen prîs beneme, diu lûter und diu blîde, und allez lop daz im gezeme von fluche er ïmmer lîde" (*Klage*, 29,5-8). Reinmar von Zweter (71,3-6) associates Êre with a similar list of personified virtues.
⁷ "ein slac sîner êren" (*Iwein*, v. 3204).
⁸ Henry Wittenwiler echoes this view by saying that we should not live like dogs, "den kain er ist worden chunt" (*Ring*, v. 2850).

conflict of duties, or, to use Schiller's terminology, a struggle of duty (*Pflicht*) against inclination (*Neigung*). As the prime example of this tragic conflict they often cite a scene in the *Lay of the Nibelungs*, in which Rüdeger's fealty to Kriemhild compels him to fight against the Burgundians, who are now his kinsmen, because one of them has just married his daughter. Rüdeger's dilemma is surely great when he begs Kriemhild to free him from his obligation and even offers to return all her gold and silver and castles. When she persists, he has to fight his kinsmen and is killed by the very sword he has given his new son-in-law.

But is this really a conflict of duties, as so many scholars maintain, or even a choice between duty and inclination? Rüdeger's real dilemma lies in the fact that he will lose his good name, no matter what he does, since it was dishonoring to break either feudal or familial bonds. He himself acknowledges this fact when, in his anguish, he says, "All people will reproach me".[1] This situation may be typically Germanic, but it is to be noted that Friedrich Panzer traced this whole episode to a French source. Ogier, Rüdeger's prototype, is afraid he will never have honor again in any land [2] and thus suffer like Beowulf's faithless followers. Hartmann's Iwein suffers a similar dilemma when he is honor-bound to remain and defend his host from a giant but also to hurry to the aid of Lunete, whom he has promised to champion in a trial by combat. He will be dishonored if rides away, yet he will be disgraced if he remains, and in either case he will be considered a coward.[3]

Whether *triuwe* was due, in modern parlance, to ethical motivation or to hope of acclaim and fear of reproach, it was nevertheless a deterrent to misdeeds. In Gottfried's *Tristan and Isolde*, the heroine's mother says that by killing Tristan they will violate their *triuwe* and their *êre*.[4] In this case *triuwe* probably means reputation for trustworthiness, for the word was often used, along with *êre*, to designate a good which one must forfeit if one breaks one's word.[5] Gradually the term *triuwe*, under influence of religious concepts, acquired

---

[1] "mich schiltet elliu diet" (*Nibelungenlied*, 2154, 3). Cf. "in schalt diu werlt gar" (*Erec*, v. 2988).
[2] "Jamais honor n'auroie nul jor en nul pais, Ains seroie honis, dolereus et mendis" (cited from Panzer, *Studien*, p. 67).
[3] "ich bin, als ez mir nû stât, gunêret ob ich rîte und geschendet ob ich bîte" (*Iwein*, vv. 4884-4886). "sô hânt sî des iemer wân daz ich dês lîbes sî ein zage" (*Iwein*, vv. 4912-4913).
[4] *Tristan*, vv. 10,211-10,215. The mother says they cannot kill him because she has taken him into her *fride* (v. 10,220).
[5] Rüdeger uses the word this way when he says that he will lose his *triuwen* and *zühte* if he attacks the Burgundians (*Nibelungenlied*, 2153, 3). According to Werner Bopp (p. 33), the word *tugent* could mean praise or public recognition for praiseworthy behavior. In this case it was a synonym of *êre* and an antonym of *schande*.

sentimental and spiritual overtones. In religious and amatory verse it gradually lost its primary meaning of truce, oath, or feudal bond and began to connote loyalty, devotion, sincerity, and sympathy.[1] These new meanings are particularly frequent in Wolfram's works; yet he too continues to use the word in its older feudal sense as well.

We have seen that every Christian had to maintain his *triuwe* to God as his liege lord; and therefore it followed that he should maintain his *triuwe* to God's other vassals too. Thus *triuwe* could be considered a service to God, no matter to whom it was shown. Rudolf lets William of Orléans remind his vassals that they owe him fealty and that they cannot be esteemed of God or of the world for half a day without *triuwe*.[2] This helps explain Rüdeger's great dilemma at the close of the *Lay of the Nibelungs*. If he fulfills his feudal *triuwe* to Kriemhild by fighting the Burgundians, he will break the *triuwe* which he owes to them as friends, guests, and kinsmen; and thus he will lose his soul,[3] since God has granted him *triuwen* and *zühte*.[4] Wolfram confirms the religious sanction of *triuwe* by saying that, although many believe that poverty has no value, "if anyone suffers it through *triuwe*, his soul will escape hell's fire."[5] Because breach of faith brought loss of good name, one could validate an oath by pledging either his *triuwe* or his *êre*.[6] In formulas meaning "on my honor", honor was understood as an external yet very real possession, more important than life itself, which was forfeited by a breach of faith.

Largess remained an important virtue in the High Middle Ages, and poets continued to stress its practical function. Time and time again the poets tell that the admirable donor is distributing his wealth to impress and obligate the recipients. When King Arthur celebrates Lanzelet's victory over Valerun, much is consumed for the sake of *êre*; and the same thought is expressed more explicitly

---

[1] Vollmer, p. 141.
[2] "Ir herren, ir sint gemant Der truwe das ich bin genant Iuwer herre, ir mine man, Und gedenket wol dar an Das niemen ainen halben tac Ane truwe werden mac Gotte noch der welte wert" (*Willehalm von Orlens*, vv. 8695-8701). The poet of the *Klage*, a sequel to the *Lay of the Nibelungs*, says of Kriemhild: "sît si durch triuwe tôt gelac, in gotes hulden manegen tac sol si ze himile noch geleben. got hât uns allen daz gegeben, swes lîp mit triuwen ende nimt, daz der zem himelrîche zimt" (*Diu Klage*, vv. 571-576).
[3] "daz ich die sêle vliese, des enhân ich niht gesworn" (*Nibelungenlied*, 2150, 3).
[4] "Aller mîner êren der muoz ich abe stân, triuwen unde zühte, der got an mir gebôt" (*Nibelungenlied*, 2153, 2-3).
[5] "swer die durch triuwe lîdet, hellefiwer die sêle mîdet" (*Parzival*, 116, 17-18). Cf. "îr vil getriulîcher tôt der vrouwen wert die hellenôt" (*Parzival*, 128, 23-24).
[6] "Ich gibe iu mîne triuwe und sicherlîche hant, daz ich mit iu rîte heim in iuwer lant. ich leit' iuch nâch den êren oder ich gelige tôt" (*Nibelungenlied*, 2340, 1-3).

when Arthur opens his treasure rooms so that people might praise him all the better.[1] Lanzelet and Guinevere also spend generously for praise and fame.[2] In the *Lay of the Nibelungs*, Siegfried's parents can well acquire *êre* with *guote*.[3] One might contend that *guote* in this context meant goodness, but the succeeding verses make it clear that the *guote* was material wealth. The same can be conjectured of similar passages in other works in which this fact is less evident, as, for example, in *Moriz of Craun*, whose exemplary hero bought praise and *êre* with many kinds of *guot*.[4] Like many other poets, Walther praised this practice by stating that King Philip should know how one wins praise and *êre* with gifts.[5] As we shall see, a worthy knight was expected to give the minstrels wealth in return for praise, that is, *guot umbe êre geben*.

Poets often revealed the commercial nature of *milte*. We have seen that Kriemhild's uncle advised her to buy *êre*; and it is clear that her lavish gifts are given in return for service. The *Lay of the Nibelungs* presents numerous passages which show that all service is in direct return for previous gifts; and even Rüdeger must fight his friends because he has received gold, silver, and castles.[6] In *Salman and Morolf*, a twelfth-century minstrel epic, Morolf wisely advises his king, "Give the heroes your red gold, and then they will follow me into peril wherever I carry the flag."[7] In *Duke Ernst*, another minstrel-epic of the time, the generous duke gives treasures freely and thus makes everyone beholden (*hold*).[8] Although the word *hold*

[1] "dâ wart durch êre vil verzert" (*Lanzelet*, v. 5404); "der künic Artus wolte brechen sîne treskammeren umbe daz, daz man in lobete dester baz" (vv. 5596-5598).
[2] "er hâte vil durch ruom gegeben" (*Lanzelet*, v. 5670); "dâ mite beharte siu wol ir êre ze vlîze" (v. 5742).
[3] "die mohten wol bejagen mit guote michel êre; des teilte vil ir hant" (*Nibelungenlied*, 29, 2-3).
[4] "mit maneger slahte guote er koufte lop und êre" (*Moriz von Craun*, vv. 1642-1643).
[5] "dir ist niht kunt wie man mit gâbe erwirbet prîs und êre" (Walther, 19, 21-22).
[6] Seeing Rüdeger approach, Hagen says: "an uns wil dienen Rüedeger sîne bürge und sîniu lant" (*Nibelungenlied*, 2173,4).
[7] "gip den helden dîn golt sô rôt: war ich den vanen kêre dar volgent sie mit in die nôt" (*Salman*, 376, 3-5).
[8] "machte er im die werlt holt er ensparte silber noch daz golt vor keinen sinen eren" (*Herzog Ernst*, v. 153). The same sentiment is expressed in *König Rother* (vv. 146-148): "sie waren dem kuninge alle holt; daz machete silber unde golt daz er in kunincliche gab". King Oswald also reminds his vassals that they owe him allegiance because he has rewarded them well: "ir sult mir triuwe erzeigen wande ir sit alle min eigen – darzuo gibe ich iu richen solt, beide silber unde daz golt, ich wil iu lihen unde geben, die wile ich han daz leben" (*Oswald*, vv. 1551-1556). In *Lanzelet* (vv. 1212-1216), when Galagandreiz has been killed by his daughter's lover, she assembles his vassals and says: "sît mîn vater nu ist tôt, sô ist daz erbe an mich komen. ich schaffe gerne sînen vromen, swer mir triuwe erscheinet und mich von herzen meinet".

had begun to acquire sentimental and spiritual overtones, it still meant basically "obliged" and remained the usual term to designate the obligated status of those who accepted *milte*. It is not merely their rime that makes the words *hold* and *gold* appear together so painfully often in MHG poetry, for example, not less than nineteen times in the *Lay of the Nibelungs*.

Germanic hospitality remained famous in Germany long after it was praised by Tacitus. In his essay *Of Honour* of ca. 1596, Robert Ashley wrote that in "Germanie, and in the low Countreyes to banquett and feast their friends often ys thought a great and magnificent thing, though not so in other places."[1] The German poets of the High Middle Ages revealed the practical purpose of hospitality, and without disapproval. In *Lanzelet*, when Gilimar escorts his guests from his castle, as Tacitus said a Germanic host should do, he does so "for his own honor".[2] In Wolfram's *Willehalm*, when the noble merchant Wimer invites Willehalm to stay with him, he frankly says that he is doing it so that his peers will praise him;[3] and, when Willehalm takes his leave, he assures his host that he will have honor.[4] Later he says it is difficult to find hospitality because his pack horses have brought no gold, or else people would be better disposed (*hold*) toward him.[5] In the *Lay of the Nibelungs*, Gunther serves good food to his guests in order to avoid reproach;[6] and, after the Burgundians have visited Rüdeger, the host's generosity is related far and wide.[7] When Liudeger's ambassadors dare not refuse Gunther's gifts, this suggests that his generosity was motivated in part by a will to superiority.[8] Hospitality enhanced the prestige of the host at the expense of the guest, and therefore Erec, being a most shamefaced young knight, blushes with shame when

---

[1] Ashley, p. 53.
[2] "durch sîn selbes êre" (*Lanzelet*, v. 6630).
[3] "mich dunket unverlorn, swaz ich iu zêren biute: gewert ir mich des hiute, her nâch giht ieslîch mîn genôz, daz mîn prîs sî worden grôz" (*Willehalm*, 131, 2-6). Cf. 135,15.
[4] "iuwer güete ist an mir worden schîn: des wirt gehoehet noch iuwer prîs" (*Willehalm*, 135, 14-15). Thomasin says, if a guest is not worthy of hospitality, at least the hosts have honored themselves: "ist sîn ein vrömeder man niht wert, si habent sich selben geêrt" (*Welscher Gast*, vv. 379-380).
[5] "trüegen mîne soume golt, sô waeret ir mir alle holt" (*Willehalm*, 140, 1-2).
[6] "In der hôhgezîte der wirt der hiez ir pflegen mit der besten spîse. er hete sich bewegen aller slahte scande" (*Nibelungenlied*, 309, 1-3).
[7] "dô wart dâ getân von des wirtes milte daz verre wart geseit" (*Nibelungenlied*, 1691, 3). The *Spruchdichter* Spervogel later alluded to his generosity by saying, "Dô der guote Wernhart an dise werlt geborn war;, do begonde er teilen al sîn guot. do gewan er Rüedegêres muot, der saz ze Bechelaeren und pflac der marke mangen tac: der wart von sîner frümekeit so maere" (*Minnesangs Frühling*, 25,34-26,5).
[8] "dine torsten niht versprechen" (*Nibelungenlied*, 166, 3).

he has to ask Enite's father for hospitality.[1] Walther also declared that a guest must be ashamed of his dependent position.[2]

The poets of the High Middle Ages often attest the public nature of honor and disgrace. Brunhild is not dishonorable when Siegfried deflowers her, but only after Kriemhild reveals the fact in public. Tristan and Isolde do not lose their honor when they commit feudal and marital infidelity, but only after their misbehavior becomes generally known. Even the little lass in Walther's *pastourelle*, "Under the Linden", would be ashamed of her folly only if someone knew.[3] As Friedrich Maurer mentions, one could be dishonored only in public;[4] or, as Walter Gehl said of the ancient Teutons centuries before, the basis of all morality was society.[5] The external nature of medieval honor is suggested by the etymology of the German word *unbescholten*, which now means "irreproachable" but originally meant "unreproached". A knight with a quick sword was seldom reproached, regardless of his conduct; and he remained *unbescholten* as long as no one dared offend him. The same is suggested by the French term *sans reproche*, which now means "irreproachable" but formerly meant "without reproach". The same is true of "blameless", which now means "not meriting blame" but formerly meant "not suffering blame, unblamed".

In the twelfth-century Latin dialogue *Salomon et Marcolfus*, it is the wise Salomon, not the facetious Marcolf, who says, "It is better to suffer damage in secret than disgrace in public."[6] Elsewhere he says, "There are many who do not know how to feel shame."[7] Such indifference to public opinion struck the Germans as the most grievous character fault possible; and their greatest opprobrium was the epithet *verschamt* (shameless), which, strangely enough, had the same meaning as the modern word *unverschämt*. The most virtuous man was the one most concerned with his reputation, since it was his concern with fame and good name that made him practice the virtues.

[1] "'her, mir waer herberge nôt' diu bete machte in schamerôt" (*Erec*, vv. 302-303).
[2] "wirt unde heim sint zwêne unschamelîche namen: gast unde herberge muoz man sich vil dicke schamen" (Walther, 31,25-26).
[3] "Daz er bî mir laege, wessez iemen (nu enwelle got!), sô schamt ich mich" (Walther, 40,10-12).
[4] "...zur Entehrung gehört die Öffentlichkeit..." (Maurer, *Leid*, p. 19); "Zur *ere*, zum Ansehen, zur Anerkennung des Ritters (und der Dame) gehört die Gesellschaft, die Öffentlichkeit" (p. 49).
[5] "Die Gesellschaft ist die selbstverständliche Grundlage altgermanischer Sittlichkeit" (Gehl, p. 20).
[6] "Melius est habere dampnum in abscondito quam verecundiam in publico" (*Salomon et Marcolfus*, p. 8, line 8).
[7] "Multi sunt qui verecundiam habere nesciunt" (*Salomon et Marcolfus*, p. 10, line 18).

Scholars often minimize the thirst for fame in the Middle Ages in comparison with that in the Renaissance. In his edition of Chaucer's *House of Fame*, F. N. Robinson says that Chaucer's "concern with the behavior of Fame and the circumstances of human reputation is something different from the craving for worldly immortality which is held, rightly or wrongly, to have distinguished the men of the Renaissance."[1] C. W. Previté-Orton seems to accept the importance of fame in the Renaissance; for he says that the humanists of the Renaissance considered fame among men "the best reward and the desire for it no excusable infirmity but the most laudable of motives."[2]

On the other hand, Frederick Artz claims that "Petrarch is modern in his almost childish desire for earthly fame."[3] Thus he considers modern the very desire for fame that Previté-Orton considers a most laudable motive among the Renaissance humanists, of whom Petrarch was surely one. As we shall see, a craving for wordly immortality was common to the entire Middle Ages, and the desire for fame was no excusable infirmity, but the most laudable of motives. Castiglione's *The Courtier*, perhaps the best expression of Renaissance attitudes, contains scarcely a statement about honor that had not been anticipated in the thirteenth century.

Artz's belief that Petrarch was "modern" in his desire for earthly fame seems to echo Jacob Burckhardt's misleading chapter on "Modern Fame" in his *Civilization of the Renaissance in Italy*, which declared such a desire to be an innovation of the Renaissance.[4] Actually, most of the phenomena that Burckhardt thought characteristic of the Renaissance had appeared in medieval Europe too, as this study has shown. Dante's yearning for the poet's laurel wreath was nothing new; for Gottfried had been concerned with it a century earlier.[5] Likewise, German poets had long looked upon themselves as the proprietors and propagators of their lieges' honor and fame.[6] Because Burckhardt claimed that northern Europe had

[1] *Chaucer*, ed. Robinson, p. 331.
[2] C. W. Previté-Orton, *The Shorter Cambridge Medieval History*, Cambridge, 1952, II, p. 1108.
[3] F. Artz, *The Mind of the Middle Ages*, New York, 1953, p. 342. Elsewhere he says, "A youth who joined the order of chivalry... (had to have)... a high sense of honor, a conception unknown to the ancients" (p. 344). Here it would appear that Artz is referring to inner integrity. However, on the same page he says that a knight often had "an absurd desire for glory and sense of honor that made him haughty and contentious," and this would suggest that he used the term "sense of honor" in an objective sense.
[4] Burckhardt, pp. 170-180.
[5] "lôrzwî" (*Tristan*, v. 4637); "lôrschapelekîn" (v. 4641); "loberîs" (v. 4647).
[6] Illustrated in subsequent notes. Franz Settegast (p. 7) says that the twelfth-century troubadours of Provence "lived in a time when the pursuit of honor and glory was as strong and general as in any other time. Therefore they soon had to realize that they could not win their patrons' favor more surely in any other way than by proclaiming their fame."

had only saints' legends and legend-like stories of princes and clerics, which were independent of fame in the sense of personally achieved notoriety,[1] one might suspect that he had never read of Beowulf, Siegfried, or Dietrich of Bern. That the desire for individual self-aggrandizement was not new to the Renaissance is indicated in Hartmann's *Iwein* when the hero sneaks away from Arthur's court to fight the keeper of the magic well. Although Arthur has announced his intention to visit the well, Iwein surreptitiously steals a march on the rest in order to win all the honor for himself rather than wait and let his friends have a chance. Incidentally, his behavior was considered highly admirable. Jan Huizinga came nearer the truth than Burckhardt when he said, "The thirst for honour and glory proper to the men of the Renaissance is essentially the same as the chivalrous ambition of earlier times, and of French origin." [2]

Johannes Bühler states that the aristocratic concept of honor during the Middle Ages "is to be distinguished from the thirst for fame of the Renaissance. It is already a transition to the modern sense of duty, and the nobleman is the first who begins to have any notion of what it means to do a thing, a good thing, for its own sake." [3] Unfortunately he does not prove this statement; and I have been unable to find any evidence for it in medieval literature. Nearly all chivalric poets maintain that good deeds are done for fame, even though the Church objected to such motivation.[4]

Henry Teichner expressed the usual medieval view when he said, "a worthy man does good works so that people will praise him";[5] and poets often gave their heroes epithets expressing a desire for fame.[6] Eilhart of Oberge lets Isalde say that Tristrant strives gladly for *êre*,[7] and Wolfram maintains that Kiot of Catalonia "aimed at high praise, undaunted by cost or deed" and that "he won praise

---

[1] "Der Norden aber besass, bis Italien auf seine Autoren... einwirkte, nur Legenden der Heiligen und vereinzelte Geschichten und Beschreibungen von Fürsten und Geistlichen, die sich noch deutlich an die Legende anlehnen und vom Ruhm, d.h. von der persönlich errungenen Notorität wesentlich unabhängig sind" (Burckhardt, pp. 177-178).

[2] Huizinga, p. 59.

[3] Johannes Bühler, *Die Kultur des Mittelalters*, Leipzig, 1931, p. 182.

[4] "Non tamen est vere virtuosus qui propter humanam gloriam opera virtutis operatur" (*Summa Theologiae*, II, II, 132, 1, ad. 2).

[5] "darumb tut ein pider man guteu dinch, daz man in preis" (Teichner, 1, vv. 10-11).

[6] Tristan says you should give *êre* to "den êre gernden" (*Tristan*, v. 227). Tristan (v. 4999) is *êregire;* and Rüdeger (*Nibelungenlied*, 2218, 3) is *êre gernde*. Cf. "den êre gernden soltû geben ze rehte dînen werden gruoz" (*Winsbekin*, 5, 5-6).

[7] "he wirbet gerne umme êre" (*Tristrant*, v. 2427).

with largess and prowess."[1] Rudolf of Ems dedicated his poem *William of Orleáns* to Conrad of Winterstet, because "his disposition and his thoughts and all his virtues were aimed at the world's praise";[2] and his *Alexander* indicates that a purpose of virtuous behavior is to protect a man from reproach.[3] Where then are the good deeds done for their own sake, which Johannes Bühler claims were not done from a thirst for fame?

Fame being the chief incentive to good deeds, people urged good actions by appealing to desire for praise. Lanzelet promises that anyone who fights successfully for the queen will be well spoken of; and Sir Kay tells the queen that it would become her name better if she refrained from reproaching him.[4] When Gernot asks Etzel to let the Burgundians fight in the open, he assures him that it will bring him honor; and Dietrich reminds Kriemhild that it will bring her little honor if she attacks her kinsmen, who have come in good faith.[5]

Just as hope of honor incited men to good, fear of shame deterred them from evil; for honor and shame flee one another.[6] As a result, a well developed sense of shame was a guarantee of winning honor. When Erec forces Yders to the ground in their fight, he withdraws to let his enemy stand up, because he does not want people to say that he has shamed himself by killing a man while he is down.[7] The ancient Teutons would have agreed with Aristotle that warriors "face dangers because of the penalties imposed by the laws and the reproaches they would otherwise incur, and because of the honors they will win by such action; and therefore those people seem to be bravest among whom cowards are held in dishonor and brave men

---

[1] "sîn herze was gein hôhem prîs ie der kost und der tât unverdrozzen" (*Titurel*, I, 14, 4); "mit milte unde ellen" (I, 16, 2). In *Lanzelet*, the hero leaves the mermaids' country "durch niht wan umb êre", Kurâus sets out "durch ruom und durch vermezzenheit", and he "erwarp niht wan um êre" (*Lanzelet*, vv. 351, 686, 1256). In *Willehalm*, Count Landrîs raises the banner high "durch sînen prîs" (373, 2) and many princes follow Poidjus "durch rîcheit und ouch durch ruom" (379, 1).

[2] "wan sîn gemüet und ouch sîn sin Und aller sîner tugende rât Gar nâch der welte prîse stât" (*Willehalm von Orlens*, vv. 2326-2328).

[3] "ein man der ganzer tugent phligt und alles valsches sich bewigt, des tugent schirmet sînen lîp umb werde man und werdiu wîp, daz er scheltens wirt erlân" (*Alexander*, vv. 1505-1509).

[4] "dem wirt dicke wol gesprochen" (*Lanzelet*, v. 5023). "daz zaeme iuwerm namen wol" (*Iwein*, v. 163).

[5] "daz ist iu êre getân" (*Nibelungenlied*, 2096, 4); "Diu bete dich lützel êret" (1902, 1).

[6] "êre unde schande vliehent einander" (*Moriz von Craun*, vv. 93-94). Peter of Stauffenberg says God should help him who "kan schande fliehen und wil sich lan beziehen zuht trüwe milte êre" (*Rittermaeren*, vv. 21-23).

[7] "daz tete er umbe daz daz ie man des möhte jehen daz im diu schande waer geschehen daz ern ligende het erslagen" (*Erec*, vv. 827-830).

in honor."[1] This is practically what Tacitus said of his fearless barbarians.

Whereas the ancient Teutons had usually equated disgrace with cowardice, the poets of the High Middle Ages also associated it with non-conformity to accepted conventions, be they social or moral. Thus Wolfram could say that Parzival was never lost because a sense of shame (*scham*) gives praise as a reward and is yet the crown of the soul."[2] Parzival had to be sensitive to shame, since a pure heart ceases to feel shame only when it dies.[3] Reinmar of Zweter said that a sense of shame is fitting for a nobleman, together with *triuwe* and good breeding.[4] St. Ambrose, the fourth-century bishop of Milan, had already made shame a Christian virtue by saying that *verecundia* is the ally and friend of a tranquil mind, that it flees impudence, is foreign to all luxury, loves sobriety, cherishes honesty, and seeks propriety.[5] Walther maintains that if any man has intelligence, manhood, silver, and gold, yet remains in disgrace, he will lose the reward of the heavenly emperor and also of the ladies.[6] It seems a safe conclusion that fear of disgrace was accepted as a Christian virtue even before love of honor was so recognized.

Honor and disgrace were important not only in this life, but even afterwards. Ulrich of Zatzikhoven states that "praise lasts when the body perishes."[7] This probably reflects the ancient Germanic belief in the immortality of earthly fame; yet it could just as well echo a passage in *Sirach*, which says of famous men: "Their bodies were buried in peace, and their names live to all generations."[8] Hartmann

---

[1] Aristotle, *Ethics*, III, 8 (trans Rose).

[2] "wan scham gît prîs ze lône und ist doch der sêle crône" (*Parzival*, 319,9-10). Cf. "verschampter lîb, waz touc der mêr? der wont in der mûze rêr, dâ im werdekeit entrîset unde in gein der helle wîset" (*Parzival*, 170,17-20).

[3] "sol lûter herze sich niht schemen, daz muoz der tôt dervon ê nemen" (*Parzival*, 358,19-20). Parzival prays that he be saved from "werltlîcher schame" (*Parzival*, 269,12).

[4] "waz einem rehten hêrren zimt ze tuonne unt ouch ze lâzen, swer daz gerne wol vernimt, dem nenne ich triuwe vor unt dar nâch zuht mit eigenlîcher schame" (Reinmar von Zweter, 68,1-3). "der êren spiegel ist diu scham" (*Der Marner*, XV, v. 10,181).

[5] "verecundia est socia ac familiaris mentis placiditati: proterviam fugitans, ab omni luxu aliena, sobrietatem diliget, et honestatem fovet, et decorem requirit" (cited in *Summa Theologiae*, II, II, 144,1,3). Cf. "inter pudentem et verecundum hoc interest, quod pudens opinionem veram falsamque metuit: verecundus a autem non nisi veram timet" (Isidore, *Etymologiae*, from Leo Spitzer, *Modern Language Notes*, 62, 1947, p. 508).

[6] "Witze unde manheit, dar zuo silber und daz golt, swer diu beidu hât, belîbet der mit schanden, wê wie den vergât des himeleschen keisers solt! dem sint die engel noch die frowen holt. armman zuo der werlte und wider got, wie der fürhten mac ir beider spot!" (Walther, 13,6-11).

[7] "der lop wert sô der lîp zergât" (*Lanzelet*, v. 8680).

[8] "Corpora ipsorum in pace sepulta sunt, et nomen eorum vivit in generationem et generationem" (*Ecclesiasticus* 44,14).

expresses the same view in a passage at the beginning of his *Iwein*, which deserves to be quoted in full: "If anyone applies himself to true virtue (*rehte güete*), fortune and honor will follow him. Sure proof of this is given by good King Arthur, who knew how to strive for praise with knightly disposition. He lived so well during his life that he bore the crown of honors then, and his name still bears it. His countrymen are right in this: they say he is still alive. He has achieved renown. Even though his body has died, his name still lives. Anyone who conducts himself as he did will guard himself from reproach (*lasterlîche schande*)." [1]

Like children today, the knights of old still insulted their enemies to make them lose face, and the insulted party lost not only public but also personal esteem until he avenged the insult. Courtly poets, like Hartmann, often composed rhetorical invective to serve as a model for their noble young audience in their own squabbles.[2] Perhaps one of the most eloquent displays of gentlemanly vituperation is found in the abusive charges made by Bolingbroke and Norfolk in the opening scene of Shakespeare's *Richard II* before their trial by combat. Insults are not limited to words alone. The action of Hartmann's *Erec* begins when Yder's dwarf slaps the unarmed hero, who, like the relentless heroes of the sagas, must stalk his enemy until he finally obtains satisfaction. Although many medieval poets like Hartmann knew the Stoic writings, they could not presume to tell their courtly audiences to ignore a slap, as Seneca had advised.

A particularly grievous type of insult was that suffered by the husband of an unfaithful wife or by the father or male guardian of a seduced or abducted woman. The woman too lost her honor, whether seduced or raped, yet her husband or guardian suffered even more, since men had more honor to lose. No one was more dishonorable than a cuckold. When Parzival, who is still a pure fool, enters the tent of the sleeping Jeschute and kisses her and takes her ring, she is dishonored. When her husband returns and suspects infidelity, he complains that his knightly honor has been changed

---

[1] "Swer an rehte güete wendet sin gemüete, dem volget saelde und êre. des gît gewisse lêre künec Artûs der guote, der mit riters muote nâch lobe kunde strîten, er hât bî sînen zîten gelebet alsô schône, daz er der êren krône dô truoc und noch sîn name treit. des hânt die wârheit sîne lantliute: sî jehent er lebe noch hiute: er hât den lop erworben, ist im der lîp erstorben, sô lebet doch iemer sîn name. er ist lasterlîcher schame iemer vil gar erwert, der noch nâch sînem site vert" (*Iwein*, vv. 1-20). Henry of Meissen also mentions Arthur's immortality: "Künc Artûs mit der rîchen tât vil hôhen prîs erwarp; wie daz er ouch erstorben sî, sîn reinez lop doch nie verdarp" (Heinrich von Meissen, 329, 13-16).

[2] For a good example of invective, see the altercation between Kalogreant and Sir Kay in *Iwein* (vv. 113-221). Because Sir Kay is not a man of honor, nothing comes of this.

to disgrace.¹ In *Tristan*, Isolde's infidelity harms King Marke's honor,² and Hagen partially vindicates Gunther's honor as a husband when he kills Siegfried. This kind of "point of honor" reached its most extreme expression in Spain, where it may have been influenced by Arabic customs. However, old Gothic survivals would have been enough to explain the tradition.³

In studying the value code of the court poets, one must remember that people and things were judged by their repute rather than by their intrinsic values, even though some clergymen saw the danger of error in such judgments.⁴ As in the case of the Romans, *dignitas* depended upon the honors received rather than upon those merited. Wolfram of Eschenbach describes this process by saying that, if *dignitas* (*werdekeit*) is the most splendid praise (*prîs*) and if praise is *werdekeit*, the two are a single thing, so great that it fulfils happiness.⁵ One might argue that *prîs* (from *pretium*) meant worth as well as repute (i.e., value as well as price); but Wolfram, like most *MHG* poets, invariably uses *prîs* in the sense of praise, fame, or public acclaim.

The most usual synonym of *prîs* was *lob*, which also rendered Latin *laus*. Conrad of Würzburg, writing nearer the end of the thirteenth century, used *wirde*, *werdekeit*, *prîs*, and *lop* practically as synonyms of *êre*.⁶ Some years earlier Rudolf of Ems had written, "In India a wise king turned his thoughts to the praise of this world. His excellence (*tugent*) enhanced his *werdekeit* in foreign lands. Through his excellence he prepared for himself great *wirde* beyond other kings".⁷ This is only one of many bits of evidence that *werdekeit* was felt to be an external possession rather than an internal quality. Modern editors, wishing to attribute incentives other than fame, often see fit to interpret *MHG* words too freely. When the *Lay of the*

---

¹ "wer hât mich entêret?" (*Parzival*, 131,8); "mir ist nâch laster gendet manec ritterlîcher prîs" (133,8-9).
² "an sin e und an sin ere" (*Tristan*, v. 13,652).
³ Stuart, p. 251.
⁴ St. Martin had said that you will show prudence, which is a means to the honest life, "si omnia prius aestimes et perpenses et dignitatem rebus non ex opinione multorum sed ex earum natura constituas" (Martin, *Formula* 2,2). St. Thomas Aquinas expressed a similar belief in his *Summa Contra Gentiles* (III,29): "Cognitio autem famae, in qua gloria humana consistit, est imperfecta; est enim plurimum incertitudinis et erroris habens".
⁵ "ist werdekeit von prîse hêr und ist der prîs die werdekeit, diu zwei sint einez wol sô breit, dâ von gelücke wirdet ganz" (*Willehalm*, 14,16-19). Thus the heathen Morgowanz has complete praise with dignity: "des prîs mit werdekeit was ganz" (32,18).
⁶ *Partononier*, 16,030-16,046.
⁷ "in Indîâ ein künic wîs, der gar an dirre welte prîs sîn gemüete kêrte: in vremeden landen mêrte sîn tugent sîne werdekeit. er hâte sich dar zuo bereit mit tugentlîchen dingen daz man sîn lop sach dringen vür ander künege wirde grôz" (*Barlaam*, 6,19-27).

Nibelungs says that Rüdeger refuses Etzel's gifts because it would be unpraiseworthy (*unlobelich*) to accept them, the editor of the most popular edition explains the word to mean improper (*unangemessen*),[1] even though the characters are motivated elsewhere almost exclusively by other people's opinions rather than by absolute standards of right and wrong.[2] Likewise, when Kriemhild marries Etzel to enhance her power, her uncle advises her to give lavishly and thus to buy honor just as Etzel's first wife had done. The same editor explains the word "buy" (*koufen*) to mean "acquire" or "earn", although the transaction is clearly to be a purchase of *êre* in return for *guot*.[3] Conrad of Würzburg states this commonplace by saying that *milte* buys popular favor.[4]

[1] Footnote to strophe 1153, in *Das Nibelungenlied*, ed. H. de Boor, Leipzig, 1949.
[2] Several passages illustrating this fact have appeared in the preceding notes.
[3] "unt daz sie ir êre koufte als Helche hete getân" (*Nibelungenlied*, 1330,3). De Boor says "erwerben, verdienen".
[4] "der liute gunst die milte koufet" (*Leiche*, 18, v. 7).

CHAPTER FIVE

KNIGHTLY HONOR - REFINING INFLUENCES

He who has a good woman's love is ashamed of any misdeed. WALTHER, 93, 17-18.

In contrast to the warrior code of honor inherited from their Germanic forebears, the thirteenth-century German knights developed a chivalric code of honor somewhat refined by foreign influences. Naturally the greatest of these influences was the Christian Church, whose teachings had been universally accepted, at least nominally, centuries earlier. Perhaps the next most important influence was classical antiquity: Greek thought reached medieval Europe first through derivative Latin works and later, during the thirteenth century, via the Arabs of Spain. Another refining influence upon literature was the greater participation of women at the courts, particularly as patrons of the poets. One might say that warriors became gentlemen when women began to preside at court.

We have seen that Christianity ran counter to the Germanic concept of honor. Although the Church taught men to turn the other cheek, even the most gentle of the court poets could not demand this of their heroes. Nevertheless, they were able to teach men to look upon revenge as just punishment, not merely as personal satisfaction. Unlike their Germanic ancestors, the knights of the High Middle Ages were expected to avenge themselves on the individual offender rather than on just any member of his kinship. Still, the older idea of vicarious revenge still appears. In the *Lay of the Nibelungs*, when Hagen finally admits killing Siegfried, he says that Siegfried had to pay because Kriemhild had insulted Brunhild.[1] Since a women was not capable of giving satisfaction, Germanic custom demanded that revenge be taken on some important member of her *vridu*, preferably her nearest kinsman or her legal guardian. Because a dwarf is by nature incapable of satisfaction, Erec cannot take revenge on the dwarf, but must defeat his master and have the dwarf thrashed.

---
[1] "wie sêre er des engalt daz diu vrouwe Kriemhild die schoenen Prünhilden schalt" (*Nibelungenlied*, 1790, 3-4).

In spite of a half millennium of Christian preaching about forgiveness, homicide was still demanded of so-called Christian knights when their honor was impugned. Gurnemanz, Parzival's courtly mentor, tells him he should show mercy and accept surrender provided his enemy has not committed a heartfelt injury (*herzen kumber*) against him.[1] This reservation, which put the final decision entirely at the discretion of the victor, explains the cruel vengeance wreaked by the saintly crusader Willehalm in Wolfram's other great epic. When Willehalm downs Arofel, the latter begs for mercy and offers ransom; yet, after much deliberation and discussion, Willehalm kills his defenseless victim in cold blood because of the heartfelt injury (*herzeser*) which Arofel had caused him by killing his sister's son. Wolfram seems to approve Willehalm's act because he has preferred revenge to rich ransom, even though he then despoils and beheads the corpse.[2] His deed is naturally *herzeser* for Arofel's kinsman, Terramer.[3] When Erec defeats Yders, the defeated knight begs for mercy, in the name of God and all women, on the grounds that he has not caused Erec enough *herzenleit* to require fatal vengeance.[4] After gloating a while in his victory, Erec deigns to spare his life. In many Crusade epics revenge is consistently brutal in all episodes until the very end, at which point the hero forigives some minor character so that the clerical author can sermonize on the virtue of forgiveness. A similar situation obtains in the *Lay of the Nibelungs* when Siegfried, following courtly innovations, pardons the captured kings Liudeger and Liudegast, whereas the older ethos prevails in the gory revenge wreaked at the end of the poem. Gurnemanz's advice about killing prisoners was repeated two centuries later, with somewhat less refinement, by Henry Wittenwiler, who said you should spare your prisoner unless he is a whore's son, in which case you should wring his neck.[5]

Whereas the Church could not persuade men of honor to forgive insults, it did succeed in making it honorable for victors to spare the vanquished, provided these had committed no heartfelt injury. Courtly epics give many examples of clemency, usually performed ostentatiously, like Siegfried's liberation of Liudeger and Liudegast. Although Siegfried renounces ransom in order to enhance his and

---

[1] "an swem ir strîtes sicherheit bezalt, ern habe iu sölhiu leit getân diu herzen kumber wesen, die nemt, und lâzet in genesen" (*Parzival*, 171,27-30).
[2] *Willehalm*, 79,15-81,18.
[3] *Willehalm*, 204,16.
[4] "durch got erbarme dich, edel ritter, über mich. êre an mir elliu wîp unde lâz mir den lîp, und gedenke dar an, daz ich dir, tugenhafter man, solch herzenleit niht hân getân, du maht mich wol bî lîbe lân" (*Erec*, vv. 956-963).
[5] "Einn hüerrensun den schol man vahen, Wie man mag, und dar zuo gahen Und würgen im den drüssel ab, Wie wol man im verhaissen hab, Mocht er an versichern nicht Gevangen werden" (*Ring*, vv. 8483-8488). Again, it is left to the victor's discretion to decide whether his victim is a "whore's son".

Gunther's prestige, hope of ransom was one of the chief causes of medieval wars. Whereas knights were not allowed to forgive insults to their honor, ladies sometimes were. Iblis, a lady in *Lanzelet*, at once forgives the hero for having killed her father;[1] Laudine, the heroine of Hartmann's *Iwein*, promptly forgives the slayer of her husband;[2] and even Isolde forgives Tristan for killing her uncle. All these ladies are moved by love. The poet is not minimizing the importance of revenge: quite to the contrary, he is using its omission as proof of love's overwhelming power.

The Church taught not only mercy and forgiveness, but also charity in the sense of alms to the poor. While the code of knighthood encouraged men to give in return for praise, the Church taught that they should give in return for God's favor and rewards in the world to come. Wishing success both here and there, the perfect knight gave for both purposes simultaneously. The popular epic *Hugdietrich* says that its hero could both bestow and give for God and for *êre*,[3] and *Duke Ernst* says that its hero distributed everything he had for *êre* and for God.[4] Whether God or *êre* came first in this cliché seems to have depended only upon the need of the rime. Conrad of Würzburg states that *milte* can buy people's favor and God's grace and that *miltekait* enhances one's honor.[5]

In all these cases the *do ut des* relation was frankly expressed. Henry Teichner says that gluttons eat their substance instead of buying heaven by feeding the poor.[6] Walther considers it very commendable that Duke Leopold has gone on a crusade to win future *êre* in heaven, and Hartmann says that those who take up the cross will win both the world's praise and the soul's salvation.[7] Wolfram's *Willehalm* often refers to the practicality of fighting for God. The Christians struggle for "everlasting glory", whoever suffers for Christ will receive eternal reward, and the Franks will receive peace of soul and buy seats in heaven. Gyburg will be repaid for the poverty of her body with the wealth of the soul, etc.[8] Since medieval

---

[1] "wan si so schiere vergaz daz er ir vater het erslagen" (*Lanzelet*, vv. 4600-4601).
[2] *Iwein*, vv. 2039-2050.
[3] "durch got und durch ere beide lihen unde geben" (*Hugdietrich*, 7,4).
[4] "beide durch ere und durch got teilte er swaz er mohte han" (*Herzog Ernst*, vv. 98-99).
[5] "der liute gunst die milte koufet unde gotes hulde wizzent daz diu miltekeit hoher eren spiegel breit" (*Leiche*, 18, 7-10).
[6] "wolt man daz himelreich erchramn" (Teichner, 53, v. 31).
[7] "der werlte lop, der sêle heil" (*Minnesangs Frühling*, 210,10). Walther says that Duke Leopold went on a crusade to earn future glory: "Dô Liupolt spart ûf gotes vart, ûf künftige êre" (Walther, 36, 1-2. Cf. 125, 5-8).
[8] "nâch dem êweclîchen prîse" (*Willehalm*, 19, 28); "swer sich vinden lât durch in in nôt, der emphaeht unendelôsen solt" (31,12-13); "der sêle vride" (32,6); "die stuol ze himele kouften" (16, 24); "der mac michs wol ergetzen und slîbes armuot letzen mit der sêle rîcheit" (216, 27-29). See also 37,20-21.

man believed in the resurrection of the body, it was an advantageous exchange, because the heavenly wealth would last somewhat longer.

Rudolf of Ems lists the medieval reasons for charity in an ascending order: "In whosoever's name you redeem the poor and comfort them, his name will reward your heart's desire. If you do it for money, they will repay you; but if you do it for *êre*, they will praise you all the more. If you do it because of God's commandment, then know rightly that God will give you on their account the everlasting crown as a reward."[1] In other words, one could give to win wealth, fame, or God's *huld*. To give for the sake of giving would have been wasted effort.

Perhaps the greatest difference between courtly largess and Christian charity was that the former was given from one's abundance and the latter from one's scarcity. In the *Lay of the Nibelungs*, Gunther rewards the Saxon emissaries because he has so much to give; and Brunhild asks who will help her distribute her wealth, "of which I have so much."[2] Since she is giving to impress and obligate, she must make it clear that she still has sufficient wealth left. On the other hand, Thomasin followed Christian teaching by saying that, to perform true *milte*, one must suffer lack through the gift.[3]

Unlike his Germanic forebears, the medieval knight was supposed, at least in clerically inspired works, to be moderate in his largess. Quoting Aristotle, churchmen said that largess was the golden mean between prodigality and avarice.[4] As Gurnemanz tells Parzival, a knight should be neither too liberal nor too parsimonious: it is dishonorable either to give away everything or to collect too much treasure.[5] In Rudolf of Ems's *William of Orléans*, Jovrit warns the hero to give with largess of spirit, but with prudence, if he wants people to praise his ambition for honor (*êre gernden muot*), and later he says that largess with prudence brings the crown of praise.[6]

---

[1] "in welhem namen dû lôstest die armen und si trôstest, des naeme lôn dîns herzen gir. tuost duz durch gelt, sî geltent dir: tuost aber duz durch êre, man lobt dich immer mêre: tuost duz durch gotes gebot, sô wizzest rehte daz dir got gît umbe sî ze lône die immer wernden krône" (*Gerhard*, vv. 1859-1868).

[2] "der het in ze gebene Gunther genuoc" (*Nibelungenlied*, 166,2); "des ich sô vil hân" (513,3).

[3] *Welscher Gast*, vv. 6189-6200; 13,715-13,718; 14,029-14,034; 14,298-14,302.

[4] "Qui dat quibus dandum est et retinet quibus retinendum est, largus est. Et qui prohibet quibus prohibendum est et quibus non est prohibendum, avarus est. Et qui dat quibus dandum et quibus non est dandum, prodigus est" (*Disciplina Clericalis*, p. 32). See Aristotle, *Ethics*, II, 7, 4.

[5] "ir sult bescheidenlîche sîn arm unde rîche. wan swâ der hêrre gar vertuot, daz ist niht hêrenlîcher muot: sament er aber schaz ze sêre, daz sint ouch unêre" (*Parzival*, 171,7-12).

[6] "Ob du niht durch tumben mut Wilt ane ere swenden din gut Wuestende des gutes. Wis zerhaft wises mutes! Miltekait des mutes, Furbesicht des gutes, Diu zwai in ainem mute Bejagent mit dem gute Das man den ere gernden mut Lobt und hat an im vergut Sin halden und sin lazen, Kan er su baide mazen" (*Willehalm von Orlens*, vv. 3341-3357). "Milte mit beschaidenhait, Du alles lobes crone trait!" (vv. 3401-3402).

The Church taught moderation in all things, even in courage and honor. In his handbook on the honorable life, St. Martin had said that one should not seek danger like a foolhardy person, nor should he fear it like a coward.[1] Whereas this advice was largely ignored by courtly poets, they did sometimes preach against excessive ambition, especially in religiously tinged works. Hartmann says that Gregorius would have conquered all lands, had he not wished to practice moderation for the sake of God.[2] Likewise, Rudolf of Ems lets Darius tell Alexander that moderation is good even in honor.[3] In spite of these platitudes, most courtly poets described heroes of unlimited ambition. Nevertheless, moderation in honor is the moral of Hartmann's *Erec* and *Iwein*. In agreement with Aristotle,[4] Hartmann believed that a perfect man should show neither too much nor too little concern for his reputation. After restoring his injured honor by defeating Yders, Erec loses his newly restored honor by devoting himself to his wife Enite to the exclusion of tournaments. Learning that he is being reproached for his indolence, he sets out to restore his honor once more by undergoing a series of perilous adventures. Thus he goes from one extreme to the other. Eventually, although wounded, he tries to block a road to all comers. When Guivreiz, whom he has previously defeated, unhorses him, he realizes that he has erred in his immoderate desire for honor.[5] Iwein's fault is also a lack of moderation in pursuing honor: in his excessive pursuit of honor he breaks his pledge to return to his wife, and thus he loses all the honor he has won.

Another tenet introduced by the Church at this time, and perhaps also derived from Aristotle,[6] was the idea that it was praiseworthy to be humble to the weak and arrogant to the strong. Gottfried of Strassburg lets King Marke tell his nephew Tristan, "Be humble and undeceitful, truthful and wellbred. Always be good to the poor and

---

[1] "Eris magnanimis, si pericula nec appetas ut temerarius, nec formides ut timidus" (Martin, *Formula*, 3,10). See Aristotle, *Ethics*, II, 8, 7; II, 6, 12.
[2] "enhaete erz niht durch got verlân, im müesen wesen undertân swaz im der lande was gelegen, nû wolde aber er der mâze phlegen: durch die gotes êre sô engerte er nihtes mêre wan daz im dienen solde: vürbaz er niene wolde" (*Gregorius*, vv. 2269-2276).
[3] "bî der êre ist mâze guot" (*Alexander*, v. 14,989). This is found in a long discussion of *êre*, which includes many commonplaces (vv. 14,963-15,010).
[4] "With regard to honour and dishonour the mean is proper pride, the excess is known as a sort of 'empty vanity', and the deficiency is undue humility" (Aristotle, *Ethics*, II, 7, trans. Ross).
[5] "sît daz ich tumber man ie von tumpheit muot gewan sô grôzer unmâze... dô ich alters eine iuwer aller êre wolde hân" (*Erec*, vv. 7012-7022).
[6] "It is characteristic of the high-minded man... to be lofty in his behavior to those who are high in station and favored by fortune, but affable to those of the middle ranks; for it is a difficult thing and a dignified thing to assert superiority over the former, but easy to assert it over the latter" (Aristotle, *Ethics*, trans. F. H. Peters, IV, 3, 26).

haughty to the rich."¹ Similarly, the abbot in *Gregorius* tells the young hero to watch his behavior and be strong to the lords and good to the poor.² Some poets advised showing meekness in general, not only to the rich and strong; and Chaucer's perfect knight was not alone in being as "meeke as is a mayde."³

Although the thirteenth-century German courts retained the ancient virtues of courage, wealth, power, fealty, and largess, honor could also be gained from *genâde* (favor or recognition from one's lord or lady), *fröude* (joy), *trôst* (hope, confidence), *mâze* (moderation), *hövischheit* (courtliness), etc. These words owed their new meanings largely to being associated with the terms *merci, joi, solatz, mezura, cortezia*, etc., as they were understood at the courts of Provence; for Provence, having never entirely lost contact with its Greek and Latin past, was the center of the most polished courtly culture.

Throughout this study the *MHG* word *hövischheit* is rendered by courtliness, never by *courtesy* as it usually is elsewhere, since the latter word now implies a disinterested kindness or consideration not necessarily implied in the *MHG* term. Courtly poets were frank in saying that the purpose of courtly behavior was to enhance one's own *êre* or prestige. This fact is made quite clear in Wolfram of Eschenbach's *Parzival*, which is perhaps the outstanding example of German courtly epic. In this poem King Arthur says that anyone who says nice things about him is really honoring himself, since he is saying them to be courtly and not because they are merited.⁴ In Hartmann of Aue's *Iwein*, Queen Guinevere unexpectedly joins a group of Round Table knights and only Kalogreant sees her in time to jump up and bow to her. Sir Kay, the uncourtly steward, then begrudges him the honor he has won and tries to spoil it by saying that they all would have jumped up if they had seen the queen.⁵ In the *Lay of the Nibelungs*, which has an unconvincing courtly skin over its Germanic core, Volker tells Hagen that they should stand

---

[1] "wis diemüete und wis unbetrogen, wis wârhaft und wis wolgezogen; den armen den wis iemer guot, den rîchen iemer hôchgemuot" (*Tristan*, vv. 5027-5030).

[2] "wis dîner zuht wol behuot, den herren starc, den armen guot" (*Gregorius*, vv. 251-252). Cf. "sît gegen friunden senfte, tragt gegen vînden hôhgemüete" (*Walther*, 36, 12); "wis gegen den vînden hôchgemuot, den vriunden niht mit dienste laz" (*Winsbeke*, 39, 6-7). This topos must have reached even Iceland, where Snorri "was good to his friends but strict with his enemies" (hann var gôðr vinum sínum en grimmr óvinum góðr. *Brennu-Njálssaga*, CXIV, 4).

[3] Chaucer, ed. Robinson, I, A, v. 69. "Sun, wilt du genzlîch schiltes reht erkennen, sô wis wol gezogen, getriuwe, milte, küene, slecht, sô enist er niht an dir betrogen" (*Winsbeke*, 19, 1-4).

[4] "er êrte sich, der mich geprîset wider dich und gein andern liuten hât. sîn selbes zuht gap im den rât mêr dan ichz gedienet hân: er hât ez durch höfscheit getân" (*Parzival*, 767, 11-16).

[5] *Iwein*, vv. 99-135.

up when Kriemhild approaches them with her retinue. By showing honor to the queen, they will enhance their own prestige.[1]

A whole volume could be written on the significance of salutations in German literature. Greetings were more than a social nicety: they were less often tokens of friendship than conscious admissions of economic or social inferiority on the part of him who greeted first. It was customary for juniors or subordinates to introduce themselves first, as is seen in the case of Hildebrand and Hadubrand, yet Feirefiz agrees to introduce himself to Parzival first even though it will bring him disgrace.[2] Because one's worth or dignity depended upon the greetings one received, poets were most careful in recording them. As in the case of modern military salutes, the inferior was expected to salute first, and his failure to do so was construed as an attack against, or at least an affront to, his superior's higher position. In the *Lay of the Nibelungs* Kriemhild is highly indignant (i.e., loses her *dignatio*) when Hagen refuses to greet her, since this appears to be an aggression against her position as queen. The chief characters of most courtly epics are actually sovereign persons, and consequently their greetings follow a protocol as punctilious as that between diplomatic representatives of sovereign states today. Because kings were the source of honor, a nod from a king or queen brought honor to the recipient, even if it was only in return, as we saw in the case of Kalogreant when the queen acknowledged his greeting.

According to Freidank, a bad or weak person (*der boese*) must suffer indignity and a weak greeting (*swacher gruoz*).[3] Farmer Helmbrecht, of whom we shall hear later, is blinded and maimed because he has given his parents a *swachen gruoz*; in other words, he has failed to honor them as God has commanded.[4] At first, men saluted only superiors; but, as more polished customs were introduced, it became customary for knights to greet ladies, even of their own rank, first. In the make-believe world of *minnesang*, or courtly love-lyrics, the lovelorn knight dared ask his lady for no more reward than a friendly greeting or a nod of the head.[5]

Both classical and Christian influence can be seen in the thirteenth-

---

[1] "Nu stê wir von dem sedele... si ist ein küneginne; und lât si für gân. bieten ir die êre: si ist ein edel wîp. dâ mit ist ouch getiuret unser ietweders lîp" (*Nibelungenlied*, 1780).
[2] "ich wil mich nennen ê und lâ daz laster wesen mîn" (*Parzival*, 745, vv. 26-27).
[3] "Der boese dicke dulten muoz unwirde unde swachen gruoz" (*Freidank*, 89,10-11).
[4] *Meier Helmbrecht*, vv. 1690-1694.
[5] "Ich sanc hie vor den frowen umbe ir blôzen gruoz: den nam ich wider mîme lobe zu lône; swâ ich des geltes nû vergebene warten muoz, dâ lobe ein ander den sie grüezen schône..." (Walther, 49,12-15).

century attitudes toward bragging and ridicule. In most shame cultures, like that of the Teutons, the chief reward of victory is praising oneself and ridiculing the vanquished. The heroes of the court epics, on the other hand, usually refrain from boasting of their success. When Erec taunts Yders, whom he has defeated, he attributes his good fortune to God rather than to his own prowess.[1] When courtly poets do say something to their own credit, they often apologize for having to brag.[2] Likewise, the more admirable characters refrain from ridicule; and it is significant that Sir Kay, who indulges most in ridicule, is no man of honor.[3]

As feminine influence became more prominent at court, court poets began to sing their praises just as they sang the praises of their lords. That is to say, they performed *frauendienst* as well as *herrendienst*. As the knight won his lady's favor or *huld* by serving her in battle or tournament, so the *minnesinger* won it by singing her praise. Whereas, in actual practice, vassals and poets alike served in return for tangible rewards, in theory they served only for the honor of being recognized by their lords and ladies. Thus the entire fiction of literary *frauendienst* was based on an exchange of *êre* in the sense of honor or prestige. Nevertheless, the word *êre* and the concept of honor play a smaller role in court lyrics than in the court epics. Being subjective, lyrics could not by rights be greatly concerned with honor as long as honor was an objective value. Later, in the songs of the mastersingers, it played a more important role; but by then honor was becoming an inner moral value and the mastersongs (*Meistergesang*), although lyrical in the sense that they could be sung, were less subjective and were actually only versified didacticism.

Although generally considered a source of honor, women actually had little honor in themselves but merely reflected the honor of their menfolk. When a man died, his wife lost her marital status and the honor acquired by it.[4] This explains why Kriemhild must avenge Siegfried's murder even against her own brothers. If a woman's honor was publicly attacked, it could be defended only by a man: when Iwein defends Lunete in a trial by combat, her life

---

[1] "doch hât mir got die saelde gegeben" (*Erec*, v. 973) Thomasin associates *ruom* with *lüge* and *spott* (*Welscher Gast*, vv. 185-296).
[2] "Ob ich mich selben rüemen sol" (Walther, 62, 6); "daz mac ich wol ane rüemen sagen" (50, 38); "rüemaere unde lügenaere, swâ die sîn, den verbiute ich mînen sanc" (41, 25-26); "sîn rüemen daz was cleine" (*Parzival*, I, v. 6); "ob ich ungerüemet wol und âne unvuoge sprechen mac" (*Winsbeke*, 48, 1-2). See *Waltharius*, vv. 561-565.
[3] *Iwein*, vv. 113-221. Thomasin says, "boeser liute spot ist unmaere, hân ich Gaweins hulde wol, von reht mîn Key spotten sol" (*Welscher Gast*, vv. 76-78).
[4] When Alexius is buried, his wife says: "mîn vröude und al mîn êre sint versenket und begraben" (*Alexius*, 1268-1269).

and honor depend upon his prowess, unless perhaps it is God who intervenes. Whereas a woman's honor depended originally upon the rank, wealth, and power of her male guardian, she could increase or diminish it through honorable or dishonorable behavior, such as liberality or penuriousness toward minstrels.

The Church tried to brand extramarital sex as sinful; yet the Germanic peoples were not soon impressed, and secular writers scarcely stressed the point for many centuries. The damsels of the courtly epics seem to suffer no reproach for giving themselves to their lovers, provided they do so with decorum and not too much haste. Sexual reticence was due to class pride more than to religious tabu. In Eilhart of Oberge's *Tristrant*, when Kehenis attempts to force his attentions upon Gymelen without any preliminaries, the outraged young lady exclaims, "Are you out of your mind? You can well see that I am not a peasant girl. Because you ask me for love in so short a time, I believe you are a peasant." [1]

When ladies in courtly literature are ashamed of erotic behavior, their shame is usually due to the circumstances, not to the sin. In *Parzival*, Gawan tells of a damsel who has been overwhelmed by a knight and regrets that she has lost her chaste maidenhood to a man who has never served her, [2] and this seems to imply that it would have been all right if he had done so. When Peter of Staufenberg's mysterious lady refuses to grant his request in the open field, she invokes Christ to prevent it from happening there and to let no one see their first union on the green heath.[3] In other words, it was not the act, but the place, that was disgraceful. Both Peter of Staufenberg and his lady make God and the Virgin Mary confidants and helpers in their affair,[4] and Tristan and Isolde likewise see no incongruity in asking God to protect them from being taken in adultery. God, being a courtly God, does so.[5] Incredibly enough,

---

[1] "Wâ tût ir hen ûwirn sin? jâ sêt ir wol daz ich nicht bin eine gebûrinne daz ir mich bittet umme minne in sô gar korzir zît: ich wêne ir ein gebûr sît" (*Tristrant*, vv. 6679-6684).
[2] "riuwebaerec was ir site, durch daz ir hête genomen der nie was in ir dienst komen ir kiuscheclîchen magetuom" (*Parzival*, 526, 2-5).
[3] "davor behüete uns min Crist, der unser aller helfer ist, daz semlich ding iht hie geschehe und kein mensche niemer sehe unser erste hohgezit uf dirre grüenen heide wit" (*Rittermaeren*, vv. 432-437).
[4] "Maria, himelkünigin, ich bevilh dir iemer mere lip sele guot und ere, daz ich han ie an dich verlan" (*Rittermaeren*, vv. 530-533). This mysterious lady is a "frouwe clar und schanden fri" (v. 324) although she submits to her lover, and she maintains that she has preserved him from all *schanden* during his campaigns (v. 362). She also refuses to go to bed with him while he is on God's errand, because "er sünd swer dirz werte" (v. 452).
[5] "jâ, hêrre got, erbarme dich über sî und über mich! unser êre und unser leben daz sî dir hînaht ergeben!" (*Tristan*, vv. 14,657-14,660). See also vv. 14,711, 14,726, 14,730, 15,542, 15,654, 15,678, 17,683, 17,733, *et passim*. "gotes höfscheit" (*Tristan*, v. 15,556). Hartmann praises a *hövesche got*, one who lets Erec kill his enemy (*Erec*, v. 5517).

some nineteenth-century scholars refused to believe that the wanton little lass in Walther's "Under the Linden" used the Virgin Mary's name as an exclamation during her rendezvous.

A woman lost her honor, not only if seduced by an inferior man, but also if raped. In Conrad of Würzburg's *World Chronicle* Tamer regrets losing her honor after Amon has violated her.[1] Since a woman could lose her honor along with her virginity, it is easy to see how the word *honor* could acquire the added meaning of "chastity", at least in the case of women.[2] A good name, rather than moral integrity, was the most usual and most approved incentive for continence. Conrad expresses this attitude in great detail and with great clarity in his *Partonopier* in a plaint by Meliur, who is afraid she will lose her good name if people learn that she is Partonopier's mistress. People will point their fingers at her, she will suffer *laster* and lose her *êren*, and she will be *geschant* in front of all her friends.[3] Another lady expresses the same fear in Conrad's *Trojan War*.[4]

More than a century later Chaucer could still say concerning an ideal woman, "no wyght mychte do hir noo shame, She loved so wel hir owne name."[5] In ancient days women had guarded their chastity, marriage vows, and widowhood "nat for holynesse, But al for verray vertu and clennesse and for men schulde sette on hem no lak; And yit they were hethene, al the pak, That were so sore adrad of alle shame."[6] This would seem to imply that Christian women were virtuous for "holynesse", but this more likely referred to holy women who had taken vows of chastity. Although concern for reputation usually protected against inchastity, it could also cause it. In Hartmann's *Gregorius*, when the sister is about to be violated by her brother, she fails to cry out for fear that the deed will become known and they will lose their honor.[7]

Love, which had been incidental in the older Germanic literature, became essential in the literature of the courts, which were presided

---

[1] "war solich nu keren, sit du an minin eren so sere hast geswechet mich und dich selbin?" (*Weltchronik*, vv. 29,171-29,173). See *II Kings*, 13,13.
[2] *NED* honour sb. 3. "(Of a woman) Chastity, purity, as a virtue of the highest consideration; reputation for this virtue, good name." Wittenwiler says that the bath-woman can help young maids "von den eren" (*Ring*, v. 2568); and Emser says that the two elders tried to deprive Susannah of "ir eer und lobe" (Emser, v. 46).
[3] *Partonopier*, vv. 8180-8211.
[4] "mîn lop in disen landen ze tôde wirt geswachet, wirt iemer kunt gemachet, daz ich worden bin dîn wîp" (*Trojanerkrieg*, vv. 17,106-17,109). See also vv. 8699, 8705, 8724.
[5] *Book of the Duchess*, vv. 1017-1018, in *Chaucer*, ed. Robinson.
[6] *Legend of Good Women*, vv. 296-300, in *Chaucer*, ed. Robinson.
[7] "sô habe wir iemer mêre verloren unser êre" (*Gregorius*, vv. 389-390). See also vv. 461, 489, 500, 531.

over by ladies. This new cult of love and womanhood seems to have been influenced by Ovid's *Art of Love* and Christian Mariology and perhaps by contact with higher Saracen civilization during the Crusades. The apotheosis of women in love lyrics may have stemmed from the Catharist or Albigensian heresy of Provence; for the rhetoric of the troubadours and minnesingers has much in common with Catharist prayers and liturgy.[1] For the purpose of this study, women will be considered only for their effect upon the concept of honor. The Church, being dominated by celibates, took a decidedly anti-feminine position, regardless of the arguments of recent apologists. Whereas St. Jerome's tirade against women in his letter versus Jovinus may be a bit extreme, many of its views prevailed in clerical writings. Women, being a pleasure of the world, hindered a man in his quest for salvation because "he that is married careth for the things that are of the world, how he may please his wife".[2]

As a result of this anti-feminine tradition, many men considered women dangerous to a man's honor as well as to his soul. This point of view was reinforced by classical references to the softening influence of Venus upon Mars. According to the Roman historians, the Teutons considered sexual activity debilitating. In his *Gallic War* (VI, 21), Caesar states that those Germanic youths who have remained chaste the longest receive the greatest praise among the people. They think that, in this way, growth is promoted, physical powers are increased, and muscles strengthened. To be intimate with a woman before the twentieth year is considered among the most shameful acts. As we have seen, Tacitus likewise stated in his *Germania* (c. 20) that Germanic youths did not exhaust their powers by mating early. Caesar and Tacitus apparently agreed with the Teutons in believing that sexual activity detracted from virility, as Plato had done before them.[3] In the *Jómsvíkings Saga*, a hero named Vigfús whets a spear while reciting a verse stating: "We have a fierce fight to expect. While the woman's friend lies at home, the fight approaches. I think that the one fond of women enjoys a warm spot under a woman's warm arms: we get our spears ready, he expects something different from battle."[4]

Following either native or classic tradition, Saxo Grammaticus

---

[1] Rougemont, pp. 75-102.
[2] *Adversus Jovinianum Libri Duo*, Migne, *Patrologia Latina*, tom. 23, 276 ff. Many of Jerome's views, which originated with Theophrastus, appeared in medieval works, for example, in Wittenwiler's *Ring*, vv. 2688-2782. "Qui autem cum uxore est sollicitus est quae sunt mundi, quomodo placeat uxori et divisus est" (*I Cor.* 7, 33).
[3] In his *Laws* (VIII, 840), Plato told how Iccus of Tarentum owed his athletic victories to sexual restraint.
[4] Cited, in verse, in *Jómsvíkings*, p. 97. This literal prose version was kindly sent me by Professor Lee M. Hollander.

expresses the same view in telling how a hero named Hjalte leaves the embrace of a wench to come to the aid of his king as soon as he hears the sound of fighting in the palace. "Preferring courage to lechery, he chose to seek the deadly dangers of Mars rather than to indulge in the alluring enticements of Venus." [1] After cutting off the nose of his sweetheart to mar her beauty, he hurries back to the king's retainers and awakens them. While doing so, he waxes eloquent on the advantages of winning glory in battle rather than shame in love-making.[2] Also, a king named Frode won disgrace as a rover, because his sailors were newly married and preferred the pleasures of the bed at home to labors of war abroad.[3]

Geoffrey of Monmouth, whose *Histories of the Kings of England* were an important source of the Arthurian legends, had anticipated this tradition by saying, "For where the use of weapons is seen to be absent and enticements of dice and women and other amusements to be present, there is no doubt that whatever there was of virtue, honor, audacity, and fame will be besmirched by cowardice.[4] Fear of such reproach compels the Burgundians to seek certain death at Kriemhild's hands rather than stay at Worms and love the fair ladies, as the kitchenmaster Rumolt advised.[5] Geoffrey's argument, via Chrétien of Troyes,[6] found its best German expression in Hartmann's *Erec* and *Iwein*. As previously mentioned, the first of these tales concerns the loss of the hero's êre through an uxorious life and of his recovery of it through deeds of arms.[7] The hero of the second tale commits the opposite fault; in his pursuit of êre he neglects his wife and thereby breaks his *triuwe* and loses his êre.[8] Thus the two of them risk the infamy that, according to Corneille,

---

[1] *Gesta Danorum*, p. 58, vv. 23-25. Cf. *Waltharius*, vv. 150-164.
[2] *op. cit.*, p. 59, vv. 1-25.
[3] *op. cit.*, p. 216, vv. 17-18.
[4] "Quippe ubi usus armorum videtur abesse. allee autem & mulierum inflammationes. ceteraque oblectzmenta adesse dubitandum non est etiam id quod erat uirtutis. quod honoris. quod audacie. quod fame. ignauia commaculari" (*Historia*, IX, 15).
[5] "und minnet waetlîchiu wîp" (*Nibelungenlied*, 1467, 4). Heinrich von Rugge disapproved of such an attitude: "Sô sprichet lîchte ein boeser man, der mannes herze nie gewan, 'wir sun hie heime vil sanfte belîben, die zît wol vertrîben vil schône mit wîben'" (*Minnesangs Frühling*, 98, 27-31).
[6] In Chrétien's *Erec*, Enide is ashamed that Erec is *recreant* (v. 2466) and has lost his *pris* (v. 2548). She hopes he will be able to wipe out their *blasme* (v. 2567) and regain his earlier fame (*los*, v. 2568) (*Christian von Troyes, Sämtliche Werke*, ed. W. Förster, Halle, 1890, III). In his *Ywain*, Gauvain eloquently expresses the knightly view toward uxorious marriage as stultifying and making a husband unworthy of his wife's love (*op. cit.*, II, vv. 2484-2538).
[7] Erec not only vindicates himself after his uxorious life, but he also saves Mabonagrin from his oath to serve his wife at the cost of his honor.
[8] Gawan describes Iwein's ignoble life as "durch wîp verligen" (*Iwein*, v. 2790).

pursues both the cowardly warrior and the perfidious lover.¹ In Shakespeare's *All's Well that Ends Well*, the countess says of her son Bertram, who deserts his bride to seek adventure: "his sword can never win the honour that he loses," for even deeds of prowess cannot compensate for perfidy.²

Centuries later Richard Lovelace alluded to love's competition with honor in his famous lines, "I could not love thee, Dear, so much, loved I not honour more." Even though the *New English Dictionary* considers this an early use of the word *honour* in its moral sense,³ I believe that Lovelace was merely following the courtly tradition that a warrior could not be worthy of love unless he preferred his good name.⁴ Three centuries earlier Conrad of Würzburg had expressed the same thought by saying, "If anyone cannot love *êre*, how should he love a pure woman with loyal thoughts?" ⁵ Although Tennyson often seems to give modern motivation to his medieval characters, he follows Chrétien's meaning when he says that Geraint, who is captivated by Enid, is "Forgetful of his glory and his name." ⁶ Here it is clearly reputation, not moral integrity, that is at stake. This literary topos lasted to modern times. A good example appears in Ibsen's *Doll's House*, when Helmer tells Nora that "no man sacrifices his honor, even for the one he loves." ⁷

Whereas the Church taught that women were a danger to men's souls and some secular writers thought them a danger to their honor, other writers of the High Middle Ages considered them prime incentives to honor. In the animal kingdom stags, bucks, bulls, and cocks seem to fight more bravely when surrounded by their mates; and this seems to hold true of man too, perhaps through some atavistic echo of older sexual selection. When Erec is being worsted in his fight with Yders, a glance at Enite makes him fight all the more valiantly.⁸ As we have seen, Tacitus mentioned how the Germanic

---

¹ "L'infamie est pareille, et suit également Le guerrier sans courage et le perfide amant" (*Le Cid*, III, 6, vv. 39-40).
² *All's Well that ends Well*, III, 2, vv. 96-97.
³ *NED* Honour sb. 2. "Personal title to high respect or esteem; honourableness; elevation of character; 'nobleness of mind, scorn of meanness, magnanimity' (J.); a fine sense of and strict allegiance to what is due or right (also, to what is due according to some conventional or fashionable standard of conduct)."
⁴ See G. F. Jones, "Lov'd I not honour more," *Comparative Literature* Vol XI, 1959, pp. 131-143.
⁵ "swer niht ere meinen kan, wie sol der geminnen reines wip mit sinnen getriuwen" (*Leiche*, 17, 37).
⁶ *Idylls of the King*, (The Marriage of Geraint, 52).
⁷ "Men der er ingen, som ofrer sin aere for den man elsker" (Henrik Ibsen, *Samlede Digterverker*, Oslo, 1937, IV, p. 205).
⁸ "und als er dar zuo an sach die schoenen froun Enîten, daz half im vaste strîten" (*Erec*, vv. 935-936). When Partonopier's blows begin to weaken, Gaudine says: "an Meliûren kapfen sult ir mit vollen ougen: sô wirt iu sunder

women stood behind their men in battle and exhorted them to even greater effort; and we have also seen that the women in the ancient sagas shamed their fathers, husbands, brothers, or sons into wreaking vengeance. Saxo Grammaticus tells how a Hunnish princess refused a Danish suitor because, "in olden days no one was considered suitable to marry illustrious women, unless he won for himself great fame through the brilliance of his deeds. In a suitor sloth was the greatest vice. Nothing was damned more in a suitor than a lack of fame." [1] Saxo also tells of a hero who has to fight a duel to prove his valor before he can win his wife.[2]

Since only the brave deserve the fair, the ladies of courtly literature often test their lovers' courage by sending them on dangerous missions. Sometimes this backfires, as in the case of Sigune and Schionatulander, whose sad story furnishes an episode in Wolfram's *Parzival* and the central theme in his misnamed *Titurel*. To test her childhood lover's courage, Sigune sends him to retrieve the leash of a straying hound; but he dies in the quest. Whereas worthy men strove hard for the praise of other men, they strove even harder to win praise from or in the presence of women. In describing a perfect knight, Conrad of Würzburg says, "He strove diligently for honors for the sake of lovely women's reward;"[3] and Iwanete tells Parzival that, if he jousts often, people will praise him in front of women.[4] Just as honor was sweetest when witnessed by women, so too disgrace was most bitter. Erec is doubly humiliated when the queen and her lady-in-waiting see him slapped by the dwarf,[5] and Parzival's shame is all the greater when a woman sees his trousers torn.[6] Feierfiz, Parzival's brother, is motivated almost solely by love in his battle with Parzival.[7]

In Wolfram's *Willehalm*, Henry of Narbonne sends his sons out into the world without any inheritance but the advice; "In case you wish to prove yourselves, esteemed women have high rewards, and

---

lougen maht unde kraft gegeben wider. niht henket iuwer houbet nider: schouwet daz vil werde wîp, sô wächset iu muot unde lîp von ir liehten angesiht" (*Partonopier*, vv. 16,090-16,097).
[1] *Gesta Danorum*, p. 124, vv. 1-3.
[2] *ibid.*, p. 194, vv. 14-17.
[3] "der fleiz sich êren harte durch minneclicher wîbe lôn" (*Trojanerkrieg*, vv. 30,002-30,003).
[4] "man lobt dich vor den wîben" (*Parzival*, 158, 12).
[5] "ern gelebt im nie leidern tac danne umb den geiselslac und schamt sich nie sô sêre, wan daz dise unêre diu künegin mit ir frouwen sach" (*Erec*, vv. 104-108).
[6] "ob iu ist zetrant inder iuwer nidercleit, daz lât iu durch die vrouwen leit, die ob iu sitzent unde sehent. waz ob die iuwer laster spehent?" (*Parzival*, 535, 20-24).
[7] "Sîn gir stuont nâch minne... Diu minne kondewierte in sîn manlîch herze hôhen muot, als si noch dem minne gernden tuot", etc. (*Parzival*, 736, 1-8).

you will also find a man somewhere who can reward service well with fiefs and other wealth." [1] In this epic the Christians, and the Saracens to an even greater degree, fight for women's rewards, which are often no more than a gracious greeting.[2] Whereas Henry had joined women's favor with feudal rewards as compatible incentives, Wolfram also associated it with God's love; for his Christians fought "for two kinds of love, for women's reward here on earth and for the angels' chorus in heaven." [3] Many thousands of verses later they are still fighting "for God and women's reward". [4] Perhaps the pagans fight so exclusively for women's rewards because they cannot fight for God.

By inspiring her knight-errant to deeds of valor, his lady contributed to his morale, or, as Wolfram states, "women give *hôher muot*".[5] Even the *Lay of the Nibelungs* follows this courtly convention by letting Ortwin ask, "What would be man's delight, and what would give him joy, if beautiful maids and splendid ladies did not do so?" [6] Rudolf of Ems expressed this thought by saying that the world values no one unless he bears "high spirits" and "dignity" from woman's love.[7] One of the chief motifs of the courtly love lyrics was the joy or despair felt by the singer according to the favor or lack of favor shown by his lady. Goethe was but one of many poets who realized that fame and women's favor are the two chief incentives to masculine endeavor.[8] Wace, whose *Brut* influenced

---

[1] "welt ir urborn den lîp, hôhen lôn hânt werdiu wîp: ir vindet ouch etswâ den man, der wol dienstes lônen kan mit lêhen und mit anderm guote" (*Willehalm*, 6, 1-5).

[2] Willehalm's men earned women's love and their hearts' favor (wîbe minne und ir herzen gunst, 7, 4). The heathen Tibalt sought after love and lands (nâch minne und nâch dem lande, 11, 9). Noupatrîs was sent to battle by women's love, and his heart and senses strove for women's reward (dar gesant hete in der wîbe minne: sîn herze und des sinne ranc nâch wîbe lône, 22, 22-25). Many heathens had risked their lives for praise and women's reward (durch prîs und durch der wîbe lôn, 25, 9). Margot's troops strove for women's greetings or other praise (wîbe gruoz oder sus nâch anderm prîse, 36, 2-3), etc., etc., etc. Likewise, Lanzelet was ready to risk all "um êre ald umb wîp" (*Lanzelet*, v. 546).

[3] "durch der zweier slahte minne, ûf erde hie durch der wîbe lôn und ze himele durch der engel dôn" (*Willehalm*, 16, 30-17, 2).

[4] "durch got und durch der wîbe lôn" (*Willehalm*, 381, 21).

[5] "sô gebent diu wîp den hôhen muot" (*Willehalm*, 83, 11). Cf. "Diu minne condewierte in sîn manlîch herze hôhen muot" (*Parzival*, 736, 6-7).

[6] "waz waere mannes wünne, des vreute sich sîn lîp, ez entaeten scoene megede und hêrlîchiu wip?" (*Nibelungenlied*, 274, 1-2). Jousting is equal to "dienen schoenen wîben" (559, 3).

[7] "der welte ist wênec iemen wert wan der von wîbes minne treit hôhgemüete und werdekeit" (*Barlaam*, 291, 12-14).

[8] In *Tasso* (III, 4) Antonio says of the two chief rewards for service: "Der Lorbeer ist es und die Gunst der Frauen." Castiglione gives a compelling picture of the good influence of women upon men's courage and other virtues (*Cortegiano*, III, 51).

the courtly tradition of all Europe, said that amours and amorous conversation made cavaliers chivalrous.[1]

Not only could a scornful woman shame a man into action, but also the love of or to a woman could inspire him to virtue. Gottfried, the rhapsodist of love, claimed that no one can have virtue or honor without love's teaching, and Walther expressed the same idea by saying, "He who has a good woman's love is ashamed of any misdeed."[2] This topos, which lasted unbroken for centuries, appeared about the year 1400 in the *Plowman from Bohemia* as, "If anyone is in a woman's service, he must refrain from all misdeeds." Elsewhere this work says that a disapproving shake of a pure woman's finger rebukes and disciplines a worthy man more than any weapon.[3] Goethe expressed this belief in his *Tasso*, when the princess says that, to learn what is proper, one should ask noble women. It also appears in his *Iphigenie*, when Arkas says that a noble man can be led far by the good word of a woman.[4]

This mystical faith in the purifying power of a woman may have been influenced by St. Paul's dictum to the Corinthians: "For the unbelieving husband is consecrated through his wife".[5] As we have seen, Tacitus tells how the Teutons ascribed mystic powers to their women. The ennobling influence of women has been praised until modern times, finding classic utterance in the closing lines of Goethe's *Faust*: "Das Ewig-Weibliche zieht uns hinan".

---

[1] "Mult sunt bones les gaberies E bones sunt les drüeries. Pur amistié e pur amies Funt chevaliers chevaleries" (*Brut*, vv. 10,769-71).
[2] "daz niemen âne ir lêre noch tugende hât noch êre" (*Tristan*, v. 190). "swer guotes wîbes minne hât, der schamt sich aller missetât" (Walther, 93,17-18). "Wer in frauen dienste ist, der muss sich aller missetat anen" (*Ackerman*, 29).
[3] "Einer reinen frauen fingirdroen strafet und züchtiget vür alle waffen einen frumen man" (*Ackerman*, v. 29). For other examples of this topos, see *ibid.*, p. 211.
[4] "Willst du genau erfahren was sich ziemt, So frage nur bei edlen Frauen an" (*Tasso*, II, 1); "Ein edler Mann wird durch ein gutes Wort Der Frauen weit geführt" (*Iphigenie*, I, 2).
[5] "sanctificatus est enim vir infidelis per mulierem fidelem" (*I Cor.* 7, 14).

CHAPTER SIX

COURTIER, CLERIC, AND CONTRADICTION

> *One should pursue wealth and honor and yet keep God in his heart.* FREIDANK, 93, 22.

In contrast to the worldly literature of the court poets, the otherworldly tradition continued unbroken, often finding expression in the works of the courtly poets themselves. The best German version of the Gregorius legend was written by Hartmann of Aue; and the best version of the St. Alexius legend was written by Conrad of Würzburg, who also contributed works on worldly themes.[1] Even more conducive to developing public morality than the courtly and monastic romances were the collections of wise maxims like the *German Cato*, Freidank's *Bescheidenheit*, and Thomasin's *Welscher Gast*, which became popular in the thirteenth century. The wisdom in these works was mostly of clerical origin, much of it directly from Scripture, especially from the books then attributed to King Solomon; yet the references to honor, like those to moderation, came largely from Roman-Stoic tradition, since Scripture was not particularly concerned with these subjects. Much of this wisdom can be traced directly to a group of twelfth-century churchmen gathered at Chartres, among others Alain of Lille, John of Salisbury, Bernard Silvester, and William of Conches.

Of all literary traditions, the didactic tradition probably contributed the most to our present concept of honor, it being the one most thoroughly disseminated among the populace. Its short pithy proverbs were easily committed to memory and served as good nourishment for generations of school children, of souls still young enough to be molded. In addition to furnishing reading matter for scholars, these collections provided source material for the *Spruchdichter*, or popular aphoristic poets, who transmitted their wisdom even to the illiterate bulk of the population. The moralists, or didactic poets, understood the word *êre* chiefly in its external sense, that is, as the acclaim of society.[2] To be sure, like Plato before them,[3]

---
[1] ed. R. Henczynski, Berlin, 1898, *Acta Germanica*, VI, 1.
[2] This is evident in Freidank's discourse on honor, in which he collects the best-known commonplaces on the subject (Freidank, 91,12 - 93,25).
[3] Plato, *Laws*, 697 B-C (trans. R. G. Bury).

they contended that this acclaim should be won not by wealth, birth, and rank, but rather by virtue. Moreover, honor was due not only to heroic deeds, but also to loyal performance of duty and to resignation to divine will, as it had long been in the monasteries. Thus they began to distinguish between true and false honor. Worldly acclaim was still a positive goal, but only when achieved through righteous deeds and disposition.

As we have seen, both Germanic and courtly society were based on the inequality of man, and the ruling classes never questioned the value of noble birth despite all Christian teaching to the contrary. The court poets thought only wellborn persons entitled to honor, everyone else being boorish and unworthy of mention; and they used the words for noble, courtly, and honorable almost synonymously. Ancient Greek and Roman society had also been based on a caste system, which was taken for granted by most philosophers. Nevertheless, some thinkers, particularly the Stoics, questioned whether noble birth alone could make a man virtuous. Juvenal, a Roman satirist who wrote at the beginning of the second century of this era, devoted his eighth satire to attacking nobility of birth; for the only true nobility is virtue (*Nobilitas sola est atque unica virtus*).

Since honor is rightfully shown to nobility and true nobility is virtue, then honor should be shown to any virtuous man. As we have seen, St. Martin of Braga claimed that one could attain the *vita honesta* by practicing the four virtues of prudence, magnanimity, continence, and justice. Early in the twelfth century Petrus Alphonsus, a converted Spanish Jew, claimed to quote Aristotle as saying that true nobility derived not from noble birth, but from the mastery of the seven liberal arts, the seven virtues (*industriae*), and the seven accomplishments (*probitates*).[1] St. Anselm of Canterbury expressed the view as "Noble is he who shines with the virtue of the spirit, illborn is he alone who is pleased with an evil life."[2] Although these scholars knew that the word *nobilitas* literally designated a good of the body (not of the mind) as the *Moralium Dogma* quoted Cicero as saying,[3] they sometimes used the word in the transferred sense of moral excellence.

Freidank expressed St. Anselm's thought more succinctly by saying, "Whoever does right is wellborn," and Thomasin said about the same thing.[4] With this new definition of "noble" he can say that

[1] *Disciplina Clericalis*, p. 10.
[2] In *Carmen de Contemptu Mundi;* Migne, *Patrologia Latina*, 158, 695. For numerous other examples of this topos, see E. Wiessner, *Kommentar zu Heinrich Wittenwilers Ring*, Leipzig, 1935, p. 167.
[3] *Moralium Dogma*, p. 54, line 8.
[4] "Nobilis est iste, qui sectatur bona gesta", "Wer reht tuot, der ist wol geboren" (*Freidanks Bescheidenheit, lateinisch und deutsch*, ed. H. Lemke, n.d., 196b, 10. See *Helmbrecht*, vv. 506-507; *Helbling*, VIII, vv. 359-362;

all "noble" people are God's children.[1] This theme was repeated constantly during the following centuries in a myriad of variations. A good example of this topos is found in Chaucer's "Wife of Bath's Tale", which says, "Looke who that is moost vertuous alway, Pryvee and apert, and moost entendeth ay To do the gentil dedes that he can; Taak hym for the grettest gentil man."[2]

We have seen that Siegfried, after reviling Gunther for his dastardly deed, still addresses him as "noble King" and thus shows that the word applied to one's rank regardless of one's behavior. Through the efforts of the moralists the word *edel* gradually began to assume its modern meaning. The Latin word *nobilis*, which is related to *nosco*, originally meant recognizable, known, or famous. Being conventionally applied to the ruling classes, it became associated with the German word *edel*, which, as we have seen, originally referred to the owners of allodial property. These two words seem to have developed their modern ethical meaning simultaneously and perhaps through reciprocal influence.

When courtly poets and pedagogues said that true nobility derived from noble behavior, they were not attacking the social order, but merely saying that "noblesse oblige". In other words, in order to receive the honor due to noble birth, one must play the part by being brave, generous, trustworthy, and dutiful to God. Although they admitted that not all men of noble birth practiced these virtues, they often implied that only wellborn persons can do so, commoners being by nature incapable of the finer things.[3] Frederick of Sunnenberg, a thirteenth-century aphoristic poet, said, "The noble and wellborn man gladly strives for honor; likewise, a peasant naturally loves disgrace and disgraceful things. The peasant is pleased with misdeeds, that is innate in him. The noble man occupies himself with good conduct and worthiness. Whenever the peasant acts knavishly, he is happy and very contented. The nobleman strives for honor."[4] One might argue that by "peasant" he is

---

Renner, vv. 889-972; *Minnesangs Frühling*, 24, 33-34; *Ring*, vv. 4421-4422. "Nieman ist edel niwan der man der sîn herze und sîn gemüete hât gekêrt an rehte güete" (*Welscher Gast*, vv. 3860-3862); "swer rehte tuot zaller vrist, wizzet dasz der edel ist" (vv. 3923-3924); "der tugent hât, derst wol geborn und êret sîn geslehte wol" (*Winsbeke*, 28, 5-6).

[1] "Sô wizzet daz die edel sint die sint alle gotes kint" (*Welscher Gast*, vv. 3925-3926). Thomasin devotes many verses to this argument (vv. 3855 ff.).
[2] *Chaucer*, ed. Robinson, III (D), vv. 1113-1116.
[3] "bî zuht die edeln man ie kande: unzuht ist noch gebiurisch schande. gebiuwer und herren kint, swâ die glîcher tugende sint, dâ ist daz lemrîn worden bunt" (Konrad von Haslau, *Der Jüngling*, ed. M. Haupt, *ZfdA*, [1], 1851, p. 550, vv. 5-9).
[4] "Der edele wolgeborne man nach eren gerne stat. So mynnet ouch von art eyn bur diu schande unde dartzu schanden rat. Dem gebure ist wol mit missetat. Daz ist im an geboren. Der edele man der vlizet sich an tzucht, an

not referring to a particular social class, but just to depraved persons in general. Be that as it may, the very choice of this term implies that all rural commoners were scorned. When Gottfried states that he has written his *Tristan* for "noble-hearts",[1] he does not mean for all wellborn persons, but merely for the few discriminating ones. Nevertheless, even though he was a burgher himself, his epic is concerned only with people of gentle birth, in the usual meaning of the word.

The popular *Spruchdichter*, on the other hand, usually argued that true nobility derives from good behavior and is thus within the reach of everyone. As Freidank expressed the idea, "Be he serf or be he free, if anyone is not noble by birth, he should make himself noble by virtuous behavior."[2] Therefore honor, which the courts tried to monopolize for the nobility, was also attainable by any virtuous person, regardless of his birth. By such arguments the moralists acknowledged the dignity (cf. *dignitas*) of labor and the laboring classes. Perhaps one of the most touching expressions of this view is to be found in *Farmer Helmbrecht*, Germany's oldest "village tale" and one of the finest gems of medieval storytelling.[3]

This tale, avowedly an eye-witness account, tells of a peasant youth who is dissatisfied with his social station and aspires to become a knight. Against the better advice of his father he leaves his family and takes service with a robber-knight and becomes a notorious bandit. Finally he is captured and punished by the loss of his eyes, his right hand, and his right foot. Driven from his father's house, he wanders as a beggar for a year until he is finally lynched by some outraged peasants.

The father, a symbol of the contented peasant, tries to persuade his ambitious son to remain on the farm by assuring him that he can win more honor at home than at court. "Follow my advice", he says, "and you will have profit and honor, for he never succeeds who strives against his order." If the son goes to court, he will win only disgrace and ridicule from the true courtiers. If he plows his fields, he can be buried with great honors like his father, who has paid his tithes every year and lived with loyalty and reliability and

---

wirdechait. Swen der gebur schelchliche tut so ist der vro unde vil gemeyt. Der edele man nach eren steit. Diu ere hat ym gesworn" (*Die Jenaer Liederhandschrift*, ed. G. Holz, Leipzig, 1901, I, p. 115).

[1] "edelen herzen" (*Tristan*, v. 47).

[2] "Er sî eigen oder frî, der von geburt nicht edel sî, der sol sich edel machen mit tugenlîchen sachen" (Freidank, 54, 8). Similarly, Wittenwiler says, "Ein gpaur der wirt ein edelman, Der sich dar nach gewenen kan" (*Ring*, vv. 4400-4402).

[3] Cited here from *Meier Helmbrecht*, ed. F. Panzer, Tübingen, 1953, *ATB* no. 11. An English translation is available in C. H. Bell, *Peasant Life in Old German Epics*, New York, 1931.

without hate. Honor and profit come to him who follows good teaching; and harm and disgrace to him who ignores his father's advice.[1]

When the son claims that he is noble because his godfather was noble, the father answers that he prefers a man who does right and remains constant. Such a man, even if of low birth (*von swacher art*), pleases the world better than a king's descendant who has never achieved virtue or honor (*tugent noch êre*). If a virtuous man of low condition (*ein frumer man von swacher art*) and a nobly born man who has never shown any breeding or honor (*zuht noch êre*) came into a country where nobody knew who they were, people would prefer the poor man's child to the noble wellborn man who has chosen dishonor (*schande*) rather than honor (*êre*). Therefore, if his son wishes to be noble, he should act nobly; for "good behavior is surely a crown above all nobility"[2].

Although the father praises the peasantry, he never questions the sanctity of the social order. One might even say that the chief theme of the story is found in the words, "He never succeeds who strives against his order." During this period the Church agreed with the nobility in believing social boundaries divinely ordained and not to be transgressed. Even though a peasant had to remain a peasant, he was none the less entitled to honor within his group. As Freidank put it, "A peasant has enough honor if he is foremost in his village." [3]

Whereas the courtly poets scorned all productive work, as the ancient Teutons had done before them, the didactic poets praised it as the monastics had done. Father Helmbrecht followed this tradition in praising the virtue of farming.[4] Praise of the honest

---

[1] "nû volge mîner lêre, des hâstu frum und êre; wan selten im gelinget, der wider sînen orden ringet" (*Helmbrecht*, vv. 287-290); "dîn laster dû gemêrest, sun, des swer ich dir bî got; der rehten hoveliute spot wirdestû, vil liebez kint" (vv. 294-297); "swer volget guoter lêre, der gewinnet frum und êre: swelch kint sînes vater rât ze allen zîten übergât, daz stât ze jüngest an der schame und an dem schaden rehte alsame" (vv. 331-336).
[2] "mir geviele et michel baz ein man der rehte taete und dar an belibe staete. waer des geburt ein wênic laz, der behagte doch der welde baz dan von küneges fruht ein man der tugent noch êre nie gewan. ein frumer man von swacher art und ein edel man an dem nie wart zuht noch êre bekant, und koment die bêde in ein lant dâ niemen weiz wer si sint, man hât des swachen mannes kint für den edelen hôchgeborn der für êre schande hât erkorn" (*Helmbrecht*, vv. 488-508).
[3] "Ein gebûr genuoc êren hât, der vor in sîme dorfe gât" (Freidank, 122, 9-10).
[4] "sô bûwe mit dem phluoge; sô geniezent dîn genuoge: dîn geniuzet sicherlîche der arme und der rîche, dîn geniuzet wolf und ar und alliu creatûre gar und swaz got ûf der erden hiez ie lebendic werden. lieber sun, nû bouwe: jâ wirt nû manec frouwe von dem bûwe geschoenet, manec künec wirt gekroenet von des bûwes stiuwer. wan niemen wart sô tiuwer, sîn hôchvart waere kleine

husbandman became common in didactic literature, and Chaucer's idealized Plowman was but one of many. Clergymen assured the peasantry that they had an essential and honorable part to play in the divine scheme. Typical is a song by Henry of Meissen, a thirteenth-century mastersinger: "People have been divided into three classes since the beginning, as I read. Peasant, knight, and priest, each was, according to his measure, ever equal to the other in nobility and condition. What is the intent of the priests? They teach us good behavior, art, wisdom, and the power of all virtues, peace, shame, and reverence. Give knighthood to the knight. The peasant has reserved the right to produce food for the other two with profit. Now priest, worthy priest, leave the other orders alone. You, proud knight, cause knighthood to smile on you, do not assume another condition. You, peasant, should not strive higher. I teach you that for the sake of lasting glory." [1]

Because the Stoics recognized the individual but not society, they denied the value of external honor.[2] The Church Fathers, on the other hand, recognized external honor as the greatest wordly value, and for that very reason they denounced it as a worldly value that distracted men from their quest for salvation. Gradually these two traditions fused in the writings of the didactic poets. Since a purely negative view toward honor would have little appeal to men of honor, who were naturally the politically and socially leading element, the didactic writers compromised by saying that it was permissible to seek honor as long as it was sought in ways pleasing to God. The old virtues of courage, loyalty, and largess had value in so far as they served the will of God. According to Joinville, King Philip Augustus of France distinguished between a *preu home* (brave man) and a *preudhome* (brave and righteous man), that is, a man who has his prowess from God and serves God free of sin.[3] A

---

wan durch daz bû aleine" (*Helmbrecht*, vv. 545-560). The didactic poet Suchenwirt expressed the thought as: "Wenn gepawrn nicht mer ist, So wirt der schimpf entrennet: Wes denn lebent die selben frist, Die herren sint gennennet? Die fürsten nicht mit phluegen gan, Die purger sich sein schamen, So muozz man underwegen lan Auf aekcher werffen den samen" (Suchenwirt, p. 111, no. 37, vv. 21-28). Cf. "Won allü froed waer gar zenicht, Waer des bumans nicht" (*Teufels Netz*, vv. 12,414-12,415).
[1] "In driu geteilet wâren von êrst die liute, als ich las. bûman, rittaer und pfaffen, ieslîch nâ sîner mâze was gelîch an adel und an art dem andern ie. wie stêt der pfaffen sin? Si lêrent wol gebâren, kunst, wîsheit, aller tugende kraft, vride, scham und dar zuo vorhte. dem ritter lîchet ritterschaft. der bûman het sich des bewart, daz er den zweien nar schüef mit gewin. Nu pfaffe, werder pfaffe, lâz ander orden under wegen; du stolzer ritter schaffe, daz ritterschaft dir lache, niht nim and dich ein ander leben; du bûman solt niht hôher streben,,," (Leiche, 244, 1-18). In his translation of Boethius's *De Consolatione*, King Alfred had already divided a king's subjects into "men of religion, men of war, and men of work" (Highet, p. 46).
[2] Eckstein, p. 19.
[3] Joinville, *Histoire de Saint Louis*, ed. N. de Willy, Paris, 1890, p. 235.

similar distinction seems to have been made by the German didactic poet Teichner. Although the word *bider* normally meant brave, he claimed that a *piderman* is one who fears and loves God.[1]

For the sake of convenience, this study has distinguished between the court poets, who affirmed worldly honor, and the didactic poets, who negated it. Actually this distinction is too arbitrary, inasmuch as all the court poets showed the influence of didactic clerical writers, and the didactic poets in turn had to write their works to appeal to secular audiences. As we have seen, Wolfram and other court poets taught that honor can be won only through practicing moderation, moderation even in courage and largess.

We have also seen that some poets, such as Hartmann of Aue, could write either worldly or otherwordly works to suit the taste of their patrons. In the opening verses of his *Gregorius*, Hartmann explains that he has sinned in his youth by writing worldly works and that now he is going to do penance by writing a religious one. Strangely enough, many scholars have taken him at his word and have believed that this confession indicated change of heart, instead of merely conformity to literary tradition.[2] Because Hartmann wrote his worldly *Iwein* after his *Gregorius* and *Poor Henry*, it is more probable that such conversion was fictitious. Before Rousseau and Goethe, people did not insist that great literature express personal experience; and Hartmann frankly admitted that he wrote what people wanted to hear.[3]

Many poets followed Hartmann's example and treated otherworldly themes in the style and language of the court epics. Foremost among these were Rudolf of Ems and Conrad of Würzburg, who selected both secular and spiritual themes. Because they stand firmly in didactic tradition, one might expect them to use *êre* primarily in a moral sense. This is not the case. Miss Irmgard Riechert, who has made a painstaking study of Rudolf's and Conrad's many uses of the word *êre*, concludes that Rudolf scarcely ever employs it in its inner sense and that, of some 900 times it appears in Conrad's works, it has definite ethical meaning some 71 times and possible ethical meaning some 51 times more.[4] Whereas some people might be surprised that *êre* so seldom had inner meaning, I think that Miss Riechert's estimate is far too high. In fact, I find no passage where inner value is absolutely certain.

Miss Riechert herself acknowledges that there are no absolutely

[1] "ein pider man daz ist der got furichten chan und got hat lieb für allez gut" (Teichner, 252, 3-5). He devotes a whole song (no. 333) to teaching that honor can be won by practicing humility.
[2] Such credulity still appears in H. de Boor, *Geschichte der deutschen Literatur*, Munich, 1953, II, 68.
[3] "daz man gerne hoeren mac, dâ kêrt er sînen vlîz an" (*Iwein*, vv. 26-27).
[4] Riechert, p. 97.

reliable criteria for judging whether the word *êre* in a given passage designates an inner or an external value,[1] and I cannot accept any of the criteria which she uses. She thinks a good criterion to be Conrad's practice of localizing *êre* in a person's heart;[2] but medieval poets, often used the heart as the seat of desire, be it good or bad.[3] Even today we can say, "He has his heart set on riches," or "For where your treasure is, there will your heart be also." When Conrad says that someone's heart is a chest of *êren*, it need mean no more than that his heart causes him to strive for honors, as is quite apparent in one passage in his *Trojan War*.[4] Miss Riechert also thinks that *êre*, when used in connection with an oath, must have inner meaning;[5] but, as we shall see, this new value became attached to oaths only in modern times. Even when Conrad seems to be using *êre* in a moral sense, the context will often show that this is not the case. In his epic about Alexander the Great, he lets Aristotle warn against drunkenness: "Be on your guard against drunkenness, which harms virtue and *êren*." But then he continues, "It is the cause of disgrace and an opprobrius grave of worldly honors."[6]

In studies appearing between 1949 and 1952 Friedrich Maurer

[1] Richert, p. 68.
[2] Riechert, pp. 8-9. As evidence she cites, among other passages, one from Conrad's *Partonopier*. However, when read in context, it is clear that the *êren* are to be understood objectively. Partonopier says of the sultan: "benamen dirre werde man nâch hôhem prîse werben kan als ein ritter ellentrîch. kein fürste wart im nie gelîch an êren, die sîn herze birt" (*Partonopier*, vv. 16,067-16,071). Since the sultan can strive for praise, it is clear that the honors that his heart (i.e. courage) produces are merely worldly praise, not inner integrity. Likewise, Miss Riechert cites the verses, "sîn herze ist in der smitten der êren lûter worden". However, here too the nature of the *êren* is clarified a few verses later when Partonopier comes into the battle "gerennet dô nâch prîse" (vv. 21,064-21,065; 21,071). In all such passages, the word *êre* refers to the praise and prestige a man wins when his heart is set on glory.
[3] Walther says, "jâ leider desn mac niht gesîn, daz guot und weltlich êre und gotes hulde mêre zesamene in ein herze komen" (Walther, 8, 19-22). Here, either tangible wealth or intangible honor can come into the heart.
[4] "sîn herze vleiz sich alles des, daz wirde heizen mohte; swaz hôhen êren tohte, dar ûf twanc er sich alle wege" (*Trojanerkrieg*, vv. 6368-6371).
[5] She cites (pp. 53-54) this passage: "daz er mich ûz dem prîse der êren hât gevellet" (*Partonopier*, vv. 7936-7937). Judging by the strictly objective sense of *êre* in the remainder of the poem, it is clear that Partonopier merely means that he has lost the glory of a good name.
[6] "wis vor trunkenheit behuot diu tugent und eren schaden tuot. si ist der schanden urhap und ein lasterlîchez grap weltlîcher êren" (*Alexander*, vv. 1751-1754). Likewise, when Rudolf of Ems appears to be using *êre* as a moral value, it sometimes happens that he is following a Latin source where this is not the case. In *Barlaam* (218, 24-26), he says that it is an *êre* for a child to obey its father, but the Latin originel merely uses the amoral word *laus* (Riechert, pp. 135-136). Cf. "Ich trunke gerne dâ man bî der mâze schenket, und dâ der übermâze niemen niht gedenket, sît si den man an lîbe, an guot und an den êren krenket" (Walther, 29, 25-27).

convincingly showed that the word êre did not have subjective meaning in the writings of Hartmann, Wolfram, and Walther.[1] Therefore it is surprising that this pupil, Miss Riechert, claimed to find such meaning in the word as used by Conrad and Rudolf, who can scarcely be said to be very much more advanced culturally than their illustrious predecessors. Some years earlier another doctoral candidate, Hildegard Emmel, had been misled by the word êre in the works of Hartmann and Wolfram and in the *Lay of the Nibelungs*, which she defined as the "socially recognized possession of virtue".[2] In this she erred: she should have defined êre as "social recognition of the possession of virtue". This may sound like quibbling, but there is an immense cultural difference between the two definitions. When Iwein defeats Guivreiz, the victim tells the victor that his courage has restored his êre. Miss Emmel explains that Erec "is thereby again in possession of his lost virtue."[3] In other words, she believes that êre is a virtue, instead of merely the reward of virtue, as Aristotle had said of timê and as Cicero had said of honos.[4]

In a recent dissertation on the meaning of the word êre in the pre-courtly period, Lotte Norwood cites many parallels in which êre is juxtaposed with piety, chastity, humility, etc. Nevertheless, she is astute enough to observe that "in these passages the meaning of the word itself is not changed. The word still refers to the person's esteem or social position."[5] What she says about the objective nature of the concept êre in pre-courtly poetry would hold by and large for the court poets such as Hartmann and Wolfram and even for their successors such as Conrad and Rudolf.

In a dissertation written in 1957, Hans Schulz proved that the word êre still had no ethical significance in the Middle German version of the *Book of the Maccabees* or in the *Chronicle of Prussia*, both of

---

[1] Maurer, "Zum ritterlichen ‚Tugendsystem' ", p. 526.
[2] "êre allgemein formuliert meint bei Hartmann den von der Gesellschaft anerkannten Besitz der Tugend" (Emmel, p. 31).
[3] "wan daz dir diu êre geschiht von dîner manheit" (*Erec*, vv. 4451-4452). "Erec ist damit wieder im Besitz der verlorenen Tugent" (Emmel, p. 36).
[4] "for honour is the prize of virtue, and it is to the good that it is rendered" (Aristotle, *Ethics*, IV, 3, trans. Ross). "cum honos sit praemium virtutis studioque civium delatum ad aliquem, qui eum sententiis, qui suffragiis adeptus est, is mihi honestus et honoratus videtur" (Cicero, *Brutus*, 81, 281. See also *Epist. ad. fam.* X, x, 1 ff.). Cf. "cum honor sit premium virtutis, et omnis prelatio sit honor, omnis prelatio virtutis est premium" (Dante, *De Monarchia*, III, 3).
[5] "In diesen Stellen ist die Bedeutung des Wortes nicht verändert. Das Wort bezieht sich noch immer auf das Ansehen, die Stellung des Menschen" (Norwood, p. 280). In expressions such as "waz bedorfte ein gôt knecht rîchtûmes mêre, behelde er trûwe unde êre", she lists êre in the category; "der konkrete Gegenstand, die Person oder Begriff, der zur êre aller beiträgt" (P. 220). Nevertheless, she attributes to it, "ehrenhafte Gesinnung im modernen Sinne" (p. 254). Chapter III is particularly commendable.

which appeared in the early fourteenth century.¹ His thoroughly objective and convincing evidence would suggest either that the clerical authors of these two texts were culturally behind Conrad, who had written more than a century earlier, or else that Miss Riechert had misinterpreted her evidence because of being misled by her modern ideas concerning honor.

Through a queer combination of historical ignorance and wishful thinking, the German Romantics and many subsequent European intellectuals believed the High Middle Ages to have been a period of universal harmony. An extreme expression of this naive view was given by Friedrich von Hardenberg, better known as Novalis, whose essay, *Christianity or Europe*, described a golden age of happy people blissfully united by a single unquestioned faith.² Modern scholars still refer to such harmony, but they usually attribute it to some period other than their own period of specialization.³

Hardenberg's views do not concur with historical fact. The High Middle Ages, like preceding and succeeding periods, was a time of spiritual tension as well as of political discord. Officially there may have been only one Christendom in Western Europe, but that was at the cost of eradicating the Albigensians and other dissident groups. Also, men constantly found themselves torn between secular fealty and Christian obedience; whenever a Christian prince was excommunicated, his followers had to choose between following him at the cost of their eternal soul and deserting him at the cost of shame in this world. Vassals usually remained true to their liege, unless they preferred to use the excommunication as a pretext to deprive him of his power. Many poets found it difficult to reconcile their Christian faith with the political machinations of the Papacy. Perhaps the best known of these was Walther, who consistently sided with the emperor against the pope's devious conspiracies.⁴

The Romantic view of the Middle Ages was furthered by the rediscovery of medieval art and by the erroneous assumption that great art always expresses social harmony and spiritual tranquillity. It may also have been influenced by a misunderstanding of certain literary works from the age of chivalry. These works should not be taken as a picture of the times, but rather as an escape from a very contrary reality. The poets were not trying to record for us how their contemporaries lived or felt, but rather to instruct their contem-

---

[1] Hans Schulz, *Studien*...
[2] *Novalis Schriften*, ed. E. Heilborn, Berlin, 1901, I, pp. 399-420.
[3] Siegfried Puknat, in discussing the chapbooks of the 15th and 16th centuries, says, "Medieval harmony between inner life and outer activity has yielded to a sheer materialistic attitude..." ("The Volksbuch of the 15th and 16th Centuries", *Journal of English and Germanic Philologie*, 47, 1948, p. 362).
[4] Walther, 33,1 - 34, 34.

poraries in how they should live and feel. Such harmony can be found in the realm of the Holy Grail, but only because this is a never-never land where all insoluble problems are ignored.

The task of the courtly poets was to reconcile Germanic and Christian tradition into a harmonious way of life. From their heathen ancestors they inherited respect for wealth and worldly honor; and from the Christian missionaries they acquired a desire for God's grace. These values, which were the goal of every hero in courtly literature, were conventionally combined into the triad *guot, êre,* and *gotes huld,* the concept *êre* sometimes being expressed as "the world's favor".[1] On one occasion Walther associates honor with wealth and subordinates them to God's grace, and thus he confesses a guilt culture.[2] On another occasion he associates God's grace with honor and raises them above life, wife, and child, which one should sacrifice rather than lose the first two.[3] In this case he seems to equate the incentives of shame and guilt culture. In all these cases the word *êre* obviously refers to objective honor, that is, to the acclaim of society.

Nevertheless, scholars have misinterpreted *êre* in these passages ever since Gustav Ehrismann identified it with Cicero's *honestum* in his inspiring, but incorrect, article on "The Chivalrous Code of Virtues" in 1919.[4] In this article Ehrismann associated the triad *guot, êre* and *gotes huld* with the Ciceronian triad *utile, honestum,* and *summum bonum,* even in cases where *êre* is modified by the adjective "worldly" (*werltlich*) and is associated with wealth and contrasted with God's grace. As a result, Ehrismann interpreted many poems and epics falsely, and so did his disciples. Although Ernst Curtius discredited his elaborate system in 1943,[5] his views are still echoed, for example even in a literary lexicon of 1956.[6] In 1950 Friedrich Maurer convincingly demonstrated that *MHG êre* meant *honos* rather than *honestum.*[7]

---

[1] "Der wîse minnet niht sô sêre, alsam die gotes hulde und êre" (Walther, 22, 24-25). "swem ez (wealth) ist lieber danne got und werltlîch êre, ich waene, er tobe" (Winsbeke, 28, 6-7). "der werlde hulde" (*Parzival*, 827, 22).
[2] "diu zwei sint êre und varnde guot... daz dritte ist gotes hulde, der zweier übergulde" (Walther, 8, 14-17).
[3] "Der wîse minnet niht sô sêre, alsam die gotes hulde und êre: sîn selbes lîp, wîp und kint, diu lat er ê er disiu zwei verliese" (Walther, 22, 24-27). Cf. "swem ez (wealth) ist lieber danne got und werltlîch êre, ich waene, er tobe" (Winsbeke, 28, 6-7). I believe that Walther, 22, 29, is erroneous.
[4] Ehrismann, "Das ritterliche Tugendsystem".
[5] E. R. Curtius, "Das 'ritterliche Tugendsystem' ". See Wentzlaff-Eggebert, pp. 253-257, and Maurer, "Das ritterliche Tugendsystem", pp. 274-285.
[6] Hermann Pongs, *Das kleine Lexikon der Weltliteratur*, Stuttgart, 1956, col. 311, states that Cicero's *honestum* and *utile* affected the knightly ethics of the High Middle Ages, for example, in Walther's "*êre und varnde guot*".
[7] Maurer, "Zum ritterlichen 'Tugendsystem' ". In his "Das ritterliche Tugendsystem", which was first written in 1944, Maurer still interpreted *êre* as *honestum.*

Many poets found no difficulty in reconciling the unreconcilables: Eilhart of Oberge merely states that one will always prosper if he loves God with his heart and strives for honor,[1] a thought possibly derived from St. Paul's epistle to the Romans.[2] The hero of many epics merely excels in all worldly virtues and enjoys worldly honor; then, by professing allegiance to God and doing some good works, he wins God's grace and assurance of further glory in heaven. In his *William of Orléans* Rudolf of Ems lets Duke Jovrit enter a cloister with the words, "In order to preserve my soul, I wish to relinquish the honor I have had in this world." [3] Hartmann's Erec and Iwein are typical of this happy breed, but it is clear that Hartmann has evaded rather than solved the problem. In his *Gregorius* he writes from a more other-worldly view, without really trying to give this world its due. Only in his *Poor Henry* does he seem to face the problem.

The hero of Hartmann's *Poor Henry* is an ideal knight endowed with all goods of body and fortune and all aristocratic virtues. His description is so typical that it deserves to be quoted. "His heart had forsworn all falsehood and villainy and kept its oath firmly to the end. His birth and station were without shortcoming. He had been given as much as he could wish of worldly honors, which he could well increase with all sorts of pure virtue. He was a flower of youth, a mirror of wordly joy, a diamond of constant *triuwe*, an entire crown of good breeding. He was a refuge for the needy, a shield for his kinsmen, an equal scale of largess. He had neither too much nor too little. He bore a heavy burden of honors on his back.[4] He was a bridge of counsel and sang well of love. Thus he could win the world's praise. He was courtly and wise." [5]

---

[1] "swer got von herzin minnet und nâch den êrin ringet dem volgit selden unheil" (*Tristrant*, vv. 3113-3115).
[2] "iis quidem, qui secundum patientiam boni operis gloriam et honorem et incorruptionem quaerunt, vitam aeternam" (*Romans*, 2, 7).
[3] "Dar uf das ich die sel bewar, Wil ich die ere lassen gar Die ich ze dirre welte han" (*Willehalm von Orlens*, vv. 14,813 - 14,815). This was also Trevrizent's solution.
[4] The image of a man bearing a burden of honors on his back probably originated in an earlier Latin version of the story, because it was traditional to relate the words *honos* and *onus*. Marcus Terentius Varro, a contemporary of Cicero, gave this etymology in his *De Lingua Latina* (V, 73): "Honos ab onere: itaque honestum dicitur quod oneratum, et dictum: 'Onus est honos qui sustinet rem publicam." Cf. " 'tis a burden Cromwell, 'tis a burden" (*Henry VIII*, iii, 2).
[5] "sîn herze hâte versworn valsch und alle dörperheit und behielt vaste den eit staete unz an sîn ende. âne alle missewende stuont sîn geburt und sîn leben. im was der rehte wunsch gegeben von wertlîchen êren: die kunde er wol gemêren mit aller hande reiner tugent. er was ein bluome der jugent, der werltvreude ein spiegelglas, stæte triuwe ein adamas, ein ganziu krône der zuht. er was der nôthaften vluht, ein schilt sîner mâge, der milte ein glîchiu wâge: im enwart über noch gebrast. er truoc den arbeitsamen last der êren

At first sight this description seems to owe a great deal to Christianity; yet, except for his moderation, courtliness, and ability to sing of love, he had only the virtues long since praised in the heroes of the sagas. Like them, his various gifts and abilities served chiefly to win the world's praise. This was all that could be asked of a worldly knight, enough for either Erec or Iwein. However, in this poem, which was probably written for an ecclesiastical patron, Hartmann wished to show that only a fool thinks he can enjoy wealth and honor without divine aid.[1] Because Henry knows no humility before God, God smites him with leprosy, which at once deprives him of all worldly êre.[2] After at first trying to find worldly aid, Henry is at last cured when he submits to God's will and refuses the lifeblood of a young maiden who has offered to die for him. Thus Hartmann reconciles the demands of this world and the next through recourse to miracle and magic.

Other poets also expressed the opinion that it was possible to enjoy the goods of fortune and God's grace too. Thomasin, a thirteenth-century Italian churchman who wrote a didactic poem in German, said that nobility, power, pleasure, reputation, wealth, and sovereignty are not really desirable goods, since a wicked man can have them. On the other hand, they need not be bad, since a well-disposed man often has them too. Like Hartmann in his *Poor Henry*, Thomasin said that we are wrong in thinking that strength, sovereignty, nobility, reputation, and power will enable us to come to God.[3]

In other words, these poets championed the Church's view that man could avail nothing without divine aid. This was perhaps the greatest break with the Germanic past, which let the praiseworthy hero rely entirely upon his own resources. The courtly epics conventionally gave lip service to the Church's view; and the poets constantly attribute the hero's success and honors to divine favor.[4]

über rücke. er was des râtes brücke und sanc vil wol von minnen. alsus kunde er gewinnen der werlde lop unde prîs. er was hövesch unde wîs" (*Armer Heinrich*, vv. 50-74).

[1] "daz si êre unde guot âne got mügen hân" (*Armer Heinrich*, vv. 398-399).

[2] In Conrad of Würzburg's *Engelhard* people show Dietrich *smâcheite* and *unêre* (vv. 5578, 5610) after he catches leprosy. Passage 5604-5619 shows how keenly loss of face was felt. According to the *Mirror of the Saxons*, lepers could not inherit property (*Sachsenspiegel*, I, 4).

[3] "ich mein diu sehs dinc, adel, maht, gelust, name, rîchtuom, herschaft. si sint gerlîch guot niht, wan ez eim übeln manne geschicht daz er si hât, daz ist wâr. sô sint si ouch niht übel gar, wan si hât dicke ein wol gemuot" (*Welscher Gast*, vv. 5745-5751). "wir wænen daz uns gebe kraft herschaft, adel, name, maht daz wir kommen hin ze got" (*Welscher Gast*, vv. 6113-15).

[4] William of Orléans thought "an die werdekait Und an die grossen salde brait Die er uf der erde hie Von Gottes gnaden enpfie" (*Willehalm von Orlens*, vv. 15,531-15,534). Likewise, Jovrit says, "Ich waere eren also rich So

However, the hero's virtue remains the decisive factor, as it had in the older epics; and God actually plays little more of a role than that formerly played by fate. Often the author states that the hero's wealth and honors are a gift of God, since all honor comes from God; yet the hero is admired and praised for these possessions. Even the ancient concept of the king's *heil* lingered in literature. In the *Lay of the Nibelungs*, King Etzel thanks his *heil* when he escapes Volker, and he later thinks his *heil* will protect his liege man Rüdeger.[1]

Whereas some poets could not see that wealth and honor conflicted with God's grace, many saw the difficulty of achieving all three goals at one time. Wolfram pondered the problem with the words, "It is a useful travail if anyone can end his life in such a way as not to forfeit his soul to God through the guilt of his body and yet can retain the favor of the world with dignity."[2] In other words, he must meet the demands of a shame culture and of a guilt culture, even though they conflict. Wolfram succeeds in solving this problem in his *Parzival*, but only by recourse to a fantastic ivory-tower realm of the Holy Grail. Spervogel, a thirteenth-century aphoristic poet, also commented on the difficulty: "A man should enjoy *êre* and should nevertheless be good to his soul at times in order that his pride will not mislead him too far."[3] The same doubt is implied by Freidank, who says that a man should pursue wealth and honor and yet keep God in his heart.[4] In Walther's best known political poem the poet deplores the strife and lawlessness of the realm which make it almost impossible for wealth, worldly honor, and God's grace to come into one heart.[5] At least this suggests that it should be possible to combine these three values in normal times, whereas the demands of the world were actually irreconcilable with those of God.

When in a religious frame of mind or when writing for churchmen, the courtly poets let their heroes strive for both the world's praise

dehain furste min gelich: Die genade tet mir Got" (vv. 14,805-14,807). Cf. "Got ist der êren hôchstez zil, ân êre in nieman reichet; er teilt ouch êre, swem er wil: gein aller creâtiure sô ist er aller êre anevanc" (Reinmar von Zweter, 76, 4-6). Reinmar devotes several strophes to praising *êre* (71-79), which he uses almost as a synonym of righteousness.

[1] "ich dankes mînem heile, daz ich dem tiuvel entran" (*Nibelungenlied*, 2001,4); "ouch trûwe ich mînem heile daz du maht selbe wol genesen" (2165,4).

[2] "swes leben sich sô verendet, daz got niht wirt gepfendet der sêle durch des lîbes schulde, und der doch der werlde hulde behalten kan mit werdekeit, daz ist ein nütziu arbeit" (*Parzival*, 827, 19-24).

[3] "Ein man sol haben êre, und sol iedoch der sêle under wîlen wesen guot, daz in dehein sîn übermuot verleite niht ze verre" (*Minnesangs Frühling*, 29 34 - 30,2).

[4] "guot und ere sol ein man bejagen und doch got in sime herzen tragen" (Freidank, 93, 22).

[5] Walther, 8, 4-27.

and the soul's salvation.¹ There were many faults which could jeopardize both; miserliness, for example, was an offense against both heathen and Christian ethics. Walther says that, if you love wealth too much, you may lose soul and honor;² and Stricker says a wicked man gives his soul and honor for wealth.³ In such contexts, honor and soul are allies, instead of bitter enemies, as usual; and one might erroneously think they are being used as synonyms. Poets often equated *schande* and *sünde* (sin),⁴ since some evil practices, like avarice and heresy, were both; yet they could not always be equated. Avenging an insult was sinful but honorable, whereas forgiving an insult was godly but shameful. Nevertheless, the clerics considered sinful and shameful synonymous. As we have seen, a well developed sense of shame was considered virtuous by both court and cloister.

The clerical and secular attitudes toward sin and honor are neatly contrasted in the *Lay of the Nibelungs*, when Rüdeger assures Kriemhild that he is ready to risk life and honor by fighting the Burgundians in order to keep his oath to her, but that he is reluctant to lose his soul by breaking his troth to them after leading them to the Huns' land, since he has promised to protect them.⁵ Nevertheless, in spite of all his concern for his immortal soul, he is really more concerned with his worldly honor and therefore obeys

---

[1] In a song urging participation in a crusade, Hartmann says that any knight whose shield has striven for high praise is unwise if he denies it to God's service; for those who take part will win "der werlte lop, der sêle heil" (*Minnësangs Frühling*, 209,37 - 210,10). Likewise, Duke Ernst decide that he and his retainers should go on a crusade to win both honor and salvation: "sô komen wir sîn mit êren abe, ê wir uns sus vertrîben lân. wir haben wider gote getân daz wir im billîch müezen ûf sîn hulde büezen, daz er uns die schulde ruoche vergeben her nâch" (*Herzog Ernst*, vv. 1816-1822).
[2] "wilt aber dû daz guot ze sêre minnen, dû maht verliesen sêle unt êre" (Walther, 23, 5-6). Cf. "Der wîse minnet niht sô sêre, alsam die gotes hulde unt êre: sîn selbes lîp, wîp unde kint, diu lât er ê er disiu zwei verliese" (Walther, 22, 24-27). Compare with Luther's "A Mighty Fortress".
[3] "der gît sêle unde êre umbe guot" (Stricker, XII, v. 300).
[4] Wolfram invokes St. Willehalm: "mîns sündehaften mundes galm dîn heilekeit an schrîet: sît daz dû bist gevrîet vor allen hellebanden, sô bevogete ouch mich vor schanden" (*Willehalm*, 4, 14-18). Notice how the word *heilekeit* could still be understood in its pagan and practical sense. Cf. "sündebaeren schanden" (*Parzival*, 471, 10). For several examples from a single work, see Wittenwiler's *Ring*, vv. 663, 695, 735, 785, 800, 6732. A possibly authentic folksong in Theodor Storm's *Immensee* says: "Was sonst in Ehren stünde, Nun ist es worden Sünde".
[5] "Daz ist âne lougen, ich swuor iu, edel wîp, daz ich durch iuch wâgte êre und ouch den lîp: daz ich die sêle vliese, des enhân ich niht gesworn. zuo dirre hôhgezîte brâht' ich die fürsten wol geborn" (*Nibelungenlied*, 2150). "Owê mir gotes armen, daz ich ditz gelebet hân. aller mîner êren der muoz ich abe stân, triuwen unde zühte, der got an mir gebôt. owê got von himele, daz mihs niht wendet der tôt" (2153).

his feudal obligation. Thus he is like the ancient ruler mentioned in the *Gospel of St. John* who "loved the praise of men more than the praise of God."[1] It is not surprising that he is called an "honor-thirsting" man,[2] since he cares more for fame than salvation. In other words, he acknowledges the older shame culture more than the new guilt culture.

Since good behavior brings *êre* and bad behavior brings *schande*, it is possible to extend the meaning of these two words to include the behavior by which they are won. By using the words in such an extended sense, Teichner could claim that one can win heaven through *êre* and hell through *schande*.[3] On the other hand, *scham*, or the desire to avoid disapproval, is actually a Christian virtue, provided one's peers disapprove of sin.[4] Although at first glance it appears that *êre* and *schande* had acquired Christian significance among the courtly poets, these poets generally used them in their external sense. Hartmann reveals this fact by saying that the world "has many a man who was never concerned with any *êre*, yet has more salvation (*heil!*) than one who has *êre* and whose heart tends toward virtues."[5] It is to be noted that the word virtue (*tugent*) here clearly means virtues in the older sense, as was no doubt the case in his description of Poor Henry, who could increase his worldly honors through all sorts of pure virtues. Walther also uses *êre* exclusively in the external sense; for example, when he says that no one has honor and wealth except him who does evil.[6]

The objective nature of *êre* is indicated by the traditional complaint that honor is often undeserved; for it was a commonplace to distinguish between merited and unmerited honor.[7] In Gottfried's *Tristan* the steward wins unmerited honor when he returns to the Irish court with the head of the dragon slain by Tristan.[8] Likewise,

---

[1] "Dilexerunt enim gloriam hominum magis quam gloriam Dei" (*John*, 12, 43).
[2] "êre gernde" (*Nibelungenlied*, 2218, 3).
[3] "dew werlt ist nur schant und er. mit schanten gewint man hell ser, mit eren gewint mans himelreich" (Teichner, 250, 15-17).
[4] "zwô tugende hân ich... scham unde triuwe" (Walther, 59, 14-15); "Schame deist ein grôziu tugent, sie bezzert alter unde jugent" (Freidank, 52, 24-25). The thought is repeated in a dozen variations in the following few verses, with numerous parallels in the notes. See *Ring*, vv. 4919-4934.
[5] "Ouch hât diu werlt manegen man, der nie ahte gewan ûf dehein êre, und hât doch heiles mêre dan einer der die sinne hât und dem sîn muot ze tugenden stât" (*Büchlein*, vv. 755-760).
[6] "êr unde guot hât nû lützel ieman wan der übel tuot" (Walther, 90, 29-30).
[7] Shakespeare expresses the thought as: "for who shall go about To cozen fortune, and be honourable Without the stamp of merit? Let none presume to wear an undeserved dignity. O that estates, degrees, and offices Were not deriv'd corruptly, and that clear honour Were purchas'd by the merit of the wearer!" (*Merchant of Venice*, II, ix, vv. 37-43).
[8] *Tristan*, vv. 9097 ff.

Sir Kay tries to gain unmerited honor by bringing the wounded Erec back to King Arthur's court.[1] As Thomasin said, Sir Kay strove for honor with lies and inconstancy, with scorn and villainy.[2] Whereas *êre* was actually a good of fortune, it was nevertheless a most admirable one; and therefore medieval man considered a concern for it to be a virtue, just as the Greeks had done. As we have seen, Geoffrey of Monmouth listed *honores* along with *virtutes*, *audacia*, and *fama*. In other words, honor and fame are virtues in so far as a concern for them inspires good works, even though the good works are done in hope of acclaim rather than for their own sake.

The Romantics' image of knighthood was largely due to the ideal that the Church concocted for it. In his *Policraticus*, John of Salisbury said that the function of the knights was "to protect the Church, fight against wickedness, venerate the priesthood, repel injustices to the poor, pacify the province, shed their blood for their brothers as the conception of their oath teaches, and, if necessary, lay down their lives."[3] This is very fine, but we must remember that this was an ideal *for* the knights, not the ideal *of* the knights. The Boy Scout Law, similarly, is an ideal *for* our youth, but not necessarily the ideal *of* our youth; and we may be sure that most of our youngsters judge their peers by a somewhat different set of standards, such as athletic prowess, impudence to teachers, and possession of expensive clothes and fast cars.

Feirefiz, Parzival's half-brother, is the son of a French father and a Moorish mother, and as a result he is half white and half black. These colors do not blend into grey but remain in spots of pure and distinct color. Being piebald, he might well symbolize his age, an age of unreconciled contradiction. As we have seen, our poets profess the ideals and values of their Germanic forebears almost unaltered, and at the same time they profess the ideals and values imported by the Christian church. Many see no contradiction: they let their heroes ask God's help in achieving revenge and thank him for his aid in despoiling their victims. Now the poet praises the world, now he damns it and praises heaven. Today he praises worldly honor as

---

[1] *Erec*, vv. 4628-4632.
[2] "wan der her Key nâch êren strebet mit lüge und mit unstaetekait, mit spotte und mit schalkeit" (*Welscher Gast*, vv. 1068-1070).
[3] "Quis est usus militiae ordinatae? Tueri ecclesiam, perfidiam impugnare, sacerdotium venerari, pauperum propulsare injurias, pacare provinciam, pro fratribus, ut sacramenti docet conceptio, fundere sanguinem et, si opus est, animam ponere" (*Policraticus*, VI, 8). *Winsbeke* (19, 1-4) says to the aspirant to knighthood: "Sun, wilt du genzlîch schiltes reht erkennen, so wis wol gezogen, getriuwe, milte, küene, sleht, sô enist er (the shield) niht an dir betrogen". This churchly admonition to meekness is also expressed in Chaucer's idealized knight, who was "of his port as meeke as is a mayde." Cf. "Was never Prince so faithful and so faire. Was never Prince so meeke and debonaire" (*The Fairy Queen*, II, 23).

the purpose of life, tomorrow he damns it as a snare of the devil.

The dualism of the Middle Ages explains the anagogical method of writing, the custom of writing on different levels of meaning. When the *sensus*, or apparent meaning of a literary work, is completely worldly, there may be more hidden *sententia*, or esoteric moral significance. Modern readers are often tempted to consider the *sententia* a mere excuse for the poet to tell an entertaining tale; because the Church taught that literature should serve only to glorify God and instruct mankind. Even when the poets were in a pious frame of mind, they could use holy conventions in a way that strikes modern man as frivolous. Walther, for example, varies the old triad of wealth, honor, and God's grace as God's grace, his lady's love, and the delightful court of Vienna, where Duke Leopold was so liberal.[1] Hartmann, like other secular poets, saw no offense in using Christian symbolism in narrating the worldly affairs of his chivalrous heroes. He even likens Erec's liberation of Mabonagrin to Christ's redemption of the world.[2]

It is difficult for modern man to understand how medieval writers could be both pious and blasphemous, and even the most callous student is shocked by the abuse of holy language and liturgy in medieval parody, such as that collected by Paul Lehmann.[3] It is especially difficult for a modern man to see how his ancestors could serve both Venus and the Virgin Mary simultaneously, as they often did.[4] Consequently, historians of the Middle Ages have peopled twelfth-century Europe with a race of goliards, or wandering scholars and defrocked monks, who journeyed from university to university singing the praises of Venus and Gula.[5] As charming as this fiction is, one needs no such race of vagabonds to explain away such blasphemies. Perhaps it would be safer to say that most goliards were merely pious monks in moments of relaxation. Bored by the tedium of copying monkish lore, a restless cleric may well have remembered his Ovid and put down his Augustine long enough to give vent to his pent up urges, before dutifully returning to his task of damning all such thoughts as works of the devil.

Although so many medieval scholars seemed untroubled by contra-

---

[1] "gotes hulde und mîner frowen minne... der wünneclîche hof ze Wiene" (Walther, 84, 7-10).
[2] See H. B. Wilson, "Sin and Redemption in Hartmann's Erec", *Germanic Review*, 33, 1958, pp. 5-14.
[3] Paul Lehmann, *Die Parodie im Mittelalter*, Munich, 1922.
[4] Wittenwiler dedicated his *Ring*, replete with pornography, to the Virgin (Marien, muoter, rainen mait, v. 2). It includes a love letter invoking both Jesus and Venus to aid the lover (Euch geseg in steg und weg Jesus in seinr güeti! Ewer phleg in leb und sweb Venus in irm gmüeti!, vv. 1909-1912).
[5] Helen Waddell, *The Wandering Scholars*, London, 1932, accepts this tradition.

diction, some seemed aware of the dualism of their society and felt crushed by its contradictory demands. In spite of its duplicity, medieval society can be safely considered, by and large, burdened by sorrow and disillusion.[1] The poets conventionally set their idealized stories into a vague past, an age far happier than their own. Ask any medieval poet you wish, and he will assure you that the world is now sad and confused, whereas it was joyful and carefree in his youth. On the other hand, if you ask earlier poets, who wrote during the age he remembers so fondly, they will assure you that that age was sad and confused, in comparison with the golden years of their own youth.[2] And so *ad infinitum*. Even modern historians fall into this trap. It is not unusual for a historian, in describing a rough and brutal episode during the Middle Ages, to assure his readers that this was after, or perhaps before, the "age of chivalry", an age which no one is quite willing to date. Perhaps William Cory was right when he suggested that "Bayard was the first rather than the last of true knights." [3]

[1] Walther's disillusioned poem to Dame World, although following literary conventions, seems convincing (100, 24 - 101, 22). Dame world was often presented as a woman with a beautiful front, but with a back putrid and devoured by worms and serpents.
[2] The era described so idyllically by Meier Helmbrecht senior (vv. 913-983) was approximately the same era so damned by Walther (124, 18-40) in comparison with the happy days of his own youth.
[3] Cory, p. 460.

CHAPTER SEVEN

THE ORIGINS OF BOURGEOIS HONOR

Whence came the best culture, if not from the burgher?
GOETHE.

Most of the didactic poets discussed so far, including Spervogel, Freidank, Stricker, and Hugo of Trimberg, were clearly commoners, as were the pseudo-courtly poets Rudolf of Ems and Conrad of Würzburg. Although popular fancy later ennobled some of these worthies, it is unlikely that many if any wandering or professional poets or singers were of genuine noble rank. As a general rule of thumb one might say that modern scholars attribute noble birth to medieval minstrels in direct proportion to their obscurity. Some people seem misled by the preposition *von* found in names like Conrad von Würzburg, but this preposition indicated only domicile, not noble rank,[1] for it would be absurd to suppose that Conrad or his ancestors ever owned that famous ecclesiastical city. Probably most of the didactic poets, like ninety-five per cent of their compatriots, were of peasant birth. However, since they did not till the soil, we can include them in the general term burgher, which will designate everyone not a priest, nobleman, or peasant.

Although many patrician families claimed descent from urbanized noblemen, their claims were largely fictitious; nearly all burghers were descended from peasants and rural laborers who had left the soil. No doubt many of them were descended from runaway serfs, who had become free by escaping to a city, where urban air emancipated them (*Stadtluft macht frei*). Consequently, the nobility drew no social distinction between burghers and peasants and excluded both from their code of honor. As the saying went, "Nothing distinguishes a burgher from a peasant but the city wall." The very pillars of bourgeois life, namely productive work and trade, were beneath the dignity of the gentry.[2]

---

[1] See George F. Jones, "Heinrich Wittenwiler - Nobleman or Burgher?" (*Monatshefte*, 45, 1953, pp. 67-68).
[2] *ibid.*, pp. 71-74. Johannes Rothe says of the knight: "Sal her danne eyn hantwerg dinge? daz geborit eme doch nicht zcu" (*Ritterspiegel*, vv. 2175-2176).

Being excluded by birth and profession from the aristocratic code of honor, the burghers developed their own criteria for judging their peers. Like the aristocracy, they admired wealth, which now took the form of cash and credit rather than lands and rents; and it became just as respectable to earn wealth as to inherit, seize, or extort it. Even though sumptuary laws forbade them to wear the expensive finery of the ruling classes, the burghers could nevertheless flaunt their prosperity by maintaining fine houses and furnishings.

Being unable to win acclaim in battle, the burghers took especial pride in their professional prowess, be it commerce or handicraft. As a result, they aspired to those virtues that bring financial success, such as sobriety, industry, thrift, and providence, all of which had been preached in the cloisters but largely ignored at the courts. Respectability and uprightness thus began to displace courage as the highest virtue, as is indicated in the semantic development of *biderbe* (brave) into *bieder* (upright), of *tühtic* (doughty) into *tüchtig* (hard working), and of *wacker* (valiant) into *wacker* (honest). In other words, in bourgeois circles *ein braver mann* gradually changed from *un homme brave* into *un brave homme*. The word *honesty* (*Ehrlichkeit*) slowly acquired a sense expressed by our term "middle class respectability".

The ancient Germanic virtue of *triuwe* retained its meaning of oathkeeping but was now concerned more with commercial than feudal contracts. Having no vassals, the burghers did not have to practice *milte* as such; yet they were expected to perform charity not only to buy salvation and win glory of men, as the nobility had done, but also to prove their financial solvency. Being a new order without ancient traditions, the bourgeoisie were more receptive to the teachings of the Church, which was their chief protection against the rapacious nobility. Being enclosed by the same wall with church and churchmen, the burghers had closer contact with them than the rural aristocracy had; and it became a sign of bourgeois respectability to take active part in church affairs as a layman.

Having little military power, at least in their beginnings, the bourgeoisie agreed with the Church in questioning the tenet that might makes right; and, at least in theory, they were more willing to live in accordance with God's *recht* or justice. To enjoy complete respect, a burgher had to profess a certain regard for the personal property rights of other people, at least of his peers and superiors. Consequently, the bourgeois ideal of honor gradually became a life of "secular piety" (*Weltfrömmigkeit*). Although the Sermon on the Mount had praised poverty and trust in God's bounty, the bourgeoisie put more faith in treasures safely stored on earth; and gradually the belief developed that making money was not only permissible but even pleasing to God.

This mercantile value code, which suggests Max Weber's anachronistically termed "Protestant Ethic", lasted almost unchanged until modern times. In his *Der Bourgeois*, Werner Sombart traces this attitude to the fifteenth century, when it was found in the writings of the Florentine merchant Leon Battista Alberta.[1] He could have gone back fully two centuries earlier to a work called *De Cura et Modo Rei Familiaris*, which was formerly attributed to St. Bernard of Clairvaux and later to Bernard Silvester, one of the scholars of Chartres. Even though it may not have been written by Bernard, it was doubtlessly written during his lifetime and expressed the values of his circle. This letter explained the art of housekeeping from a practical and therefore uncourtly point of view. It is ironic that it was purportedly written to a knight (*miles*), but this was probably a subterfuge to give it social respectability.[2]

The middle-class attitudes in this letter, such as that thrift and productivity are respectable, can be traced directly to ancient philosophers. Xenophon himself saw fit to devote an entire work, the *Oeconomics*, to the art of practical living. In his *De Officiis*, Cicero quotes Xenophon in saying that it is a virtue to make money, but only by honorable means, and that it is also a duty to save it and increase it by care and thrift.[3] Seneca himself must have seen no dishonor in speculation, since he was one of the wealthiest businessmen of his day. The bourgeois attitude toward business, particularly toward investment, seems to have been justified and even furthered by a literal interpretation of Christ's parable about the talents.[4] Success in business became an indication of the amount of God's grace that men enjoyed, just as success in warfare had been for the aristocracy. The Old Testament itself had praised diligence by saying, "A man skillful in business, he shall stand before kings."[5]

In nearly all bourgeois writings, as in the aristocratic literature before it, *honestum* and *êre* usually referred to the respect or recognition which one enjoyed, rather than to the virtues or dispositions through which they were won. Also, good behavior and attitudes were usually a means to an end, not an end in themselves. The ultimate goal was now more modest, being social recognition and

---

[1] Sombart, p. 242. Cf. "Never let your expenditures be greater than your income."

[2] *Migne, Patrologia Latina*, 182, 647-651. This is echoed in Wittenwiler's *Ring*, vv. 5019-5200. Wittenwiler advises such thrift and frugality to one who wishes to keep house "mit eren".

[3] "Res autem familiaris quaeri debet iis rebus, a quibus abest turpido, conservari autem diligentia et parsimonia, eisdem etiam rebus augeri" (*De Officiis*, II, 24, 87).

[4] For an example of this interpretation, see *Wittenwiler's Ring, etc.*, ed. G. F. Jones, Chapel Hill, 1956, pp. 226-227.

[5] "Vidisti virum velocem in opere suo coram regibus stabit" (*Proverbs*, 22, 29).

approval, rather than awe, fear, or superior status, as in the aristocratic code.

The bourgeoisie identified feminine honor with chastity. That is to say, they accorded honor only to maids and faithful wives. As we have seen, the ancient Teutons demanded marital fidelity; and marriage was guaranteed by oath and sealed with material gifts. Moreover, in the case of the ruling classes, with whom most literature was concerned, there was the great problem of legitimacy; for accusations of infidelity against a queen might cause violent political repercussions. Even though marital fidelity was demanded of women, the matter did not play a great role in medieval literature; and poets and minstrels generally assigned the epithets "good" and "bad" to courtly ladies according to their generosity to poets and minstrels.

According to Montaigne, when his contemporaries spoke of a "good woman" or a "woman of honor and virtue", they meant no more than a chaste woman. To bind women to chastity, people seemed to ignore all other duties and to give them free rein to commit any other fault provided they would remain chaste.[1] This explains why, in Shakespeare's *All's Well that Ends Well*, Mariana can tell Diana that, "the honour of a maid is her name, and no legacy is so rich as honesty." [2] It was not a woman's behavior that counted, but rather her good name. As Castiglione explained in his *Courtier*, "whereas a dissolute life is neither a vice, nor a fault, nor a disgrace for a man, it is such utter infamy and shame in a woman that, once spoken against, she is disgraced forever, whether the calumny be true or false." [3] Since feminine morality was one of the few fields in which the burghers could compete on equal terms with the aristocracy, they made the most of it; and fallen women were subjected to great cruelty. Still, if a fallen woman had a sufficient dowry, she could always find a man to "make an honest woman of her". Also, it was no dishonor for a maid to sell her chastity for a

---

[1] "Tout ainsi que notre passion, et cette fievreuse solicitude que nous avons de la chasteté des femmes, fait aussi qu'une bonne femme, une femme de bien et femme d'honneur et de vertu, ce ne soit (en effaict) à dire autre chose pour nous qu'une femme chaste; comme si, pour les obliger à ce devoir, nous mettions à nonchaloir tous les autres, et leur lâchions la bride à toute autre faute, pour entrer en composition de leur faite quitter cette-ci" (Montaigne, II, 7).
[2] *All's Well*, III, 5, v. 13.
[3] "e questo perché noi stessi avemo fatta una legge, che in noi non sia vicio né mancamento né infamia alcuna la vita dissoluta e nelle donne sia tanto estremo obbrobrio e vergogna, che quella di chi una volta si parla male, o falsa o vera che sia la calunnia che se le dà, sia per sempre vituperata" (*Cortegiano*, II, 90, ed. Maier, p. 322). According to Cervantes, "El honor de las mujeres consiste en la opinión buena que dellas se tiene" (*Don Quixote*, cited from Américo Castro, *Semblanzas*, p. 365).

high enough price, and a royal mistress was held in esteem, in contrast to her sisters on the street.

As we have seen, the ancient Teutons had divided society into two sharply separated groups: the free and the unfree. Later, perhaps under the influence of Romance customs, the Germans began to divide secular society into two orders: the nobility and the peasantry, the latter being despised and oppressed whether of free or unfree origin. When the burghers began to assert themselves, they too were included in the term "peasant", even in the case of wealthy and powerful commoners like Philip van Artevelde.[1]

While acknowledging the social superiority of the aristocracy, the bourgeoisie had the satisfaction of feeling superior to their country cousins, whom they scorned as unworthy of honor. Before telling the story of Cincinnatus, the seventeenth-century writer Hans Kirchof found it necessary to explain that in Rome it was quite honorable to cultivate the fields, and this indicates that the burghers of his day would not have thought so.[2] The burghers took the peasants' dishonorable status so completely for granted that they seldom mentioned it in their literature; yet it does appear occasionally. In a Shrovetide play by Hans Sachs, the shoemaking mastersinger of Nuremberg, a country bumpkin named Hans Dolp knocks at the door of a rich burgher, who has just welcomed a nobleman as guest; and the burgher refuses him on the grounds, "I receive only honorable people."[3] This remark naturally referred to Dolp's social status rather than to his moral behavior, there being no evidence of bad character on his part.

It is significant that Hans Sachs found it fitting for a nobleman to accept a burgher's hospitality, in view of the fact that the burghers refused to consort with the peasants. The dishonorable status of all peasants is suggested in Wittenwiler's *Ring*, which on two occasions alludes sarcastically to the honorable status of its villagers.[4] The chief purpose of declaring all peasants dishonorable was to exclude them from the guilds, which the artisans and merchants had formed to protect themselves from fair competition.

Professing to be Christians, the burghers sought divine sanction for their scorn and mistreatment of the peasantry. For this purpose they adopted the very arguments used against them by the nobility. Among these were the Biblical stories of Adam's unequal children, Esau's sale of his birthright, Abraham's begetting Ishmael by his

---

[1] Huizinga, p. 90.
[2] "denn zu Rom hielt man gar für ehrlich, wer das felt bauwet oder der ritterschaft pflegte" (*Wendunmuth*, I, p. 27).
[3] Hans Sachs, 15, v. 52.
[4] "erbrer leuten" (*Ring*, v. 2640); "erber leut" (v. 3624). Likewise, they are "namhaft" (v. 3645).

bondswoman Hagar, and many more. At the beginning of the fifteenth century Henry Wittenwiler related the story of Noah's cursing of Canaan as proof that the classes were separated by divine will. When one of the peasants in his *Ring* asks if all men are not Adam's children, another explains, "It is quite true that everyone has come from Adam and his wife Eve; yet some individuals were so worthy that they were chosen by the people and elected as lords. Some were good and some were bad; goodness always made its way inside and wickedness begged at the door, just as it happened to Sir Noah's sons. When one of them saw his father drunk, he began to ridicule him and therefore became a bondsman; but those who honored their father then became honorable free men. Therefore we are not equal. One is poor, the other rich, one a peasant, the other noble." [1]

It will be noted that Wittenwiler does not differentiate between the two dutiful sons, a fact which suggests that he felt no barrier between burgher and nobleman. In any case, everyone except the peasant is honorable. It will be remembered that the Norse *Lay of Rig* had accounted for three classes, of which the two free classes appeared to be honorable. It seems strange that people still cited the curse of Canaan in the fifteenth century, in view of the fact that Eike of Repgau had discredited it so thoroughly a century and a half earlier.

Of all country dwellers, perhaps the lowliest were the herdsmen, no social distinction being made among shepherds, cowherds, and swineherds. Herdsmen were scorned because they owned no property and tended other people's beasts. Because they lived apart from other people, they were suspected of occult powers and communications with evil spirits. Rightfully or wrongfully they were accused of stealing the animals entrusted to them and, having no recognized honor, they could not defend themselves from such accusations. The profession required little skill or intelligence and was open to the dregs of society; and open competition kept the wages low. In spite of a fiction of genteel swains and shepherdesses

---

[1] "Es ist wol war, daz iederman Chomen ist von Adams leib Und von Evan, seinem weib! Doch sein etleich sunderbar, So from gewesen (daz ist war), Daz seu von dem volk derwelt Sein ze herren und gezelt. Etleich warent tugenthaft, Etleich auch gar ungeschlacht. Die tugend die prach alweg für, Die bosshait chrangelt vor der tür, Sam her Noes sünen gschach: Do einr sein vater trunken sach, Do huob er sein ze spotten an; Dar umb ward er ein aigen man; Und die den vatter erten so, Die wurden erber frien so. Also sein wir nicht geleich: Einr ist arm, der ander reich, Einr ein gpaur, der ander edel" (*Ring*, vv. 7225-7244). It is interesting that the words *from, tugenthaft, ungeschlacht, tugent,* and *bosshait* (which had formerly meant useful, strong, illborn, strength, and weakness) are used here in a moral sense. This explanation of the origin of the social classes would be correct if these words were read in the amoral sense.

in pastoral literature, actual shepherds were always shunned. Ronsard later expressed the prevailing view when he described some make-believe shepherds: "Those are not shepherds from a country cottage who, for pay, lead their sheep to the fields to graze, but from a high and noble family." [1]

In addition to rural laborers, the burghers excluded certain other social and professional groups whom they branded as "dishonorable people" (*unehrliche Leute*). Having no honor and therefore no civil rights, these pariahs were beyond the pale of good society. Their number included Wends, priests' children, wandering minstrels, millers, bath attendants, barbers, linen weavers, skinners, tanners, bailiffs, and executioners.[2] Not only these individuals, but also their families and descendants were scorned and ostracized by decent people. No distinction being made between being morally and socially dishonorable, people tended to consider them infamous in both meanings of the term. According to Otto Beneke, "between 1472 and 1525 master artisans had to swear that their guild candidate was of honorable (*namhaft*) parents, that he was free and no one's serf, nor the son of a bather, barber, linen-weaver, or minstrel."[3]

The dishonorable groups derived from both native and classic tradition. In native tradition, all captives and serfs had been without honor, and their curse remained upon their descendants beyond the proverbial third and fourth generation. After the Germans began their drive toward the East, most prisoners were Slavs, particularly Wends; and, as a result, the Wends and their descendants remained stigmatized, even after they had become legally free, just as the American Negroes continued to suffer the handicaps of slavery long after their emancipation. According to Wilhelm Raabe, "down into the eighteenth century no German guild accepted a Wend. The members of that despised race were dishonorable like the executioner and other infamous people. No one received them as guests under his roof, no one sat at table with them. In the thirteenth century 'Wendish dog' was the worst reproach that one Germanic Christian could offer another." [4] The Wends were eventually absorbed into the German majority and have therefore played a minor role in modern German literature. Even in *MHG* literature they played a minor role, since this literature was written mostly in southern and central Germany, whereas the Wends lived in the northern districts where the vernacular was Low German. Raabe

---

[1] "Ce ne sont pas bergers d'une maison champestre Qui menent pour salaire aux champs les brebis paistre, Mais de haute famille et de race d'ayeux" (Ronsard, *Eclogues*, I, first speech).
[2] See Otto Beneke, *Von unehrlichen Leuten*, Hamburg, 1863, and C. von Schwerin, *Germanische Rechtsgeschichte*, Berlin, 1944, p. 169.
[3] Beneke, pp. 79, 11.
[4] Raabe, p. 189.

describes their sad plight vividly in a short story explaining the origin of the legend of the Pied Piper of Hamlin. Although he wrote his story in the nineteenth century, he claimed that it was based on authentic records. According to him, the Pied Piper was actually a thirteenth-century minstrel whom the young men of Hameln mistreated because he was a Wend. In revenge, he led the youth of the city into an ambush laid by their enemy, the Bishop of Minden, from which not one returned.[1]

As we have seen, a Teuton owed his honor and legal rights to his membership in a clan, all outcasts and exiles being without rights or honor. For this reason illegitimate children did not enjoy complete honor. In order to prevent priests from trying to transmit ecclesiastical property to their children, priests' children were particularly severely treated. According to the *Mirror of the Saxons*, the blood money of priest's children was set at as much hay as two year-old oxen can pull;[2] in other words, their death could not be legally avenged, and thus they had no honor. Ridicule of priests' children is reflected in Chaucer's *The Canterbury Tales*. Symkyn, the hero of the "Reeve's Tale", married a wife of "noble kyn", whose father was the parson of the town.[3] Thus both spouses were "dishonorable", regardless of their pretentions.

As long as honor depended upon ownership of property, all unpropertied people were refused social recognition. This condition lasted until modern times, being maintained by property qualifications and poll taxes; and all vagrants and vagabonds were denied civil rights.[4] As long as good behavior was motivated chiefly by what one's neighbors and kinsmen might say, people without neighbors and kinsmen could not be trusted, and it was assumed that people who leave home must have some reason for doing so. As Joseph de Maistre expressed this international prejudice, "the man who has property, family, morals, and reputation stays in his own country."[5] When honorable people traveled, they needed recommendations to honorable families in order to be socially accepted.

The term "vagabonds" included all wandering minstrels, these

[1] Raabe, pp. 171-207.
[2] "Paphen kindere unde die unecht geboren sîn, den gibt men zu bûthe eyn vûder howis, alse zwêne jârige ossen gethên mugen" (*Sachsenspiegel*, III, 45, 9).
[3] Chaucer, ed. Robinson, *C.T.*, A. 3942-3943.
[4] Lisei's father was accused of theft with little evidence because, "Ach, wir haben kei Heimat, kei Freund, kei Ehr; es kennt uns niemand nit" (*Pole Poppenspäler*, p. 72), Pole's mistress is surprised that he is in jail, because she thought his child was "ehrlicher Leute Kind" (p. 71). Later Lisei says she should not marry Pole because "wir sind landfahrende Leut. Was werden sie sagen bei dir daheim" (p. 78). They are not "zunftberechtigt" (p. 37).
[5] Cited in Coulton, p. 542.

being lumped together under the terms "poor people" (*arme liute*) and "traveling people" (*varendiu diet*). These two epithets alone were enough to assure them social opprobrium, for vagrancy was as detestable as poverty. For centuries one of the worst insults was to call someone a vagrant.[1] It is not surprising, therefore, that the *Mirror of the Saxons* allowed minstrels to avenge themselves only on a man's shadow.[2] Minstrels were forced to be vagabonds by the very nature of their profession, which required them to move to newer fields as soon as their repertory was exhausted in a given area. They were scorned not only for their poverty and vagrancy, but also for their practice of taking wealth for honor (*guot umbe êre nemen*). The mastersinger Michel Beheim described this function with the words, "The prince had me in servile pay, I ate his bread and sang his song. If I come to another, I shall write for him too. If he rewards me for it, I shall praise his name."[3] Helbling tells of a minstrel who says, "Sir, give me something and I shall spread your fame."[4] Because of this practice, minstrels were accused of giving unjust praise and thus contributing to unmerited honor. A thirteenth-century poem complains that, for gifts, a minstrel "praises him who should be reproached and reproaches him who should be praised."[5]

The expression *"guot umbe êre nemen"* had the further meaning of selling one's honor for pay, since the Germans had always scorned persons who accepted compensation for entertainment. In describing the sword dances of the ancient Germanic youths, Tacitus had made it clear in his *Germania* (c. 24) that they would not accept pay but performed to increase their skill and to entertain. The ancient prejudice against paid entertainers is reflected in the *Lay of the Nibelungs*, which states that Volker the Fiddler was really a free and wealthy lord, and was called the Fiddler only because he

---

[1] Cf. "herverlauffner buob" (*Ring*, v: 456) with *harverloufen, verlüffner buobe, her verloufer böser wiht, herkumer schalk*, and *hergeloffenen Weib* (documented in Edmund Wiessner, *Kommentar zu Heinrich Wittenwilers Ring*, Leipzig, 1935, p. 41).
[2] "Spellûten und alle den, die sech zu eigene geben, den gibt men zu bûthe den scheden eynis mannis" (*Sachsenspiegel*, III, 45, 9).
[3] "Der furst mich hett in knechtes miet, ich ass sein brot und sang sein liet. ob ich zu einem andern kum, ich ticht im auch, tut er mir drum. ich sag lob sinem namen" (*Reimchronik*, strophe 1485). Cf. "cuius enim panem manduco, carmina canto". This was still quoted by Otto Ludwig: "Wes Brot ich esse, des Lied ich singe" (*Erbförster*, I, 9). The Provencal troubadour Peire Vidal had said of the king of Hungary: "Et aurai gran honor, Si m'a per servidor, Qu'eu posc far sa lauzor Per tot lo mon auzir E son pretz enantir Mais d'autr'om qu'el mon sia" (cited from Settegast, p. 8).
[4] "herre, gebt mir eteswaz sô mach ich iuwer êre breit" (*Helbling*, II, v. 1312).
[5] "der spilmann, der um gâbe lobet den, der da zu scheltende ist, unn den schiltet, der do zu lobende ist" (cited from *Grimms Deutsches Wörterbuch*, X, 1, column 2409).

could play a fiddle as well as fight.[1] To symbolize the dishonorable status of minstrels, the *Mirror of the Saxons* denied the right of revenge to "minstrels and all those who give themselves into bondage." [2]

Ever since the Romantic Movement poets have tried to glorify the minstrels of old and put them on an equal footing with their aristocratic audiences. It is true that noblemen often dabbled in music, which was an acceptable leisure-class pastime; but they scorned the professional minstrels who sold their honor. Gentlemen like Hartmann and Wolfram made it clear that they were primarily knights and wrote only in their spare time, and they did not beg their patrons for donations. Walther, on the other hand, was no "man of honor", no matter how noble his sentiments may have been; for he was not ashamed to beg for gifts. Although he rode a horse, dressed as a courtier, and received honor in the villages, he was proably treated as a lackey by his courtly patrons.

Walther's designation *von der Vogelweide* (from the bird meadow) was likely fictitious and scarcely suggests noble birth. He himself admitted being a mendicant on many occasions; and the only historical document concerning him records that he received a gift.[3] One of his poems begins, "Could anyone now alive say that he ever saw greater gifts than we received in Vienna in return for praise?" [4] Later generations assumed that Walther was of noble birth and depicted him with a coat of arms. In the seventeenth century Martin Opitz mentioned Walther, "Emperor Philip's privy-counselor", in order to prove that aristocrats had once engaged in poetry in spite of their noble birth.[5] Today, if an irate citizen addresses an editorial to the president, we do not call him a "presidential advisor". In actuality, professional musicians were not accepted socially by their patrons until Beethoven won that honor. Even Mozart had been carried on the archbishop's rolls as a valet de chambre.

The minstrels also suffered the animosity of the clergy, who resented their competition. Not only did their flattery lead to pride, but also their music incited men to dancing and other sins. Besides that, the public devoted their time and money to music rather than to sermons. Saxo Grammaticus followed clerical tradition in reproaching

---

[1] "durch daz er videlen kunde" (*Nibelungenlied*, 1477).
[2] "kempen und ir kinder, spellûde, unde alle die uneht geboren sîn... die sin alle rehtelôs" (*Sachsenspiegel*, I, 38, 1).
[3] "sequenti die apud Zeize Walthero cantori de Vogelweide pro pellicio V solidos longos".
[4] "Ob ieman spreche, der nû lebe, daz er gesaehe ie groezer gebe, als wir ze Wiene haben dur êre enpfangen?" (Walther, 25, 26-28).
[6] "Walter von der Vogelweide, Keyser Philipses geheimen rahte... wie hoch sich selbige vorneme Männer, ungeachtet ihrer adelichen ankunfft und standes, der Poeterey angemasset" (*Buch von der deutschen Poeterei*, IV).

an ancient king for giving gifts to jugglers and minstrels;[1] and Berthold of Regensburg preached against giving money to flatterers and minstrels for the sake of praise or fame.[2]

The dishonorable people included not only unrooted or unpropertied persons, but also several gainfully employed professional groups, which, along with their children, were excluded from all honorable guilds. Among these were the millers, who were accused of robbing both clients and employers. Millers may have originally owed their dishonorable condition to their servile status as employee of the feudal lord, but later they were scorned because of their purported dishonesty. Since the seigneur could force his peasants to grind their grain at his mill, his miller had a monopoly and was not subject to the peasants' choice. Moreover, the exactions of the seigneur were naturally blamed on the miller. In any case, the miller's dishonesty and rascality were a popular theme in medieval literature, as I have shown elsewhere.[3]

Bathers or bath attendants were likewise in ill-repute either because their predecessors in the Roman world had been public slaves or because their services were intimate and personal. Moreover, the baths also served as brothels, and the proprietors were procurers and the female attendants were often prostitutes or, if superannuated, procuresses. Consequently, female bath attendants played a comical stock role in medieval literature. In describing a bath woman who is acting as a go-between in a peasant courtship, Henry Wittenwiler says, "She could wash and also massage and do business with sluts and thereby help young maids from their honor. And if one could do no better, she would fall on the grass herself."[4] The author of the *Devil's Net* says, "The bathers and their assistants are gladly whores and knaves, thieves, liars, and panders, and they know all the gossip. They can do business with laymen and priests too. They can also procure young ladies for those who want to indulge in lechery."[5]

According to legend, Emperor Wenceslas was rescued from captivity by a heroic bath maid; and, filled with gratitude, he not only

---

[1] "mimos ac ioculatores" (*Gesta Danorum*, p. 186, v. 5).
[2] "gîst aber dû ez den lotern unde den gumpelliuten durch lop oder durch ruom, dar umbe muostû gote antwürten" (Bertold, I, p. 25).
[3] "Chaucer and the Medieval Miller", *Modern Language Quarterly*, 16, March, 1955, pp. 3-15.
[4] "Die chond waschen und auch reiben, Chauffmanschaft mit schloern treiben, Da mit jungen mägetein Helfen von den eren sein; Und moht man nicht gevaren bas, So viel sei selber in daz gras" (*Ring*, vv. 2566-2570).
[5] "Der bader und sin gesind Gern huoren und buoben sind,... Dieb, lieger und kuppler, Und wissend alle fremde maer. Och kunnend si wol schaffen Mit laigen und och mit pfaffen, Die ir uppkait wend triben, Und kunnend die fröwlin zuo in schiben Und denn aber in daz bad gan" (*Teufels Netz*, vv. 10,277 - 10,286).

rewarded her for this service but also granted a charter to the bathing guilds in 1406. This charter forbade people to scorn the bath attendants or to belittle their honorable service.[1] Since tolerance cannot be legislated, people continued to shun the bathers long after they had been officially declared honorable. The socially, even if no longer legally, dishonorable status of bathers and surgeons explains why the Bavarians could not tolerate the morganatic marriage of their young duke, Albert, with the bather's daughter, Agnes Bernauer, whose sad fate was so convincingly dramatized by Friedrich Hebbel in 1851.[2]

Weavers were in ill repute because their sedentary occupation made them unsuitable for military service, as the Roman military historian Vegetius observed.[3] In one of Seifried Helbling's allegories, Manliness says "I will chase cowardice from me into a weaver. He always sits without a loin-cloth, and by that his cowardice is recognized."[4] Of all the weavers, the most scorned were the linen weavers, who were legally dishonorable. Because they had no guild, they could not protect themselves from free competition, and thus they usually had to work under sweat shop conditions. Because of their poverty, it was jocularly said that "the linen weavers accept no apprentice who can't fast for six weeks."[5] Their pitiful condition lasted until the mid nineteenth century, if we may trust Gerhard Hauptmann's play *The Weavers*, in which the avaricious entrepreneur Dreissiger threatens to beat down his weavers' poor wages by warning them how much worse off the linen weavers are.[6]

Skinners and tanners owed their dishonorable status to tabus against blood and to the accusation that they misappropriated parts of the hides entrusted to them; for, like the millers and tailors, they processed other people's goods and were therefore suspected of dishonesty. A popular rime declared that skinners were first cousins of the shepherds,[7] who were also accused of theft. These

---

[1] Beneke, pp. 57 ff.
[2] Although Hebbel set his play in the years 1420 to 1430, he let Caspar Bernauer, the heroine's father, tell her that she has an honor to lose, even though fifty years earlier she would not have been tolerated at a tournament.
[3] Vegetius, I, 7. See J. Petersen, *Das Rittertum in der Darstellung des Johannes Rothe*, Strassburg, 1909, p. 67.
[4] "diu Manheit sprach: 'ich wil den zagen von mir in einen weber jagen: der sitzet ân schamgewant, dâ bî sîn zagheit ist erkant'" (*Helbling*, VII, vv. 791-794).
[5] "Die Leineweber nehmen keinen Lehrjungen an, Der nicht sechs Wochen hungern kann" (S. Liptzin, *The Weavers in German Literature*, Göttingen, 1926, p. 15).
[6] Gerhard Hauptmann, *Die Weber*, Act One. "Sie sollten mal die Nase hübsch wo anders 'neinstecken und sehen, wie's bei den Leinwandwebern aussieht. Die können von Not reden".
[7] "Schäfer und Schinder - Geschwisterkinder".

two groups were declared honorable by the same law and were among the last to be vindicated. Article 4 of the Imperial Law of August 16, 1731, decreed that the dishonorable status of skinners should continue for the first and second generation, but that succeeding generations should be admitted to every honorable handicraft and profession.[1] As we shall see, Heinrich von Kleist saw fit to allude to the dishonorable status of the skinner in his story Michael Kohlhaas, which was set in the sixteenth century.

Executioners were also dishonorable until the eighteenth century, as one can see in the case of Karl Huss, an acquaintance of Goethe, who was born in Bohemia in 1761. Although he was an exemplary pupil, he had to withdraw from school when the parents of the other pupils discovered that his well educated father was an executioner; and eventually he had to follow the profession of his father, no other being open to him.[2] Scorn for hangmen appears in German literature from the Middle Ages down to the present.[3] Court deputies and bailiffs were also social outcasts until the nineteenth century. Friedrich Hebbel's *Maria Magdalene*, which appeared in 1844 and described a contemporary milieu, ends tragically because the self-respecting cabinet-maker, Master Anton, once refused to drink with the bailiff and advised him to drink with his confrere, the skinner.[4]

Thus we see that most of the dishonorable professions were shunned even after they had been officially declared honorable. As Otto Beneke says, "When the division into seven honorable social classes (*Heerschilden*) had long been forgotten, the stigma of these people remained so well in the memory of the guilds that had flourished meanwhile that they refused them and their sons entry into their honorable corporations".[5]

It is often claimed that, after its brief flourish during the age of chivalry, German literature degenerated in the hands of the bourgeoisie. Be that as it may, the bourgeoisie were not to blame as long

---

[1] Beneke, p. 91.
[2] *Briefwechsel und mündlicher Verkehr zwischen Goethe und dem Rathe Grüner*, ed. J. S. Grüner, Leipzig, 1853, pp. 61 ff.
[3] *Meier Helmbrecht* (vv. 1013-1019) says that the virtuous ways of old are now as unwelcome as a hangman (*hâhaere*). In Clemens Brentano's Kasperle und Annerl of 1817 an old peasant woman asks the narrator if he is an honorable man or perhaps a *Henker* (*Kasperl und Annerl*, p. 100). In *Aquis Submersis* Theodor Storm says, "denn ein Ehrsamer Rath hatte dermalen viel Bedrängniss von einer Schinderleichen, so die ehrlichen Leute nicht zu Grabe tragen wollten." According to Van Eerden & Ulmer, *Deutsche Novellen*, Holt, 1942, p. 272, a *Schinderleichen* was the "corpse of a person executed or of the executioner himself. The hangman, his assistants, and his relatives were formerly considered 'dishonorable' ".
[4] "Gevatter Fallmeister" (*Maria Magdalene*, II, 3).
[5] Beneke, p. 11.

as the courts continued to exist and had every right to foster first-rate literature. Besides that, there is no proof that the writers of courtly literature were mostly gentlemen. Gottfried, the most courtly of all, is generally assumed to have been a burgher, and it is possible that some of the so-called "ministeriales" poets only acted the role in order to be presentable at court.

Medieval aristocrats were fighting men and, as such, unproductive. According to accepted belief, the function of the nobility was to protect Christendom; but, except on the frontiers of heathendom or during crusades, the nobles could protect their coreligionists only from the other Christian knights. In other words, they remained parasitical and furnished the kind of "protection" given by gangsters during our era of prohibition. After the invention of firearms, the mounted knight had less advantage over the burghers, who could now employ mercenary artillerymen to destroy the castles of the knights who pillaged their convoys. As the burghers attained economic and political leadership, they also became the bearers of culture. Their new values gradually set the standard for society in general, even if the displaced aristocracy tended to retain their old value code. Honor, in the sense of social position and public esteem, was still the reward for virtue; but bourgeois virtue differed greatly from the old virtues of courage, prowess, fealty, and largess.

Although there were a few educated noblemen like Ulrich von Hutten, most education was in the hands of the bourgeoisie, often of the petty bourgeoisie, like Conrad Celtis and Luther, who were the sons of peasants. Being a gentleman was a full-time occupation, what with its demands of fighting, hunting, dressing, dancing, and taking one's genteel pleasures; and little time was left for study.[1] Likewise, the nobility are usually conservative and have little desire for social progress or other change. Consequently Goethe was right in asking, "And whence came the best culture, if it was not from the burgher?" (Wo kam die schönste Bildung her, Und wenn sie nicht vom Bürger wär?)

Germany's literary output was of poor quality during the fourteenth and fifteenth centuries; and most of what appeared had been written before and better. Even the few good works, such as the *Plowman from Bohemia* (*Ackermann aus Böhmen*), were largely compiled from traditional materials.[2] In general the mastersingers

---

[1] In her introduction to *The Vulgaria of John Stanbridge*, London, 1932, Beatrice White shows that the sixteenth-century English gentry in general had little respect for the study of letters. This would have held also of the German nobility of the time. In spite of their leisure and educational advantages, the German nobility have contributed but an infinitessimal part of German culture.

[2] For the traditional nature of such literature, see the sources traced in the notes to *Johannes von Tepl, Der ackerman*, ed. W. Krogmann, Wiesbaden, 1954.

repeated the formulas of the *Minnesinger* and *Spruchdichter* but did not achieve their excellence. This holds especially true of literary expressions of honor, which scarcely made any progress during the period. Even works as late as the *Ship of Fools* of 1496 and the plays of Hans Sachs a half century later show no real advance over the didactic writers of the thirteenth century.

The *Ship of Fools* repeats the old clichés found in *Farmer Helmbrecht* in these words: "All nobility is made of virtue. If one has good behavior, honor, and virtue, I consider him a nobleman; but, if anyone has no virtue, breeding, shame, honor, or good behavior, I consider him void of all nobility, even though his father were a prince. All nobility comes from virtue." [1] The tenacity of these commonplaces is shown by their appearance in Molière's *Dom Juan*, which was written a century and a half after the *Ship of Fools* and nearly four centuries after *Farmer Helmbrecht*: "And finally know that a nobleman who lives badly is a monster in nature; that virtue is the first title of nobility; that I have far less regard for the name that one signs than for the deeds that one does, that I would value the son of a porter who was an honest man more than the son of a monarch who lived like you." [2]

Nevertheless, these fallow centuries were not entirely lost, since they provided time for the good seed to take root and begin to grow. The new ideas introduced by the clerics and didactic poets in the thirteenth century were novel and not always convincing; but centuries of repetition made them so commonplace that they gradually won over the public at large, even if only in theory. The invention of printing naturally helped disseminate the new values.

[1] "Uss tugent ist all adel gemacht Wer noch gut sytt, ere, tugent kan den haltt ich fur eyn edel man. Aber wer hett keyn tugent nitt Keyn zucht, scham, ere, noch gute sytt Den haltt ich alles adels laer Ob joch eyn fürst syn vatter wer Adel alleyn by tugent stat Vss tugent aller adel gat" (*Narrenschiff*, 76, 56-64).

[2] "Apprenez enfin qu'un gentilhomme qui vit mal est un monstre dans la nature; que le vertu est le premier titre de noblesse; que je regarde bien moins au nom qu'on signe qu'aux actions qu'on fait, que je ferais plus d'état du fils d'un crocheteur qui serait honnête homme, que du fils d'un monarque qui vivrait comme vous" (*Dom Juan*, IV, 6).

CHAPTER EIGHT

HONOR IN REFORMATION AND BAROQUE LITERATURE

The fame of lofty deeds must perish as a dream.
GRYPHIUS.

In countries to the west and south of Germany external honor or personal reputation was perhaps the most popular subject for dramas. Today this subject is most often associated with the Baroque dramas of Spain, particularly with those of Lope de Vega and Calderón, such as *El médico de su honra* and *A secreto agravio, secreta venganza*. As the principal characteristics of such dramas, D. C. Stuart summarizes these facts: "honor is a pure crystal belonging to man and woman; it is not acquired, but is conferred upon them at birth; the slightest breath of scandal dims it; any stain upon it must be kept hidden at all cost; if the stain becomes visible it must be washed out with blood; a woman's transgression, or merely suspected transgression, is enough to wound the honor of a man connected with her by blood or by marriage. The cruelty of the law of honor is realized and bemoaned. *Dura lex, sed lex.*"[1] Stuart also shows that sources of the Spanish concept of honor, especially with regard to vengeance wreaked by a husband on his wife or her lover, can be found in ancient Gothic survivals and need not be attributed to Moorish influences.[2]

Nevertheless, even though all the elements were present in Spain, it so happens that the first drama of this tradition, Torres Naharro's *Imenea* of 1517, was written, played, and published in Italy, albeit its author was a Spaniard. Whereas Stuart believed the Spanish honor-dramas to be the direct result of Italian models, Américo Castro doubts this and contends that the Spanish ideal of honor, as expressed in the dramas, could have developed independently from medieval precedents and international humanistic theories, especially those from Seneca.[3] In order to be popular, the dramatic action had to glorify external honor and revenge; yet the authors could

---
[1] Stuart, p. 248.
[2] *op. cit.*, p. 251.
[3] Castro, p. 330.

also cite Stoic ideas opposing the point of honor.[1] Italian influence is obvious in Shakespeare's *Othello*, and it is indirectly present in the honor-dialectics of his *Richard II* and *Henry IV*.

Perhaps the best known of all honor-dramas is Corneille's *Le Cid* of 1636, which was based on a drama of the same name written a few years earlier by the Spaniard Guillen de Castro. Corneille's version presents a true psychological conflict, or one should say conflicts, since both the hero and heroine must choose between love and honor. The hero's father, a meritorious but aging statesman named Don Diegue, has a rather undignified altercation with a younger rival, Count de Gormas, concerning their relative honor and merit; and, after much abuse on both sides, Gormas slaps the old man. Mortally grieved by this affront, which makes him feel ineligible for holding high office, Don Diegue draws his sword; but Gormas easily disarms him and does not deign to pick up his sword as a trophy.

Don Diegue then implores his young son, Don Rodrigue, to remove his infamy and repair his honor by killing Gormas, even though Gormas is the father of Don Rodrigue's fiancée, Chimène. After much inner struggle and rhetorical monologue, Don Rodrigue decides to answer the call of honor and avenge his father, even at the cost of losing his love. When Gormas falls in their duel, Chimène demands justice of the king, since she too puts her honor above her love. Because the king delays in avenging her, Don Rodrigue offers to let her kill him in order to restore her honor, but she refuses the offer and persists in demanding lawful justice. The king decrees a trial by combat and adds the stipulation that Chimène must marry the victor. Don Rodrigue defeats Chimène's champion ,much to her joy, and thereby wins her hand.

Except for omitting the theme of revenge for adultery, this play includes most of the motifs popular in the Italian and Spanish honor-dramas, which seem to have preserved chivalresque situations and adorned them with classic commonplaces. Don Rodrigue's dilemma reminds one of that of Rüdeger in the *Lay of the Nibelungs*, and Chimène's dilemma is like that of Laudine, who loved her husband's slayer. Just as Wolfram von Eschenbach reproved Laudine for forgiving and marrying Iwein,[2] so too Jean Chapelain, speaking for the French Academy, called Chimène a "denatured girl" for marrying Don Rodrigue.[3] In this play we find many familiar commonplaces: An insult can be washed off only with blood; a man who lieves infamously is unworthy of the day; the code of honor is a hard law; if one conquers without peril he triumphs

---

[1] *op. cit.*, pp. 354-382.
[2] *Parzival*, 253, 10-18.
[3] In his *Sentiments de l'Académie sur "le Cid"* of 1637.

without glory; a man without honor does not merit a noble woman; infamy pursues a cowardly warrior and a faithless lover; dying for one's country is not a sad lot because such a death brings immortality; and many more.[1]

One might contend that Corneille has deepened the motivation of this play by associating honor with duty. On one occasion Don Diegue states that, whereas love is only a pleasure, honor is a duty;[2] and he tries to persuade his son by appealing to his filial piety. Because such an appeal is not enough, he also convinces him that he must fight to avenge not only his father but also his own honor, and his son accepts this double motivation.[3] Throughout the play people seem anxious about external appearances, and their chief concern is their *gloire, honneur, fame, renommée, nom, mémoire, honte, infamie, blâme*, and *médisance*. When Don Rodrigue visits Chimène after the duel, her only worry is that she will lose her honor if people see him leave.[4] Likewise, Don Rodrigue knows that he can voluntarily lose the trial by combat without any danger to his glory, because people will say (*on dira*) that he did not try to resist because of his love for Chimène.[5]

According to modern standards, these noble characters are extremely selfish. Just to save his own reputation, Don Diegue goads his dutiful but inexperienced son to challenge the realm's most famous warrior; and later he sends him to seek glory, and an honorable death if necessary, in a campaign against the Moors. Likewise, Chimène greatly inconveniences the king with her selfish demands for vengeance.

Contemporary with these honor-dramas there appeared a flood of learned disquisitions on honor, good examples being Giovanni Battista Possevino's *Dialogo dell' honore*, written in 1555, and Robert Ashley's *Of Honour*, written in or soon after 1596. Closely following classical sources, Ashley neglects the "point of honor",

---

[1] "Ce n'est que dans le sang qu'on lave un tel outrage" (I, 5, v. 14); "qui peut vivre infâme est indigne du jour" (I, 5, v. 24); "Noble et dure contrainte, aimable tyrannie" (I, 6, v. 22); "Trop peu d'honneur pour moi suivrait cette victoire: A vaincre sans péril, on triomphe sans gloire" (II, 2, vv. 37-38); "Qu'un homme sans honneur ne te méritait pas" (III, 4, v. 40); "L'infâmie est pareille, et suit également Le guerrier sans courage et le perfide amant" (III, 6, vv. 39-40); "Mourir pour le pays n'est pas un triste sort; C'est s'immortaliser par une belle mort" (IV, 5, vv. 31-32).
[2] "L'amour n'est qu'un plaisir, l'honneur est un devoir" (III, 6, v. 35).
[3] "D'un affront si cruel, Qu' à l'honneur de tous deux il porte un coup mortel" (I, 5, vv. 7-8). Later the son states, "j'ai vengé mon honneur et mon père (III, 6, v. 29). Gormas also looks upon Don Rodrigue's challenge as a duty (*ton devoir*, II, 2, v. 27).
[4] "Dans l'ombre de la nuit cache bien ton départ: Si l'on te voit sortir, mon honneur court hasard" (III, 4, vv. 127-128).
[5] "Rodrigue peut mourir sans hasarder sa gloire..." (V, 1).

which, although of Germanic origin, was discussed in most of the classically inspired works about honor written on the Continent. Although he acknowledges his debt to both the Academic and Peripatetic philosophers, Ashley actually owes most of his ideas to Aristotle.[1] Like Aristotle, he considers the desire for honor a virtue, provided it is moderate and provided one seeks true rather than false honor. Although he distinguishes between true and false honor and between glory and honor, he does not realize that he is using the word "honor" to denote two separate concepts. He begins his work by saying that honor must spring from the Godhead, "since we find no Originall thereof in the earth neither in things without soule, neither in brute beastes, not in men themselves: but only in one onely God alone." Honor must be good, since God demands it of us. This thought could be pagan as well as Christian, since it is proved by a reference to the temple the Romans built to commemorate Honor.

We have seen that many thirteenth-century German courtly and didactic poets believed, in agreement with Aristotle, that the pursuit of true honor leads to virtue; and thus they believed that it made men more pleasing to God, from whom all true honor comes. This view remained popular for centuries, finding perhaps its best expression in Spenser's *Fairy Queen*. Nevertheless, most clergymen followed the other-worldly tradition of damning wordly honor as a temptation of the devil. As Bossuet declaimed in his funeral oration for Henriette of England in 1670: "Glory! What is more pernicious and more mortal for a Christian? What bait more dangerous? What smoke more capable of turning the best heads?"[2]

In his treatise *The Courtier*, written in 1528, Baldesar Castiglione discussed the ways and means by which a courtier could win the favor of his liege and the admiration of his peers. This work, which was translated into most European languages, including German, remained a handbook on courtly behavior for generations. Most of its admonitions reappeared intact a century later in Nicolas Faret's *L'honneste Homme*.[3] According to Faret, to be an "honest man" one should be born to a noble and distinguished family, since noblemen withdraw from wickedness through fear of "infamie"; yet, although desirable, noble birth is not absolutely necessary. The military career is the most suitable profession, and courage is even more important than deportment or wealth. An honest man must defend

---

[1] Ashley, p. 24.
[2] "La Gloire! Qu'y a-t-il pour le chrétien de plus pernicieux et de plus mortel? quel appât plus dangereux? quelle fumée plus capable de faire tourner les meilleures têtes?" (Bossuet, *Oraison funèbre d'Henriette d'Agleterre*, cited from Highet, p. 657).
[3] ed. M. Magendie, Paris, 1925.

his honor; but he should not be quarrelsome, vain, or coarse. He should be physically attractive and excel in leisure-class sports, including moderate gambling. He should avoid avarice, indolence, despondence, affectation, calculation, excessive make-up, and vice. He should pursue virtue, learning, modesty, and good deeds; and he should be graceful, well dressed, and sweet-breathed. In other words, Faret has retained not only the ideals of Castiglione's courtier, but practically those of the thirteenth-century knights. Although he has added a few social graces, honor remains an external possession which one earns through good behavior. Aptly enough, the sub-title of the book is "the Art of Pleasing at Court." Faret's apparent cultural advance in this work over Castiglione can be attributed to his social class: Faret was a bourgeois trying to write for noblemen, whereas Castiglione was born an aristocrat.

Objective honor was ordinarily eulogized by laymen only; yet one of the most amazing and original arguments on the subject was written by a clergyman. In a sermon delivered in or about 1667 on I Samuel 2,30 (For them that honor me I will honor), an English divine named Isaac Barrow argued that honor must be a good thing, since God sees fit to bestow it on men. First he praises honor as the goal and therefore source of every worthy deed; and for this purpose he complies a veritable commonplace book of ancient wisdom. Next he shows that desire for honor is rooted in man's very nature, for without it we would be but brutes. Then he lists the many passages in Scripture where honor is mentioned as a desirable good or as a gift of God.[1] This remains perhaps the most successful attempt to reconcile love of God and love of honor.

While secular poets, and Isaac Barrow, glorified objective honor, most clerical poets, or poets in clerical employ, continued to belittle it. Even poets who often praised it sometimes damned it. According to Tasso, "Fame, which entices you proud mortals with a sweet sound and appears so beautiful, is an echo, a dream, even the shadow of a dream that faints and fades away into every wind."[2] Montaigne expressed this thought somewhat later with the words, "Of all the dreams of the world, the most universally accepted is the concern for reputation and glory, which we espouse to the point of quitting riches, repose, life, and health, which are real and substantial, in order to follow that vain image and simple voice that has neither body nor substance."[3]

---

[1] Barrow, pp. 74-101.

[2] "La fama che invaghisce a un dolce suono voi superbi mortali, e par sí bella, è un'echo, un sogno, anzi del sogno un'ombra, ch'ad ogni vento si dilegua e sgombra" (Torquato Tasso, *Gerusalemme Liberata*, ed. L. Bonifigli, Bari, 1930, XIV, 63).

[3] "De toutes les resveries du monde, la plus receué et plus universelle est le soing de la reputation et de la gloire, que nous espousons jusques à quitter les

In contrast to Norfolk's encomium of honor in Richard II, Shakespeare also presents Falstaff's monologue: "What is honour? A word. What is that word honour? Air. A trim reckoning! Who hath it? He that died a Wednesday. Doth he feel it? No. Doth he hear it? No. 'Tis insensible then? Yea, to the dead. But will it not live with the living? No. Why? Detraction will not suffer it. Therefore I'll none of it. Honour is a mere scutcheon – and so ends my catechism."[1] A century and a half later Albrecht von Haller, a Swiss scholar, repeated the commonplace by calling honor a "valued nothing,... a bewitching fantom."[2] A century later the Austrian dramatist Grillparzer, following Spanish baroque tradition, wrote: "What is the world's fortune? – A shadow! What is the world's fame? – A dream!"[3] It is generally recognized that baroque civilization was dualistic, but we should remember that this dualism was a heritage from the Middle Ages, despite current beliefs about medieval harmony. At about the same time as Grillparzer, the German-Hungarian poet Nikolaus Lenau similarly deprecated ambition: "Cease your struggle for honor; rather turn your hot striving into your own heart, and you will live a beautiful life."[4]

While the Renaissance and Baroque poets of Italy, Spain, France,

richesses, le repos, la vie et la santé, qui sont bien effectuels et substantiaux, pur suyvre cette vaine image et cette simple voix qui n'a ny corps ny prise" (Montaigne, ed. Armaingaud, I, 41).

[1] *King Henry IV*, Part I, V, 1, vv. 135-143. Iago follows either tradition, depending upon his need. To Cassio he says, "As I am an honest man, I thought you had receiv'd some bodily wound. There is more sense in that than in reputation. Reputation is an idle and most false imposition, oft got without merit and lost without deserving. You have lost no reputation at all unless you repute yourself such a loser" (*Othello*, II, 3, vv. 266-272). To Othello he says, "Good name in man and woman, dear my lord, Is the immediate jewel of their souls. Who steals my purse steals trash; 'tis something, nothing; 'Twas mine, 'tis his, and has been slave to thousands; But he that filches from me my good name Robs me of that which not enriches him And makes me poor indeed" (*Othello*, III, 3, vv. 155-161).

[2] "Geschätztes nichts der eitlen Ehre! Dir baut das Alterthum Altäre; Du bist noch heut der Gott der Welt. Bezaubernd Unding, Kost der Ohren, Des Wahnes Tochter, Wunsch der Thoren, Was hast du dann, das uns gefällt?" (Haller, p. 9). In forty more strophes he heaps classical commonplaces and historical illustrations to show that worldly honor is a fleeting and useless thing.

[3] "Was ist der Erde Glück? - Ein Schatten! Was ist der Erde Ruhm? - Ein Traum!" (*Das goldene Vliess. Medea*, V, vv. 2366-2367). Cf. "Und die Grösse ist gefährlich, Und der Ruhm ein leeres Spiel" (*Der Traum ein Leben*, IV, vv. 2653-2654). Grillparzer vacillates in his views on honor like his heroine Sappho. First she says, "Weh dem, den aus der Seinen stillem Kreise Des Ruhmes, der Ehrsucht eitler Schatten lockt!"; but then she says, "Es schmähe nicht den Ruhm, wer ihn besitzt. Er ist kein leer-bedeutungsloser Schall, Mit Götterkraft erfüllet sein Berühren!" (*Sappho*, I, 5).

[4] "Lass das Ringen nach der Ehre; Lieber all dein heisses Streben In den eigenen Busen kehre, Und du lebst ein schönes Leben" (Lenau, I, p. 125).

and England were devoting so much of their time to discussing honor, German writers almost entirely ignored the subject. Their lack of interest can be explained by their religious urges, which caused them to expend their energies in mysticism and theology, and then with reformation, counter-reformation, and the political and military struggles resulting from them. The Christian tradition of inwardness, which had flourished with the mystics, was handed down to the Reformers and passed on by them to the Pietists and other sects. Naturally these inner-directed people were less anxious about the opinions of other people than about the salvation of their souls. To use medieval terminology, they longed more for God's grace than for man's favor. The theocentric teachings of the early missionaries had at last borne abundant fruit. The attitude of the whole Reformation Era toward honor can be summed up in the verse of the Protestant anthem, "A Mighty Fortress", which says we should have no thought for "life, wealth, honor, child, and wife."[1] In other words, as during the Cluny Reform, the values of this world are nought in comparison with the values of Heaven. In such an atmosphere, honor could not inspire great literature.

To be sure, the ruling classes still cherished military renown, as can be seen in their constant dynastic struggles. Consequently, some poets continued the heroic tradition. In his "Battle Song" Jacob Vogel claimed that there is no happier death than that before the enemy, since it brings immortal fame.[2] Nevertheless, such sentiments were rare compared with concern for salvation. Andreas Gryphius was more representative of his time, at least of the literature of his time, when he said, "The fame of lofty deeds must perish as a dream."[3] Johann Scheffler, better known as Angelus Silesius, championed such a view in his *Cherubinischer Wandersmann*. Typical is his epigram: "The honor of this world perishes in a short time; Alas, seek the honor of eternal bliss."[4]

---

[1] "Nehmen sie den Leib, Gut, Ehr, Kind und Weib." Seen clerically, this is much more advanced that Walther's similar passage contrasting life, wife, and child to God's grace and honor (Walther, 22, 24-27).

[2] "Davon tut haben Unsterblichen Ruhm Mancher Held frumm" (*The Oxford Book of German Verse*, Oxford, 1946, No. 26). Note that, at this late date, the word *frumm* still meant brave, as had been usual centuries earlier. In other words, a courageous man was still a useful man.

[3] "Der hohen Taten Ruhm muss wie ein Traum vergehen" (*The Oxford Book of German Verse*, Oxford, 1946, No. 41).

[4] *Cherubinischer Wandersmann*, VI. At first glance, one of his statements appears to anticipate the internalization of honor discussed in the next chapter: "Wer in sich Ehre hat, der sucht sie nicht von Aussen; Suchst du sie in der Welt, so hast du sie noch draussen" (VI, 24). A comparison with some other passages (e.g. VI, 25, 26, 27, 76, 209, 210 *et passim*) shows that he uses the word *Ehre* to mean future glory in heaven, in other words *gloria*, not *honestum*.

The most typical, and the best, German literary product of this theocentric age was Grimmelshausen's *Simplicissimus* of 1668, which described the brutality and violence of the Thirty Year's War. Although it poses initially as an autobiographical picaresque novel, this work is really a sermon in disguise, a sermon against the vanities of life – one might even say against life itself. Simplicissimus, a war orphan, lives first with a peasant and then, after his home has been destroyed by pillagers, with a hermit who teaches him to see the vanity of life. Carried away by soldiers, he experiences all the horrors of war, forgets the hermit's teaching, and lives a wicked and wordly life as a soldier. At last, upon reading a religious tract by a Spanish Franciscan named Guevara, he sees the vanity of the world and retires to the Black Forest as a hermit.

Such a plot naturally leaves little room for honor. Whereas Simplicissimus does not read Guevara's other-wordly tractate until the end of the book, it is apparent that the author had read it before hand; because his whole book stresses the emptiness of wordly joys, including wealth and honor. Grimmelshausen used the word *Ehre* almost exclusively in its objective sense, as, for example, in the formula *Ehre und Reputation* and in the statement that a fallen girl regains her *Ehren* when married and is *entunehrt* when raped.[1] Although it might appear that subjective value is intended in the expression "incapable of honor", this is not likely the case, for this is said of Simplicissimus while he is playing the role of a calf.[2] As we have seen, it had been conventional since Xenophon to say that animals are incapable of honor, in the sense of *timê*.[3] On the other hand, when reflecting about his wasted life, Simplicissimus once regrets that he has not paid attention to his honor for its own sake but only for his own exaltation;[4] and this suggests that honor is used here in the sense of honorable behavior. Also, the pair *Ehre und Tugend* appears in its old sense of female chastity;[5] but *Ehre* is used objectively in nearly all other cases.

Whereas Grimmelshausen usually uses *Ehre* in the sense of Latin *honor* rather than *honestum*, the adjectives *ehrlich* and *ehrbar* always mean *honestus*, in either its objective or subjective meaning. Natu-

---

[1] "Ehre und Reputation" (*Simplicissimus*, II, p. 48; III, 310); "ehrbar und reputierlich" (II, p. 237); "Ehren" (II, p. 227); "entunehrt" (II, p. 242).
[2] "keiner menschlichen Ehre würdig noch fähig" (I, p. 172); "keiner Ehre fähig" (I, p. 177).
[3] Cassio alludes to this belief when he exclaims: "I have lost my reputation! I have lost the immortal part of myself, and what remains is bestial." (*Othello*, II, 3).
[4] "Ich nahm meine Ehre in acht, nicht ihrer selbsten, sondern meiner Erhöhung wegen" (III, p. 129).
[5] "Ehre und Tugend" (II, p. 209).

rally they always have objective meaning when applied to objects,[1] in which case Grimmelshausen often uses them facetiously. In some cases, however, the words are used in their moral sense, as when it is said that an honorable (*ehrlicher*) man keeps his word.[2] Both *ehrlich* and *ehrbar* appear often as standing epithets for clergymen and good Christians in general;[3] and, as in medieval didactic verse, virtues are *ehrlich* and vices are *schändlich*.[4] As heir to a clerical tradition, Grimmelshausen thinks the stars show honor to God, as the old hermit sings in one of his hymns.[5] Grimmelshausen himself was *honestus*, or invested with civil rights, if we may trust the notice of his death made in his parish register.[6]

Following clerical tradition, Grimmelshausen lets his hero sing a song in praise of the peasantry, its ten strophes summarizing all the arguments presented in *Farmer Helmbrecht* in very much the same language and sequence. Even though this poem praises the peasant for nourishing Christendom, it still reveals some upper-class rationalization by saying that God puts an especial cross on the peasants to protect them from pride and lets the soldiers despoil them to protect them from arrogance.[7] These last two thoughts had often appeared in satirical poems directed against the peasantry and justifying the status quo.[8] Grimmelshausen also praises the ancient artisans and inventors just as highly as ancient conquerors,[9] and thus he evinces clerical-bourgeois rather than aristocratic tendencies. In spite of such praise for productive work, he nevertheless reveals some of the current prejudices against the "dishonorable" people and common laborers by ridiculing people who try to win nobility even though their ancestors were day-laborers, carters, carriers,

---

[1] "der ehrliche Tanz" (I, p. 135); "ehrlicher Ort" (I, 136); "ehrbare Früchte" (I, p. 137); "ehrliches Stier" (I, p. 158); "ehrliche Übungen" (III, p. 174); "ehrbarer Bart" (III, p. 81), *et passim*.
[2] "ein ehrlicher Mann hält sein Wort" (I, p. 124).
[3] "ehrbarer Domine" (II, p. 234); "ehrlicher Christenmensch" (III, p. 44); "ehrliche Christen" (III, p. 282); "ehrliche Christenmenschen" (III, p. 283); "ehrbares christliches Tun" (III, p. 108); "ehrliche Übungen" (III, p. 174); *et passim*.
[4] "ehrlichen Tugenden, schändlichen Lastern" (III, p. 178).
[5] "Ehre ihm beweisen" (I, p. 26).
[6] The notice of Grimmelshausen's death in his parish register states that he was *honestus* (cited in *Simplicissimus the Vagabond*, ed. A. T. S. Goodrich, London, 1912, p. xxii).
[7] *Simplicissimus*, I, p. 12.
[8] Hugo von Trimberg states: "Der maniger vil trazmüetic wêre: Wêren in die herren niht ze swêre, Sô möhte man ir vil manigen vinde Bî der hôchferte ingesinde" (*Renner*, vv. 1311-1314). In a satire of the Reformation period St. Peter says: "Denn wo kein straf an den baurn geschicht, So wirt fürwar kein bauer selig nicht" (O. Schade, *Satiren und Pasquille aus der Reformationszeit*, Hannover, 1856-58, I, p. 167, vv. 474-475).
[9] *Simplicissimus*, I, pp. 176-177.

washerwomen, jugglers, bailiffs, constables, and other scorned people.[1] On another occasion, he lets Simplicissimus say that no recruiting officer would take him because he looks shabbier than a linen weaver.[2]

Grimmelshausen also follows clerical tradition in preferring nobility of behavior to nobility of birth. A young nobleman and a sergeant have a long argument in which numerous biblical and classical commonplaces are mustered to prove or disprove the military superiority of better-born people. The nobleman, in agreement with Castiglione, argues that wellborn people are more respected and therefore can be better leaders and that they are by nature more avid for glory. The sergeant, on the other hand, argues that no army can fight well unless its common soldiers have some hope of rising through their own merits.[3] It is not difficult to see that Grimmelshausen favors the more democratic view, especially since he knows that children do not always resemble their parents and therefore do not deserve their titles.[4] Nevertheless, he follows the time-worn tradition of letting his well-endowed hero be a person of gentle birth, like Paris, Siegfried, Gregorius, and many other foundling heroes. Later, while pretending to believe himself a calf, Simplicissimus preaches his master, the military governor of Hanau, a sermon on the vanity of titles and honor. This lecture, which lasts a whole chapter, argues that a man who holds titles, authority, and honor suffers many trials and tribulations and is in constant danger of losing all his treasures in this world, to say nothing of those in the next. Simplicissimus then cites numerous Greek and Roman writers to prove that great men always suffer from envy, enmity, and backbiting.[5] It is to be remembered that seventeenth-century writers like Grimmelshausen did not have to be widely read in the classics in order to flaunt classical knowledge. This was readily available in commonplace books, for instance in Tobias Magirus's *Polymnemon*, which was printed in Frankfurt in 1661 and included numerous classical quotations on the subject of honor.

Naturally Grimmelshausen, who considers forgiveness better than revenge, cannot appreciate the "point of honor".[6] Simplicissimus's only affair of honor is not an honorable affair, for it begins in drunken boasting and ends in deceit. Incited by wine and esprit de corps, Simplicissimus challenges a cavalryman who has spoken disparagingly of the musketeers. The cavalryman takes up the guantlet

---

[1] *op. cit.*, I, p. 3.
[2] "Leineweber" (*op. cit.*, II, p. 174).
[3] *op. cit.*, I, pp. 63-68.
[4] *op. cit.*, I, p. 173.
[5] *op. cit.*, I, pp. 178-184.
[6] The older Herzbruder is clearly expressing Grimmelshausen's views when he preaches against revenge (*op. cit.*, I, p. 240).

and agrees to meet him in an open field where each will use his own weapons. Seeing Simplicissimus's musket misfire, he charges down upon him, only to be shot down. The apparent misfire was a ruse. Simplicissimus had merely touched off a little powder on top of his powder pan.[1] Unlike his courtly predecessors, Grimmelshausen considered duels both stupid and sinful. Like the virtuous heroes of the courtly epics, Simplicissimus resolves to win esteem and praise through liberality; yet Grimmelshausen makes it clear that he does not consider this a virtuous resolve.[2] As he often stresses, thirst for fame is a vice rather than a virtue.[3]

[1] *op. cit.*, II, p. 48.
[2] "Ansehen und guter Lob" (*op. cit.*, II, p. 91).
[3] "Ehre und Ruhm zu erjagen" (*op. cit.*, II, p. 3).

CHAPTER NINE

INNER HONOR

The honor of the world can give you no honor.

THEODOR FONTANE.

We have seen that the Renaissance and Baroque "honor-dramas" of Italy, Spain, France, and England were primarily concerned with "objective" honor and that Germany contributed little to this tradition. Germany's first notable honor-drama was not a tragedy involving the loss of one's good name, but rather a comedy discussing the relative value of personal and public honor. Gotthold Ephraim Lessing, a leader of the Enlightenment in Germany, wrote his *Minna von Barnhelm* soon after the Seven Year's War, which ended in 1763. Its hero, Major von Tellheim, has been dismissed from the Prussian army at the close of the war with suspicions cast at his previous conduct. During the war he had been stationed in the conquered province of Saxony, where he won the respect and affection of the occupied populace by his leniency in exacting contributions. He not only exacted the least amount permitted him but even advanced a large sum of his own money to mitigate the collections. However, at the close of the war his leniency is attributed to bribery, and the Prussian authorities refuse to return the funds he has advanced.

Feeling his honor impugned, Tellheim thinks he has no right to claim his fiancée, a beautiful Saxon heiress whose heart and hand he won through the nobility of his character and conduct during the occupation. When he fails to write her after the war, the fiancée, Minna von Barnhelm, comes to Berlin to look for him; and by chance she stops at the very hotel where he has been lodging. Preferring a solvent guest, the avaricious host removes Tellheim's belongings to a less desirable room and lets his suite to the young lady. As the play opens, Tellheim's man of all work, Just, is cursing the host for evicting such an honorable man.

And an honorable man Tellheim is, in every sense of the word, as several people in the play attest. The meaning of *ehrlich* is somewhat clarified by the fact that he is elsewhere called *brav* and *edel* and is included in the term *honnête-homme*. It is further clarified by being attributed to Tellheim's former sergeant-major, Werner, who is elsewhere called "excellent" (*vortrefflich*) and who shows many of the admirable character traits shown by Tellheim. Werner uses the word in saying that, if they were "honorable fellows and good Christians", they would go fight the Turks; and the host uses the word in assuring Minna that he has acquired Tellheim's ring in the most honorable manner. Riccault de la Marlinière, a rather questionable French adventurer, states that his fellow gamblers are "honorable people" (*ehrlike Leut*), but apparently he is referring to the proverbial honor among thieves.[1] In any case, it is clear that Lessing uses the word *ehrlich* to mean socially and morally respectable, that is to say *honnête*, as the French translation of 1772 consistently renders it.

Tellheim's nobility of soul is revealed not only by what the others say, but even more by his generous acts. In spite of his financial embarrassment, he has refused to touch a large sum of money entrusted to him by Werner. He also refuses to allow the widow of an old colleague to pay a debt owed him by her late husband, and he tries to convince her that her husband owed him nothing. Later he destroys the receipt and even tells Werner that the debt has been paid. He likewise refuses money from Just, whom he once supported in a hospital at his own expense. Unlike his predecessors in chivalric literature, Tellheim gives anonymously and from his scarcity, rather than from abundance. Minna reveals Tellheim's true character when she says that he is brave but never speaks of bravery and that he would never regret a good deed because of its bad consequences.[2] That he is above seeking revenge is revealed when he protects the host from Just, who wants to thrash him for insulting his master.

Tellheim does not treasure his reputation for his own sake. Werner tries to persuade him to accept his money by warning that people will talk about him if he falls into debt; yet Tellheim replies that he does not care if people know he has no money. He refuses the money on the grounds that it is wrong to borrow money if you are not sure you can return it.[3] In other words, Lessing indicates that Tellheim is motivated by feelings of right and wrong, not by the opinions of people. Tellheim believes that one should be a soldier only in order to serve his country or a cause, even though the authorities think soldiers fight for their own glory rather than out of duty. He confesses to Minna that he became a soldier not only because of

---

[1] Tellheim is *ehrlich* (*Minna von Barnhelm*, I, 1; II, 2; III, 12), *brav* (III, 5), *edel* (III, 12), and an *honnête-homme* (IV, 2). Werner is *ehrlich* (IV, 8) and *vortrefflich* (III, 4). *ehrliche Kerls und gute Christen* (I, 12). *ehrlichste Weise* (II, 2). *ehrlike Leut* (IV, 2).
[2] "Sie sind der Mann nicht, den eine gute Tat reuen kann, weil sie üble Folgen für ihn hat" (IV, 6).
[3] "Man muss nicht borgen, wenn man nicht wiederzugeben weiss" (III, 7).

political principles but also because of his belief that every honorable man should test his mettle in danger; and he assures her that his only desire is to be a quiet and contented person as soon as the war is over.[1] Thus, we see that Tellheim is the very paragon of an honorable man, in the Christian-Stoic sense of this term.

Nevertheless, despite his steadfastness of character, Tellheim is the victim of linguistic ambivalence. As an officer and a gentleman, he is dedicated to the ideal of honor, even though uncertain of its meaning. His own actions are motivated by an innate sense of right and charity; yet he can not escape the traditional belief that only a man with a spotless reputation has a right to court an honorable woman. In other words, his trouble is actually semantic: he uses the word *Ehre* in both its subjective and objective meanings, without distinguishing between the two contrary concepts.

Like other people in the play, Tellheim uses the word "honor" with objective meaning as in "to have the honor" or "to promise on my honor". In trying to explain to Minna why he cannot marry her, he reminds her that he is no longer the vital and glory-seeking (*voller Ruhmbegierde*) man for whom the barriers of honor and fortune were open; and in this case *Ehre* means fame and reputation. On the other hand, when Minna refuses to accept this argument, he sends her a letter in which he has written everything that honor commands him,[2] and in this case *die Ehre* clearly means moral rectitude or inner conscience. Nevertheless, he immediately uses the word again in its external sense by contending that he is unworthy of her because his honor (i.e., reputation for rectitude) has been impugned.

When Minna tells Tellheim that Riccaut has brought word of his vindication, Tellheim does not believe it and avers that he will starve rather than leave the city before he receives justice.

"I don't want mercy," he says. "I want justice. My honor..."

"The honor of a man like you," Minna interrupts, alluding to his sense of integrity.

"No, my dear young lady," he answer heatedly. "You can probably judge right well about all things, but just not about this. Honor is not the voice of our conscience, not the testimony of less righteous..."

---

[1] "Man muss Soldat sein für sein Land oder aus Liebe zu der Sache" (III, 7). "Die Grossen haben sich überzeugt, dass ein Soldat aus Neigung für sie ganz wenig, aus Pflicht nicht viel mehr, aber alles seiner eignen Ehre wegen tut" (IV, 6). "dass es für jeden ehrlichen Mann gut sei, sich in diesem Stande eine Zeitlang zu versuchen, um sich mit allem, was Gefahr heisst, vertraulich zu machen und Kälte und Entschlossenheit zu lernen" (V, 9). "nun ist mein ganzer Ehrgeiz wiederum einzig und allein, ein ruhiger und zufriedener Mensch zu sein" (V, 9).

[2] "die Ehre haben" (IV, 6); "auf meine Ehre" (III, 7); "voller Ruhmbegierde... Schranken der Ehre..." (II, 9); "was mir die Ehre befiehlt" (IV, 6).

"No, no," Minna answers, to help him out of his hopeless confusion. "I understand. Honor is – honor."

"In short, young lady, – you didn't let me finish. – I wanted to say: if they insult me by holding back what is mine, if my honor does not receive the most complete satisfaction, then I cannot be yours, my lady; for I shall not be worthy of it in the eyes of the world. Fräulein von Barnhelm deserves a blameless (*unbescholten*) husband. It is a despicable love that does not scruple at exposing its object to contempt. He is a despicable man who is not ashamed to owe his entire fortune to a young lady whose blind affection..." [1]

At this point Minna interrupts his outmoded argument by turning her back; and then she returns his ring. When she has departed, Franziska, her lady's maid, tells Tellheim that Minna has lost her good name and been disowned by her rich uncle for coming to him. Now that Tellheim is rich and blameless and Minna is poor and dishonored, she refuses his renewed courtship with all the arguments that he has given her. Hearing her repeat his arguments point by point, he realizes the absurdity of his exaggerated sense of honor. When she adamantly refuses to hold him to his word now that she has lost wealth and honor, he even threatens to refuse his belated justice which people have dishonored by such an insulting suspicion. When Tellheim has finally suffered enough torment and seen his errors, Minna reveals that her misfortune was a ruse. Minna, who is motivated chiefly by love, refers to honor almost only in her parody of Tellheim's argument. On one occasion she declaims against men's concern for the "specter of honor".[2]

An English translation of Lessing's comedy appeared in 1799 with the title *The School for Honor*; and that is just what it is. In addition to Minna's instruction on the true meaning of honor, there are other lectures on the subject. Franziska condescendingly asks Just why Tellheim has dismissed all of his more glamorous servants and retained only the worst one. When Just answers that perhaps he was the most *ehrlich*, Franziska replies that one is not much if one is merely *ehrlich*. Thereupon Just teaches her a lesson by telling how all the others have robbed or deserted their master or ended in prison. The valet, for example, is now enjoying great honor after stealing his master's complete wardrobe. Thus Franziska realizes that she has disparaged *Ehrlichkeit* too much.[3]

---

[1] "Die Ehre ist nicht die Stimme unsers Gewissens, nicht das Zeugnis weniger Rechtschaffenen -..." (IV, 6).
[2] "Gespenst der Ehre" (IV, 6). A few verses earlier she uses the word *Ehre* in the sense of moral duty: "Und wenn unsere Stände die geringste Empfindung von Ehre haben..." She uses *Ehre* in its objective sense, in parodying Tellheim, in Act V, Scene 9.
[3] "ein ehrlicher Kerl" (III, 2); "man ist auch verzweifelt wenig, wenn man weiter nichts ist als ehrlich" (III, 2); "sich alle Ehre machen" (III, 2); "Ich setzte die Ehrlichkeit zu tief herab" (III, 3).

Franziska herself expresses a view acceptable to King Solomon but not to most of the medieval court poets, when she says that beautiful women are most beautiful when unadorned. Tellheim also expresses a view contrary to most medieval poets when he says that Minna is not one of the vain women who see in their men only their rank and dignity (*Ehrenstelle*); for her attitude would have been unworthy of Brunhild or Kriemhild. Whereas the noun *Ehre* appears most often in its objective sense, the verb *schämen* appears most often in a subjective sense. That is to say, it usually means to be "*a*shamed" rather than "shamed". Tellheim tells his colleague's widow she should not be ashamed of her misfortune; and Franziska calls Just *unverschämt* because of his rudeness. In parodying Tellheim Minna says it is a base creature that is not ashamed to owe her entire fortune to the blind affection of a man.[1]

It is to be noted that Lessing expressed no social satire, except for following dramatic tradition in having the inn-keeper an avaricious and dishonest character. Werner calls Just a sumpter-soldier (*Packknecht*) when the latter suggests that the two of them thrash the host to avenge the insult to Tellheim, since the host is not capable of giving the major satisfaction. However, here it is the cavalryman's scorn for baggage personnel, not any prejudice on the part of the poet. The "dishonorable people" have been entirely forgotten; in fact Franziska, who is very much of a lady, is the daughter of a miller on Minna's estates.[2]

As we have seen, honors had been the wage of the soldier since the time of Aristotle. When Major Tellheim belittles this incentive, he speaks as an individual and not as a typical warrior of his time. In fact one might say that he is speaking for his creator, Lessing, who was no man of war but a man of God, albeit a rather enlightened one. Although Tellheim's king, Frederick the Great, swore by Cicero's *De Officiis*, he still found it advisable to spur his troops onward with promise of glory and eternal fame, as at the battle of Kolin in 1757.[3] About a half century later, in 1810, the Prussian dramatist Heinrich von Kleist attributed post-Kantian motives to Colonel Kottwitz, an officer serving Frederick's predecessor at the battle of Fehrbellin in 1675. Like Tellheim, this consciencious warrior denies that he is ready to shed his blood just for reward, be it money or honor,[4] even though such incentive would have sufficed

---

[1] "Wenn wir schön sind, sind wir ungeputzt am schönsten" (II, 7); "Ehrenstelle" (V, 9); "Vor mir dürfen Sie sich Ihres Unglücks nicht schämen" (I, 6); "unverschämt" (II, 6); "Es ist eine nichtswürdige Kreatur, die sich nicht schämet..." (V, 9).
[2] "Packknecht" (I, 12); "Mein Vater war Müller..." (II, 2).
[3] When his guards hesitated, he called, "Ihr Racker, wollt ihr ewig leben?"
[4] "Schütt ich mein Blut dir, an dem Tag der Schlacht, Für Sold, sei's Geld, sei's Ehre, in den Staub?" (*Prinz von Homburg*, V, 5, vv. 1588-1589).

for his Germanic ancestors. Kleist could admire such an attitude in others; yet fame was the goal of his own life,[1] which he ended because of his failure to gain recognition as a poet.

When Tellheim states that he wrote what honor dictated, he is using the word in a sense that this study has conveniently but arbitrarily termed "post-Kantian". That is to say, honorable acts are performed disinterestedly and purely through a desire to do the right thing. Of course it is to be noted that Lessing wrote his comedy more than twenty years before Kant formulated his "categorical imperative". Kant himself did not associate his moral imperative with the word "honor",[2] but it is easy to see that succeeding generations often used the word "honor" to designate a disinterested fulfilment of duty in answer to absolute moral law.

Fichte, the second great German idealist philosopher, definitely associated sense of honor and sense of duty by saying, "There is something that means more to me than anything else and to which I subordinate everything else, from the upholding of which I will not let myself be deterred by any more practical consequence, for which I would sacrifice without hesitation my entire worldly welfare, my good name, my life, the entire welfare of the universe, if it should conflict with it. I shall call it honor. I by no means place this honor in the judgment of others about my actions, even if it were the unanimous judgment of my contemporaries and of posterity, but rather in that judgment which I myself can form about them."[3] By this he seems to have meant about what St. Paul meant when he wrote to the Galatians. "But let each one test his own work, and thus he will have glory in himself and not in another." [4] For all its pompous verbosity, Fichte's definition, which appeared in 1795, well illustrated the ideal accepted by the following century. Bismark

---

[1] In a letter from St. Omer of 26 October 1803 he wrote, "Der Himmel versagt mir den Ruhm, das grösste der Güter der Erde; ich werfe ihm, wie ein eigensinniges Kind, alle übrigen hin. Ich kann mich deiner Freundschaft nicht würdig zeigen, ich kann ohne diese Freundschaft doch nicht leben: ich stürze mich in den Tod." Cf. "I could not love thee, Dear, so much..."
[2] Cf. "Die Ehre des Mannes besteht darin, was die Leute denken, des Frauenzimmers aber, was sie sprechen" (*Anthropologie*, 1798, cited from Lipperheide, p. 132).
[3] "Es gibt etwas, das mir über alles gilt, und dem ich alles andere nachsetze, von dessen Behauptung ich mich durch keine möglichere Folge abhalten lasse, für das ich mein ganzes irdisches Wohl, meinen guten Ruf, mein Leben, das ganze Wohl des Weltalls, wenn es damit in Streit kommen könnte, ohne Bedenken aufopfern würde. Ich will es *Ehre* nennen. Diese Ehre setze ich keineswegs in das Urtheil anderer über meine Handlungen, und wenn es das einstimmige Urtheil meines Zeitalters und der Nachwelt sein könnte, sondern in dasjenige, das ich selbst über sie fallen kann" (I. H. Fichte, *I. G. Fichtes Leben und literarischer Briefwechsel*, Leipzig, 1862, II, p. 45).
[4] "Opus autem suum probet unusquisque, et sic in semetipso tantum gloriam habebit et non in altero" (*Galatians*, 6, 4).

followed this tradition in 1881 by saying, "My honor stands in no one's hand but my own, no one can heap it on me. My own honor, which I carry in my heart, suffices me fully, and no one is judge of it and no one can decide whether or not I have any."[1]

However, this egocentric definition of honor was by no means new, having enjoyed uninterrupted continuity since Cicero asked whether one should do something expedient but wrong if it would remain unknown to the Gods and men.[2] St. Paul described such inner-directed pagans with the words: "When Gentiles who have not the law do by nature what the law requires, they are a law to themselves, even though they do not have the law. They show that what the law requires is written on their hearts, while their conscience also bears witness and their conflicting thoughts accuse or perhaps excuse them."[3] In the sixth century St. Martin of Braga, following Seneca, expressed Cicero's view by saying that it does not matter if no one else sees the acts of your mind and body, since you yourself see them.[4]

Even Martin Luther, despite his theocentric orientation, was not averse to extolling a disinterested love of virtue, "If you ask a chaste man why he is chaste, he should say, not on account of heaven or hell, and not on account of honor and disgrace, but solely because it would seem good to me and please me well even though it were not commanded."[5] It is easy to see how this pagan-Stoic view fitted Luther's belief that good works should be an incidental result of faith rather than a means to attain reward. Perhaps it is significant that, since Luther, most praise of disinterested virtue and honor have come from either Protestant or agnostic thinkers.

Although Luther could recognize the value of disinterested honor and virtue, not all Protestant thinkers could do so. Sir Thomas Browne, a young English doctor with a theological bent, expressed

---

[1] "Meine Ehre steht in niemandes Hand als in meiner eigenen, und man kann mich damit nicht überhäufen; die eigene, die ich in meinem Herzen trage, genügt mir vollständig, und niemand ist Richter darüber und kann entscheiden, ob ich sie habe" (Bismark's speech to the Reichstag on 28 November 1881, cited from Reiner, p. 49).
[2] "si id dis hominibusque futurum sit semper ignotum, sisne facturus" (*De Officiis*, III, ix).
[3] "Cum enim gentes, quae legem non habent, naturaliter ea quae legis sunt faciunt, eiusmodi legem non habentes ipsi sibi sunt lex; qui ostendunt opus legis scriptum in cordibus suis, testimonium reddente illis conscientia ipsorum, et inter se invicem cogitationibus accusantibus aut etiam defendentibus" (*Romans*, 2, 14-16).
[4] "Nam nihil differt, si nemo videat, cum ipse illos videas" (St. Martin, *Formula*, 4, 53).
[5] cited from John H. Randall, *The Making of the Modern Mind*, Houghton Mifflin, 1940, p. 139.

the difficulty of being honest merely for the sake of virtue. In his *Religio Medici* of 1634 he states that only memory of the Day of Judgement can make us "honest in the dark" and "virtuous without a witness." Citing the Latin adage that virtue is its own reward, he states that is "is but a cold principle, and not able to maintain our variable resolutions in a constant and settled way of goodness. I have practiced that honest artifice of Seneca, and, in my retired and solitary imaginations to detain me from the foulness of vice, have fancied to myself the presence of my dear and worthiest friends, before whom I should lose my head rather than be vicious; yet herein I found that there was nought but moral honesty, and this was not to be virtuous for his sake who must reward us at the last. I have tried if I could reach that great resolution of his, to be honest without a thought of heaven or hell; and, indeed I found, upon a natural inclination, an inbred loyalty unto virtue, that I could serve her without a livery; yet not in that resolved and venerable way, but that the frailty of my nature, upon an easy temptation, might be induced to forget her. The life, therefore, and spirit of all our actions is the resurrection, and a stable apprehension that our ashes shall enjoy the fruit of our pious endeavours: without this, all religion is a fallacy, and those impieties of Lucian, Euripides, and Julian, are not blasphemies, but subtile verities, and atheists have been the only philosophers."[1] In other words, he endorses guilt culture as the most effective guardian of personal morality.

Notwithstanding Isaac Barrow's previously cited defense of external honor as an incentive to good deeds, he too concluded that conscience is a stronger spur; for "a man of honour" is surely "the best man next to a man of conscience."[2] Schiller, with historical acumen, expressed the sixteenth-century Puritan belief that Christian conscience was a stronger incentive than external honor. In his drama *Maria Stuart*, Burleigh subtly and treacherously suggests to Paulet, who has custody of the Scots Queen, that it would be expedient if she were to die an apparently natural death; and he assures him, "Your reputation will remain clean." To that the old Puritan answers "But not my conscience."[3] William Cory, the previously cited nineteenth-century scholar, said that the sentiment of honor "is a lay thing; it is a rival of the priestly sentiment of saintliness."[4] Here it appears that Cory is using the word "honor" in the sense of disinterested response to duty or absolute moral law, as championed by Cicero, Seneca, St. Martin,

[1] Browne, p. 393 (Sect. XLVII).
[2] Barrow, p. 84.
[3] "Euer Ruf bleibt rein". - "Nicht mein Gewissen" (*Maria Stuart*, I, 8, vv. 1062).
[4] Cory, p. 460.

Luther, Kant, Fichte, and Bismark. Because such morality is independent of public opinion and fear of punishment, it represents a stage of civilization apart from shame culture and guilt culture. For want of a better word it might well be called a "duty culture". Just as shame culture could also have been called "honor culture" in the primitive meaning of the word "honor", duty culture could be called "honor culture" in its later Stoic-subjective meaning.

Although all good Christians were taught to expect reward or punishment in heaven, the pagan-Stoic belief in disinterested goodness never entirely died. To be accepted as a popular ideal, it did not require the philosophical justification of Kant's *Critique of Morals* so much as a weakening of Christian dogma. As we have seen, Major Tellheim acted virtuously without hope of recognition from God or man. Sometime after the middle of the nineteenth century Theodor Fontane expressed the idea of inner honor in a little poem, the gist of which is: "The honor of this world can't give you any honor. What exalts and maintains you in truth must live in you yourself. If you lack the supports of genuine inner pride, then it will profit you little, even if the world applauds you. To the vain you may grant fleeting praise and ephemeral fame. However, let the most sacred thing for you be to be able to stand up to yourself." [1] Shakespeare had expressed a similar sentiment some two and a half centuries earlier, when he let Polonius say, "To thine own self be true, And it must follow, as the night the day, Thou canst not then be false to any man." [2]

As we have seen, Sir Thomas Browne questioned whether virtue for its own sake was a strong enough incentive to make us honest in the dark, and in this he touched on a problem which was to be recognized by German writers too. Moral autonomy, like that practiced by Tellheim and preached by Fichte, is a sufficient safeguard in the case of a truly virtuous man. But who is to judge whether he is truly a virtuous man? Who is to decide whether his moral decisions are honest or whether they represent rationalization or wishful thinking? Lessing, whose Tellheim could do the right purely for the sake of doing the right, had previously created a character who did not deserve this moral independence and would have been a better man if he had been more concerned with public opinion, as Aristotle would have demanded. In his youthful comedy, *The Treasure*, an otherwise inconspicuous little work of 1750,

[1] "Es kann die Ehre dieser Welt Dir keine Ehre geben, Was dich in Wahrheit hebt und hält, Muss in dir selber leben. Wenn's deinem Innersten gebricht An echten Stolzes Stütze, Ob dann die Welt dir Beifall spricht, Ist all dir wenig nütze. Das flüchtge Lob, des Tages Ruhm Magst du dem Eitlen gönnen, Das aber sei dein Heiligtum: Vor dir bestehen können" (*Gedichte von Theodor Fontane*, Stuttgart, 1910, p. 24).
[2] *Hamlet* I, 3, vv. 78-80.

Lessing portrayed a thoroughly selfish character who prided himself on being independent of his neighbor's opinion. When a friend tells Philto that people call him an old deceiver, cheat, and bloodsucker because he refuses to give his ward her rightful dowry, Philto says that he does not mind their invective as long as he is convinced that they are wrong.[1] This is clearly a case where he should have listened to the public conscience, since he had no inner conscience of his own. Just two centuries later Hans Fallada created another character who prided himself on his moral autonomy, also without any right. Erwin Sommer, a chronic alcoholic, has been arrested for attempting to kill his wife. When his lawyer tries to save him from a "dishonoring prison sentence", the depraved sot says he does not fear this punishment, since his honor lies only in himself.[2]

As we shall see, by the middle of the nineteenth century German dramatists could assume that their audiences would agree that the best judge of a man's value is his inner voice, which is in no way dependent upon the opinions of other people. Therefore when, in the first year of the twentieth century, Frank Wedekind let the hero of his one-act play *The Court Singer* doubt this maxim, it is clear that he is a despicable character. While speaking to an old man who has devoted his life to composing music, but without success, the ignoble young opera singer says, "The measure of a man's importance is the world, and not the inner conviction that he has appropriated through years of brooding."[3] The public at large would have tended to agree, theoretically at least, with Wilhelm Röntgen's contradictory view on the subject. After winning the Nobel Peace Prize in that same year, the famous scientist said, "In comparison with the inner satisfaction over a successfully solved problem, any public recognition loses its significance."[4] Our court singer, who can not

---

[1] "Ich kann es niemanden verwehren, das Nachteiligste von mir zu denken, oder zu sprechen; genug, wenn ich bei mir überzeugt bin, dass man mir unrecht tut" (*Lessings gesammelte Werke*, Leipzig, 1912, II, p. 183). In a previous comedy, *Damon*, Lessing had created another morally autonomous but unjust person. Oronte, the frequent and intentional bankrupt, ridicules *Ehre*, even though he has no conscience to take its place (*op. cit.*, I, p. 361).
[2] "entehrende Gefängnishaft"; "Meine Ehre liegt allein bei mir" (Hans Fallada, *Der Trinker*, Rowohlt Verlag, Hamburg, 1950, p. 289).
[3] "Der Masstab für die Bedeutung eines Menschen ist die Welt und nicht die innere Überzeugung, die man sich durch jahrelanges Hinbrüten aneignet" (*Der Kammersänger*, Scene 8). One might almost suspect that Wedekind had read Hobbes's cynical remark: "For let a man (as most men do,) rate themselves at the highest Value they can; yet their true Value is no more than it is esteemed by others" (*Leviathan*, X). Wedekind would probably have agreed with Montaigne: "A man's value and estimation consists in heart and will: there lies his true honour" (*The Essays of Montaigne*, trans. E.J. Trechmann, Oxford, 1927, Chapter 31).
[4] "Verglichen mit der inneren Befriedigung über ein erfolgreich gelöstes Problem verliert jede äussere Anerkennung ihre Bedeutung" (cited in

appreciate such an inner reward, is clearly a scoundrel. This is later proved when his former mistress kills herself in his room; for his only concern is that the affair will make him miss his train to Brussels, where he has a singing engagement. He does not wish to break his contract, because no one will engage an artist who is *kontraktbrüchig*.[1] Here his dilemma and his motivation are much like those of Rüdeger, Iwein, and the noble heroes of the *chansons de geste*; yet the modern audience is not supposed to find it noble of him to put his professional reputation before his affection or compassion.

The preceding chapters have shown how German secular poets gradually shifted from wholehearted endorsement of wordly honor to skepticism and finally to open opposition. By the mid eighteenth century some writers like Lessing could argue that true honor was inner integrity, rather than external appearance, as Cicero and Seneca had claimed so long before. In 1847 Ernst Mortitz Arndt, a patriot and educator of his nation, wrote: "Honor? What the world usually understands by this word: titles, orders, gold, etc., that is a very petty, transitory thing. But the honor of honesty, that is something much higher. It is German honor, the honor of an entire great nation." [2] By the beginning of the twentieth century inner honor was universally extolled by German poets. The remaining chapters of this study will show how the new attitudes toward honor affected the literature of the late eighteenth and of the nineteenth centuries. It will be noted that, whereas most poets extolled disinterested performance of duty and compliance with absolute moral law, very few of them used the word *Ehre* to designate this virtue. Instead they generally used the words *Ehrlichkeit* and *Ehrsamkeit* and reserved the word *Ehre* to denote objective honor or status. [3]

M. Spann & C. Goedsche, *Deutsche Denker und Forscher*, Appleton, New York, 1954, p. 91).
[1] *Der Kammersänger*, Scene 7.
[2] "Die Ehre? Was die Welt meistens unter diesem Namen versteht: Titel, Orden, Gold, usw., ach, das ist ein gar kleines, vergängliches Ding; aber die Ehre der Ehrlichkeit, das ist etwas viel Höheres, es ist eben deutsche Ehre, Ehre eines ganzen grossen Volkes" (from Lipperheide, p. 133).
[3] Objective honor is the only meaning given for *Ehre* in as recent a thesaurus as Karl Peltzer, *Das treffende Wort*, 3d. ed., Thun, 1955, p. 150: "Ehre - Anerkennung, Lob, Preis, Ansehen, Auszeichnung, Rang, Ruf, Ruhm, Wertschätzung, Würde, - Achtung, Ehrenplatz." Compare this with: "honor: A high excellence of character tending particularly to respect of the unprotected rights of others; (honesty, respect for the property rights of others.)", *Morrow's Word-finder*, ed. P. Hugon, New York, 1927, p. 157.

CHAPTER TEN

HONOR AND THE COMMON MAN

Virtue commands respect, even in beggar's rags.
SCHILLER, *Kabale und Liebe*, II, 6.

As long as honor meant respect shown to superiority and superiority was equated with rank, wealth, and power, so long did honor remain a monopoly of the upper classes. As C. L. Barber has shown, seventeenth-century English dramas used the term "honour" only of the gentry: a commoner could aspire to no more than "reputation".[1] When honor began to be shown to moral as well as to social superiority, and when "honor" finally began to designate the moral qualities that commanded respect, then the upper classes lost their monopoly and honor became attainable by all men.

Since the days of the ancient Greeks it had been agreed that great tragedy, in fact serious literature in general, should concern itself only with aristocratic personages. This view obtained not only in the courtly literature of the High Middle Ages, but even in most bourgeois literature of succeeding centuries. Just as the medieval burghers largely overlooked their own class in seeking heroes for their romances, their descendants continued to do so through the period of Baroque. In his *Buch von der Deutschen Poeterey* of 1624, Germany's most influential seventeenth-century *ars poetica*, Martin Opitz declared that tragedy should not introduce persons of humble estate,[2] even though such a rule would have excluded commoners like himself. Andreas Gryphius, Germany's chief dramatist of that century, followed this tradition of choosing wellborn heroes, although he too was of simple birth. Even Grimmelshausen, while denying the importance of gentle birth, saw fit to let his foundling hero be the son of a nobleman.

The German bourgeoisie, who were gradually beginning to feel their own importance, could not ignore their own order forever. English writers such as George Lillo had already written dramas concerning common life, and German writers were not long in

---
[1] Barber, pp. 101-126.
[2] "ohne das sie selten leidet, das man geringen standes personen und schlechte sachen einführe" (*Buch von der Deutschen Poeterey*, V).

adopting this innovation. Twelve years before writing his *Minna von Barnhelm*, Lessing had written a bourgeois tragedy called *Miss Sara Sampson* (1755), which borrowed heavily from Lillo's *Merchant of London* (1731) and Richardson's *Clarissa Harlowe* (1748). Of more interest to our study was Lessing's *Emilia Galotti* of 1772, which is not only a bourgeois tragedy but also an "honor-drama". Lessing was less successful with this drama than with his *Minna*, its chief fault being his choice of theme, that of the father who kills his daughter to save her honor from a tyrant into whose hands she has fallen. Such motivation was credible in the ancient legend of Virginius, the Roman republican who stabled his daughter Virginia to death to save her from a lecherous decimvir; but it could no longer be presented convincingly in the year 1772. "Feminine honor" was still of great importance; yet it scarcely justified killing one's own daughter.

Lessing's dramatization of this theme is set at an imaginary Italian court at a vague time between the Renaissance and his own day. Emilia, the daughter of Odoardo Galotti, is betrothed to Count Appiani, a young nobleman in the service of the prince of that court. Knowing that the prince is enamoured of Emilia, the prince's diabolical chamberlain arranges to have the bridal procession waylaid by pretended bandits. Appiani is killed in the attack, and Emilia is ostensibly rescued by the prince's servants and brought to his summer residence. Hearing of the attack, Galotti hurries to the residence, where he learns the true state of affairs from the prince's former mistress. Unable to free his daughter from the prince, who feigns legal grounds for having to detain her, Galotti stabs her to death with a dagger given him by the jealous mistress.

Realizing that the old Roman theme was morally archaic, Lessing tried to revivify it by giving it new moral and psychological motivation. This is clearly revealed in the next to last scene, in which father and daughter realize that they cannot prevent the prince from confining her in the notorious home of Grimaldi, the chancellor. When Emilia threatens to take her own life, her father reminds her that she has "only one life to lose".

"And only one innocence," she answers.

"Which is high above all force," the father assures her.

"But not above all seduction. – Force! Force! Who cannot defy force? What people call force is nothing: seduction is true force. – I have blood, father, blood as young and warm as anyone. And my senses are senses. I stand for nothing, I am good for nothing. I know the house of the Grimaldis. It is a house of pleasure. An hour there, under the eyes of my mother, and such tumult arose in my soul that the strictest exercise of religion could scarcely assuage it for weeks. Of religion! Of what religion? In order to avoid nothing worse, thousands have drowned themselves and become saints. Give me, father, give me this dagger!"[1]

Not only Emilia's good name is at stake, as in older versions of this story, but actually her innocence, since she herself fears that she can not resist temptation. It is significant that the word "honor" does not appear, only the word "innocence" (*Unschuld*). A few lines later, when Emilia tries to provoke her father by alluding to Virginius's concern for his daughter, she uses the word *Schande*; but she probably uses it to mean shameful behavior rather than public ignominy. Moreover, the emphasis upon Emilia's piety in the first chapter suggests that she, as well as Lessing, considered such behavior a sin before God. Lessing's play, if taken at its face value, implies that he considered death with honor better than a life of shame, at least for a woman. However, it is to be remembered that honor and shame here designate inner values rather than merely good or bad reputation.

During the decade following *Emilia Galotti*, the theme of "feminine honor" furnished the motivation for many dramas, especially in the tradition of the *Kindermörderin*, the unwed and abandoned mother who kills her child to avoid disgrace. Perhaps the best known example in this category is the Gretchen episode in Goethe's *Faust*, which was more representative in the earlier version, the so-called *Urfaust*, which Goethe completed in approximately 1775. In this story Gretchen's fall brings reproach not only upon her, but also upon her brother. As a soldier and man of honor, who has already boasted of his sister at his drinking bouts, Valentin feels his honor sullied by his sister's shame. Any rascal can insult him now that his sister has renounced her honor,[2] and he does not regret dying in his attempt to gain satisfaction. His soldierly concern for his honor explains his cruel denunciation of his sister, which strikes most modern audiences as so heartless and unjustified.

Another good example of this genre, perhaps partially plagiarized from Goethe's then unpublished play, was Heinrich Leopold

---

[1] "Und nur *eine* Unschuld!" "Die über alle Gewalt erhaben ist." "Aber nicht über alle Verführung. – Gewalt! Gewalt! wer kann der Gewalt nicht trotzen? Was Gewalt heisst, ist nichts; Verführung ist die wahre Gewalt. – Ich habe Blut, mein Vater; so jugendliches, so warmes Blut als eine. Auch meine Sinne sind Sinne. Ich stehe für nichts. Ich bin für nichts gut. Ich kenne das Haus der Grimaldi. Es ist das Haus der Freude, Eine Stunde da, unter den Augen meiner Mutter, – und es erhob sich so mancher Tumult in meiner Seele, den die strengsten Übungen der Religion kaum in Wochen besänftigen konnten! – Der Religion! Und welcher Religion? – Nichts Schlimmeres zu vermeiden, sprangen Tausende in die Fluten, und sind Heilige! – Geben Sie mir, mein Vater, geben Sie mir diesen Dolch" (*Emilia Galotti*, V, 7).

[2] "beschimpfen" (*Faust*, v. 3641); "Da du dich sprachst der Ehre los" (v. 3772).

Wagner's *Die Kindesmörderin* of 1776, in which a butcher's daughter is seduced and deserted by an officer. These two works, and many other dramas of the Storm and Stress era, seem to question the ideal of honor that puts such grievous punishment on a girl only because she has loved unwisely. When Valentin curses his sister, Goethe gives a vivid picture of the future a fallen girl could expect. First she will begin with one man, then with a dozen, then with the whole city. At first concealed by darkness, her shame will eventually be revealed, and respectable people will avoid her like an infected corpse. She will no longer wear a gold chain or stand at the altar or wear a lace collar or go to dances, but hide herself in some corner with beggars and cripples.[1] Such an attitude explains why so many unwed mothers took their lives.

In 1784, some twenty-two years after *Emilia Galotti*, Germany received another bourgeois tragedy in which the ruling classes oppress the common people and refuse to respect their honor. Friedrich Schiller's youthful play, *Love and Intrigue*, is set at an imaginary German court of his day. It tells of the thwarted love a bourgeois girl named Louise and a young nobleman named Ferdinand, whose father wishes him to marry the duke's mistress. Ferdinand's father, the unscrupulous president of the ducal court, supposes that he can terminate the affair because Louise is only the daughter of a poor court musician. When he fails, he calls Louise a whore and demands to know how much his son has been paying for her favors.[2]

Imbued with enlightened views on human dignity, Schiller naturally accepted the Christian view that every virtuous individual merits respect, even if he wears rags.[3] Although he paints the president in the blackest colors, we should remember that the president's views had prevailed in good society throughout the Middle Ages, when honor was restricted to the upper classes. A vestige of the old attitude lingers in the gradual debasement of the words *wench* and *dirne*, which once meant country lass and serving girl, respectively, but have since acquired disrespectful overtones suggesting immorality. The president plans to have Louise exposed on the pillory, in the belief that Ferdinand, as an officer, will have to renounce her once she has been publicly disgraced.[4] He is justified in expecting such a reaction, since Ferdinand has convinced him

---
[1] *Faust*, vv. 3736-3763.
[2] "Sie wird Ihre Gunst nicht verschenkt haben" ... "Hure" (*Kabale und Liebe*, II, 6).
[3] "Ehrfurcht befiehlt die Tugend auch im Bettlerkleid" (*op. cit.*, II, 6). Cf. "And as the sun breaks through the darkest clouds, So honour peereth in the meanest habit" (*The Taming of the Shrew*, IV, iii, vv. 175-176).
[4] *op. cit.*, III, 1; II, 7. Luise later refers to the pillory as a *Schandbühne* (III, 6).

that he is a man of honor. He has told his father that he cannot marry Lady Milford, the duke's mistress, because he would be embarrassed before every artisan who had married an intact wife and even before the concubine who was washing the stains of her own *Schande* on his *Ehre*. "If you take my honor," he tells his father, "then it was an inconsiderate and rascally deed to give me life, and I must curse the father as well as the pander." [1] Despite this pretext, Ferdinand is really less concerned with his honor, in the sense of reputation, than with his love; and therefore he threatens to mount the pillory with Louise if she is thus disgraced. Louise claims to be unconcerned about public opinion; yet she later tells her father that she would rather leave town than suffer ridicule and loss of good name.[2]

Lady Milford, the mistress, is especially concerned with her honor, which she has inherited from an illustrious English family. Honor is her greatest possession; yet she realizes that it is a good of fortune which she contrasts with virtue, just as Ferdinand has formerly done.[3] She refuses to renounce Ferdinand because her honor will not allow her. "Our union is the talk of the whole country," she argues. "All eyes, all shafts of ridicule are aimed at me. The affront will be unquenchable if a subject of the prince refuses me." [4] Later, after Louise has appealed to her sense of decency and inner pride, Lady Milford has a change of heart and says that she will let herself be shamed (*beschämen*) but not reproached (*beschimpfen*),[5] a statement which is difficult to analyse. She seems to mean that she is willing to be socially degraded, but she is unwilling to act in such a way that anyone could reproach her moral integrity.

The bourgeoisie's emergence in literature did not indicate that the

---

[1] "Meine Ehre, Vater – wenn Sie mir diese nehmen, so war es ein leichtfertiges Schelmenstück, mir das Leben zu geben, und ich muss den Vater, wie den Kuppler verfluchen" (*op. cit.*, I, 7).
[2] "Ich verachte das Urteil der Menge" (*op. cit.*, IV, 7); "Weg von der Stadt, wo meine Gespielinnen meiner spotten und mein guter Name dahin ist auf immerdar" (V, 1).
[3] Lady Milford compares her own *Ehre* with Luise's *Tugend* (*op. cit.*, IV, 8). Ferdinand had previously distinguished between *Tugend* and *Ehre* and said that the former often survives the latter (II, 3). Cf. "Er selbst (the duke) ist nicht über die Ehre erhaben, aber er kann ihren Mund mit seinem Golde verstopfen. Er kann den Hermelin über seine Schande herwerfen" (II, 3). In view of Ferdinand's objective use of *Ehre*, his oath "bei meiner Ehre" (V, 2) is probably meant in its ancient sense of "I pledge my good name".
[4] "Meine Leidenschaft, Walther, weicht meiner Zärtlichkeit für Sie. Meine Ehre kann's nicht mehr – Unsre Verbindung ist das Gespräch des ganzen Landes. Alle Augen, alle Pfeile des Spotts sind auf mich gespannt. Die Beschimpfung is unauslöschlich, wenn ein Untertan des Fürsten mich ausschlägt" (*op. cit.*, II, 3).
[5] "Beschämen lässt sich Emilie Milford – doch beschimpfen nie!" (*op. cit.*, IV, 8).

upper classes had become more democratic so much as it indicated that the bourgeoisie had become more active as literary patrons and public. On the other hand, the subsequent emergence of the laboring classes as subjects of literature did reveal an expanding social consciousness, since these classes produced neither patrons nor public. As we shall see in the next chapter, the lowest orders of society became serious subjects in German literature soon after the French Revolution. Great passions, which had once been thought limited to the aristocracy, were now found to exist among the common people too. Although Ferdinand Freiligrath attributed this discovery to Clemens Brentano,[1] Schiller had already noted deep passions among the lowly and dispossessed, as will be shown in the discussion of his *Criminal through Lost Honor*. During the nineteenth century nearly all the scorned and oppressed classes obtained a hearing in literature and were judged by their merits rather than by the accident of their birth. Peasants were representative of mankind for Immermann, Auerbach, Bitzius, Keller, Stifter, and a host of others. Chamisso saw pure humanity in a washerwoman, Grillparzer in a poor minstrel, and Hauptmann in his weavers, draymen, flagmen, and factory workers.

Adalbert Stifter argued passionately for the innate dignity of man in the preface to his *Bunte Steine*, a collection of stories about simple people. In this preface, which was written in 1852, Stifter defended himself for always describing little people leading humdrum lives. For Stifter, the growing of the grain and the twinkling of the stars are greater than storms, volcanoes, and earthquakes; and he holds a similar view concerning human beings. "Just as it is in external nature," he argues, "so it is in the inner nature of mankind. A whole life of righteousness, simplicity, self-control, reasonableness, effectiveness in one's circle and admiration for beauty, combined with a serene and resigned death – these I consider great. Great passions, frightful thundering rage, craving for revenge, the inflamed spirit that strives for activity, tears down, changes, destroys, and often throws away its own life in its agitation – these I consider not greater, but rather smaller, since these things are merely the products of individual and onesided forces, just like storms, fire-spewing mountains, and earthquakes." [2]

[1] Concerning Brentano's *Kasperl und Annerl*, Freiligrath wrote: "Der warf zuerst aus grauer Bücherwolke Den prächt'gen Blitz: die Leidenschaft im Volke!" (cited in *Brentanos Werke*, ed. F. Bomke, Leipzig & Wien, 1892, p. 90).
[2] "Ein ganzes Leben voll Gerechtigkeit, Einfachheit, Bezwingung seiner selbst, Verstandesgemässheit, Wirksamkeit in seinem Kreise, Bewunderung des Schönen, verbunden mit einem heiteren, gelassenen Streben, halte ich für gross: mächtige Bewegungen des Gemüts, furchtbar einherrollenden Zorn, die Begier nach Rache, den entzündeten Geist, der nach Tätigkeit

What Stifter wishes to observe is "the gentle law", by which he means the moral law that guides mankind. This law is concerned with the forces that aid all mankind, not just one individual. "The law of these forces is the law of righteousness, the law of morality, the law that wishes for everyone to exist with other people, respected, honored, and without danger..." [1] The student of mankind can see this law "just as well in the lowest hut as in the highest palace, he sees it in a poor woman's devotion and a hero's tranquil scorn of death for the fatherland or for humanity." [2] Here we see the Church's ideal of honor for all men, an ideal at last accepted by a good proportion of mankind, at least in the West. Henceforth, with few exceptions, all German writers deplore and ridicule the remaining customs, prejudices, and selfishness preventing the realization of the Christian ideal.

strebt, umreisst, ändert, zerstört und in der Erregung oft das eigene Leben hinwirft, halte ich nicht für grösser, sondern für kleiner, da diese Dinge so gut nur Hervorbringungen einzelner und einseitiger Kräfte sind wie Stürme, feuerspeiende Berge, Erdbeben" (Adalbert Stifter, *Gesammelte Werke*, Bielefeld, 1956, III, p. 10). This belief suggests George Chapman's words, "They're only truly great who are truly good" (*Revenge for Honour*, V, 2).

[1] "Es ist das Gesetz dieser Kräfte das Gesetz der Gerechtigkeit, das Gesetz der Sitte, das Gesetz, das will, dass jeder geachtet, geehrt, ungefährdet neben dem andern bestehe..." (Stifter, *op. cit.*, p. 10).

[2] "Er sieht es ebensogut in der niedersten Hütte wie in dem höchsten Palaste, er sieht es in der Hingabe eines armen Weibes und in der ruhigen Todesverachtung des Helden für das Vaterland und die Menschheit" (*op. cit.*, p. 11).

CHAPTER ELEVEN

LOSS OF HONOR

Take honour from me, and my life is done.
SHAKESPEARE, *King Richard* II, I, 1.

As long as honor was more important than life itself, loss of honor was life's greatest tragedy; and therefore loss of honor has been a favorite motif in German literature from its very beginnings. We have seen the plight of Cain in ancient vernacular versions of Scripture, in which he is deprived of his honor because he has slain his brother. Likewise, we have seen the overwhelming grief experienced by Iwein, Rüdeger, and other heroes threatened with loss of honor, and we have learned to appreciate the apprehensions of unwed girls who felt their shame growing in their bodies. In reading ancient tales in which honor makes cruel demands, as when Hildebrand must fight his son or Rüdeger must fight his Burgundian friends, we sometimes feel that the poet is questioning, or at least deploring, the bitter code. As defenders of traditional values, medieval secular poets could not openly attack the sanctity of the code of honor; but, when Christian-Stoic values finally prevailed among intellectuals of the Enlightenment, even secular poets began to change sides and question this questionable tradition.

In 1787 Schiller wrote a short story, *Criminal through Lost Honor*,[1] to prove that histories of violent actions are often written wrongly and therefore not understood. A tranquil reader is so far removed from the violent emotions of a criminal that he cannot grasp the meaning of his act and is estranged rather than moved by it; for he can be moved only if he feels himself imperiled by the criminal's misfortune. Thus, instead of giving us moral instruction, history serves only to satisfy our curiosity. To profit from history, we should see not only what the criminal does, but why he does it. We must see his thoughts and their causes, not just his acts and their consequences. Only in this way can we understand and sympathize with the criminal instead of scorning and damning him. Schiller illustrates his argument as follows:

[1] *Schillers Werke, National Ausgabe*, ed. H. H. Borcherdt, Weimar, 1954, XVI, pp. 7-29.

Wolf Sonnenwirt, the son of a poor tavern-keeper's widow, becomes a juvenile delinquent as a result of poverty and physical unattractiveness. Because his ugliness repulses the girls, he tries to compensate for it by dressing elegantly and giving gifts beyond his means. When his funds are exhausted, he becomes a poacher in order to give his winnings to his sweetheart. Finally his rival, the forester, guesses the source of his money and catches him in the act of poaching; and Sonnenwirt avoids prison only by paying a large fine, which so impoverishes him that he must sell his tavern.

Driven by shame, jealousy, and hunger, he resumes his poaching until the forester catches him again; and this time he must serve a year in prison. Upon returning home he tries to find employment as a laborer or even as town swineherd, even though it is a dishonorable status. Even this is refused him, and he is again forced to poach for a living. Once more his rival catches him; and he is convicted, branded, and sentenced to three years of hard labor in a fortress. There he is completely corrupted by the other inmates, who are hardened criminals and delight in degrading him morally. Released and back at home, he finds himself ostracised; but by now he has forgotten how to feel shame and no longer minds other people's scorn. He needs no good qualities, since no one expects them of him. Despair and shame have robbed him of all ambition to go elsewhere and try to pass as a man of honor.

Reverting to his life as poacher, he soon has a chance to kill the forester who has caused his misery. Fleeing from the scene of the crime, he meets a gang of robbers and other outcasts, who immediately choose him as their leader because of his notoriety as a poacher. At first he is happy to be among peers and welcomes the honor proverbially found among thieves. After a year of successful theft and robbery, however, he tires of his life and companions and he begins to fear that one of them will betray him for the reward and pardon promised by the authorities. He tries to win a pardon in order to enlist in the Seven Years War; but his requests are not acknowledged even though he reminds the authorities that his crimes began only after he was deprived of his honor. Receiving no answer, he decides to leave the country and join the Prussian army. When detained en route by a customs official, he admits his identity and is later executed.

It is significant that this story was first called *Criminal through Infamy* (*Verbrecher aus Infamie*) and later changed to *Criminal through Lost Honor* (*Verbrecher aus verlorener Ehre*); for this shows that Schiller, like the ancient Greeks and medieval Europeans, realized that sense of honor and sense of shame are merely two aspects of a single motivating force. Although he claimed that his story served to illustrate a literary-historical and psychological point, it is clear that it also served as social protest, much as his juvenile drama *The Robbers* had done. He himself admits that, even if the reader's leniency will not help this particular criminal, a post mortem of his crime will perhaps instruct mankind and, possibly, even justice. Thus his work more or less follows the tradition of medieval sermons, in which the moral lesson is illustrated by an *exemplum*.

Schiller's advice that a narrator should describe not only a criminal's act but also his prior thoughts and feelings was best followed by Heinrich von Kleist in his story *Michael Kohlhaas*, which appeared in 1810. In this story Kleist succeeded in depicting the psychological factors that changed a righteous man into the most terrifying man of his time. Kohlhaas, a sixteenth-century Brandenburg horse-dealer, is offended by a Saxon nobleman, Squire Wenzel von Tronka, who wrongfully detains two of his horses and then allows them to be maltreated and worked nearly to death in his own service. Righteously indignant, Kohlhaas seeks justice via all possible legal channels and finally, when it is refused, resorts to self-help by arming his employees and attacking and burning the Tronka castle. Discovering that the guilty party has escaped, he declares a feud against any individual or city that gives him refuge: and soon his band, reinforced by many adventurers, wages successful and destructive war against all the neighboring authorities. Martin Luther persuades the outlaw to submit his case to due process of law; but again justice is corrupted by Tronka's kinsmen, until finally the Elector of Brandenburg appeals to the Emperor and demands that a fair trial be given.

Kleist attributed Kohlhaas's actions to his love of justice, as one might expect in the early nineteenth century; for Kleist disregarded anachronisms, as one can see in Kohlhaas's use of paper money. Nevertheless, the older motivation occasionally shows through, especially in the action itself; and it is apparent that the historical Kohlhaas was fighting not so much to establish justice (*das Recht*) as to assert his own rights (*sein Recht*).[1] In the sixteenth century there was still no one *recht* for all men, but rather a special *recht* for each social order. As a free landholder, Kohlhaas has certain inherited privileges that the nobleman violates, and thus his honor as a free man is impugned. He writes to his wife that he has not been protected in his rights; and Luther sees that he has shed so much blood because his prince has not defended his right. Although his sense of justice is often mentioned,[2] Kohlhaas seems chiefly

---

[1] The historical account given in C. Burkardt's *Der historische Hans Kohlhase und Heinrich von Kleists Michael Kohlhaas*, Leipzig, 1864, tells how Kohlhaas wished to defend his honor and good name, as became a man of honor (p. 22).
[2] *Michael Kohlhaas*, pp. 1, 162, 180, 141, 147, 157.

concerned with restoring his own prestige, or else he would have accepted compensation rather than insist that the nobleman fatten the starved horses himself. Like the ancient Germanic heroes of old, Kohlhaas was indignant in the sense that he felt his *dignatio* threatened.

An interesting motif, which is not found in Kleist's principal sources,[1] is the dishonorable status of the skinner. After the assault on the Tronka castle, one loses sight of the two horses that have caused the whole tragedy. Later it is discovered that, having little else but skin left on their bones, they had found their way to the skinner and have thus become just as "dishonorable" as he is. When a noble relative of the guilty squire, wishing to fatten the horses himself, orders his servant to lead the horses from the skinner, the servant prefers a blow from his master and summary dismissal, rather than a taint on his honor. Because the nobleman has tried to transgress the traditional tabu against the dishonorable skinner, he is set upon by the populace and severely beaten. Before his execution, Kohlhaas has the satisfaction of seeing his horses made "honorable" again by having a flag waved over their heads.[2]

After *Minna von Barnhelm, Emilia Galotti*, and *Criminal through Lost Honor*, the next important German work consciously devoted to discussing honor was *Kasperl and Annerl*, a short-story or *Novelle* written by Clemens Brentano in 1817. This is a frame-story within a frame-story: the chief action is told by a man whom we shall call the narrator; and all preceding events are told by an aged peasant woman whom the narrator finds spending the night on the steps of the ducal palace in a small German city. When asked why she wishes to speak to the duke, the old woman tells a long story about her grandson, who was the unfortunate victim of an exaggerated sense of honor.

Her grandson, Kasperl, had always been deeply concerned with honor and had always enjoyed stories with honor as a theme. He was greatly impressed, for example, by the story of a French corporal who, when commanded to whip one of his soldiers, did so because it was his duty then shot himself with the soldier's gun to end his disgrace. Kasperl's father and brother, who lack honor, laugh at such stories; and the father, with Falstaffian scorn for that virtue, suggests that he eat his honor if he is hungry. Kasperl has so indoctrinated his sweetheart, Annerl, in his code of honor that she distinguishes herself in manner and appearance from the other

---

[1] No mention is made of the skinner in any of the chronicles reproduced by Rudolf Schlösser, *Die Quellen zu Hr. v. Kleists Michael Kohlhaas*, Bonn, 1913, or in C. A. H. Burkhardt, *Der historische Hans Kohlhase*, Leipzig, 1864.
[2] *Michael Kohlhaas*, pp. 148, 197, 202, 246.

village maids and is greatly offended if any young man tries to do anything that might hurt her good name.

After serving as a cavalryman for some time in France, Kasperl is promoted to corporal and requests a leave to return home to impress family and fiancée with his new honor. Because of his exceptional reliability, his superiors even lend him the horse assigned to him. On the last leg of the journey his horse developes a saddle sore. When a tavern-keeper says "it does a rider no honor" to ride a horse in that condition, Kasperl dismounts and leads the horse the rest of the way home. Consequently, he has to spend another night en route, namely at a mill not far from home. During the night robbers break into the mill and bind the miller, but Kasperl drives them off before they get the miller's money, but not before they have stolen his own horse and knapsack. When the miller offers to pay for the horse, Kasperl refuses on the grounds that it would be against his honor. He then proceeds home on foot without money or papers with which to prove that he has been honored with a promotion.

Reaching home, he discovers that his father and brother are the thieves who stole his horse and knapsack; and, upon discovering that he is the son of a dishonorable thief, he knows his honor is irretrievably gone. Although his father and brother beg him not to report them, his sense of honor and duty require him to sound the alarm. He then goes out and shoots himself on his mother's grave, leaving a letter stating that he could not survive his disgrace and requesting that he be given an honorable grave. He also asks Annerl never to marry a man worse than himself. Kasperl's sense of shame would have been even greater if he had known thatAnnerl was then awaiting execution for killing the baby she had borne after being led astray by the ambition (*Ehrgeiz*) he had inculcated in her. In her quest for prestige and status she had been seduced by a nobleman, who had promised marriage and told her that Kasperl had died in France. Deserted by her lover, she had killed his child and surrendered herself to justice without revealing the name of her seducer.

Learning that it is only an hour before the girl is to be executed, the narrator determines to wake the duke and ask for a pardon: but Ensign Grossinger, the captain of the guard, will not let him pass, since his honor is at stake. The word *Ehre* overwhelms the narrator, who, remembering Kasperl's and Annerl's honor, damns the sense of honor that has caused the tragedy. In spite of Grossinger's attempt to interfere, the narrator gets the duke's attention and wins a pardon. He and Grossinger then rush at full gallop to the scaffold but arrive just after the word has fallen. Grossinger confesses to being the seducer and is nearly killed by the crowd before being rescued by the duke. The duke reads Kasperl's testament and orders that he and Annerl be given an honorable burial; and he further declares that Annerl has been pardoned and has died honorably. Later he commemorates the two victims of honor by erecting two statues representing false and true honor.

Although the duke's two statues represent true and false honor, Brentano has actually presented only false honor. Using Aristotelian terminology, one might argue that Kasperl's honor was a vice only because he had an excess of virtue; but it almost appears that honor is intrinsically bad, as it had been in monastic literature of past centuries. The old grandmother seems to express Brentano's true feelings when she says of Annerl, "If the child just hadn't always been chasing after honor but had only clung to God and had never let Him go in her plight and had borne shame and contempt (*Schande und Verachtung*) for His sake instead of the honor of men, the Lord would surely have had mercy on her."

The grandmother had already expressed this pious view more concisely by saying "Give honor to God alone," an admonition that served as the theme of Kasperl's and Annerl's funeral oration.[1] In spite of the old grandmother's disregard for worldly honor, she takes pride in her grandson's inordinate sense of honor; and she never stops requesting an honorable grave for her loved ones. The grandmother once asks the narrator whether he has an honorable calling, or whether he might be a hangman or a spy; and this is the only allusion to the "dishonorable" professions.[2]

Schiller's advice about portraying a criminal's motives as well as his deed was also heeded by the Westphalian authoress Annette von Droste-Hülshoff in her short story *The Jews' Beechtree*. This story, written in 1842, tells the fate of a village lad named Frederick Mergel, who, like Sonnenwirt, kills a man for taking his honor. Like Sonnenwirt, Frederick has little honor to lose and therefore zealously guards what little he has. His father, a depraved drunk, had driven his first wife to her death and would have succeeded likewise with Frederick's long-suffering mother, if he had not died first in a drunken stupor. Before dying he had let the house and garden run down and the debts run up, and his widow inherited only bitter memories and pressing mortgages. Because of his violent and contentious nature, he was reported after death to have become an evil ghost that haunted the nearby forest. Thus little Frederick was persecuted first as the son of a drunken sot and then as the son of an evil spook.

[1] "Gib Gott allein die Ehre" (*Kasperl und Annerl*, p. 98); "Gebt Gott allein die Ehre" (p. 123). Cf. "Soli Deo honor et gloria in saecula" (I *Timothy*, 1, 17).
[2] "Er ist doch nicht etwa Henker oder Spion..." (*Kasperl und Annerl*, p. 100).

Like Sonnenwirt, Frederick tries to offset his lowly status by dressing well, even though his mother is in rags. His craving for honor makes him brag and show off; and he makes every effort to avoid being shamed. Lacking true ambition, he works only as a cow-herd, a poorly paid position considered dishonorable for an adult; yet he can afford his pretences because his uncle pays him to keep watch and warn him and his notorious band of timber thieves when the foresters approach. On one occasion the uncle causes Frederick to become involved in the murder of a forester; but he shames his nephew into missing confession and overcoming his guilty conscience.

Frederick finds the greatest balm to his ego in patronizing and protecting Johannes Niemand (John Nobody), a nameless and slow-witted child who resembles him and is obviously the bastard son of Frederick's woodstealing uncle. It is this friendship that causes Frederick's downfall. There is a wedding in the village and, because many outside guests are expected, the villagers strive to uphold their community honor. In the midst of the festivities, while Frederick is dancing and acting ostentatiously, Johannes shames himself by trying to steal some butter. Feeling his dignity injured by his protegé's disgrace, Frederick tries to regain his status by showing off his gold watch, which is the envy of his colleagues. To his great humiliation, Aaron, a Jewish huckster, arrives at the wedding and demands payment for the watch; and Frederick leaves the party pursued by his creditor and by the laughter of the guests. Soon afterwards the Jew is found murdered in the forest, and it is discovered that Frederick and Johannes have disappeared. The local Jews buy the beechtree under which Aaron was murdered and carve into it a Hebrew inscription, a curse damning the murderer to die when he returns to the tree.

Twenty-eight years later Johannes returns to the village, broken in body and spirit from hard labor in Turkish slavery, which had begun within a year after he had run away with Frederick and joined the Austrian army. The lord of the manor, who had known him as a child, takes care of him and sees to his physical needs; yet the old derelict remains morose and forlorn. Eventually he disappears while on an errand, and extensive search fails to find him. Some days later his rotting body is found hanging to the Jews' beechtree, and only then do people realize that it is Frederick, not Johannes, who has returned.

Although Droste-Hülshoff does not explain it as such, her story discusses the conflict between shame culture and guilt culture. During his youth Frederick was free of any ideas of moral guilt or duty and was concerned only with his relative social status. This is understandable in view of his unfortunate heritage. When his father caused the death of his first wife, he sought solace in drink; but the authoress questions whether he was driven to it by remorse or by shame.[1] Frederick learns religious and social prejudice even from his unhappy mother.[2] As a result of his unwholesome background, he is frivolous, excitable, and arrogant; and he keeps up appearances to avoid censure and prefers inner shame to public disgrace.[3] His touchy sense of honor makes him act aggressively toward other people's disapproval,[4] as when his dignity is injured by Johannes's theft of the butter. It is no wonder that Aaron's accusation is an unbearable ignominy that causes him to commit murder.

Although Frederick had been morally delinquent in his youth, his terrible ordeal in Turkey made him recognize his guilt. Perhaps his long slavery made him forget how to feel shame or to desire honor. Perhaps his long suffering in life made him fear even greater suffering after death. Perhaps his isolation among heathens made him long for the comfort of his own religion. In any case, he did not consider more than a quarter century of back-breaking and deforming labor sufficient expiation for his crime.

Lessing's *Emilia Galotti* and Schiller's *Love and Intrigue* are conventionally classified as "bourgeois tragedies", even though they concern nobles as well as commoners. In fact it is the nobility that induces the tragedy by jeopardizing the commoners' honor. Perhaps Germany's first, and possibly best, purely bourgeois tragedy on the theme of honor is Friedrich Hebbel's *Maria Magdalene*, which appeared in 1844. As the title implies, it is the story of a fallen woman; and as such it deals primarily with the problem of lost "feminine honor". Like Emilia, the heroine of this play is killed by her father; but in this case the father uses words rather than a dagger. Unlike Emilia and Louise, her fate is not caused by the tyranny of the ruling classes: rather it results from the bigotry and

---

[1] "Ob nun den Mergel Reue qüalte oder Scham... (*Judenbuche*, p. 7).

[2] When Frederick tells his mother that a neighbor named Hülsmeyer has beaten and robbed Aaron, she says that Hülsmeyer is a man of established residence (*angesessener Mann*, cf. *angesessene, unverdächtige Leute*, p. 30) and that all Jews are rascals (die Juden sind alle Schelme). She also explains that it is all right to steal wood and game from the forest (p. 11).

[3] "...während in Friedrichs Zügen der Wechsel eines offenbar mehr selbstischen als gutmütigen Mitgefühls spielte und sein Auge in fast glasartiger Klarheit zum erstenmale bestimmt den Ausdruck jenes ungebändigten Ehrgeizes und Hanges zum Grosstun zeigte, der nachher als so starkes Motiv seiner meisten Handlungen hervortrat" (p. 18). "er gewöhnte sich, die innere Schande der äusseren vorzuziehen" (p. 33).

[4] "und da ein sehr empfindliches Ehrgefühl ihn die geheime Missbilligung mancher nicht übersehen liess, war er gleichsam immer unter Waffen, der öffentlichen Meinung nicht sowohl Trotz zu bieten, als sie den Weg zu leiten, der ihm gefiel" (p. 33).

prejudices of her own class, particularly from the self-righteousness of her father.

Master Anton, an uneducated cabinet maker, prides himself on his righteous behavior and respected place in society; and his only anxiety is his fear that his wayward son Carl will bring dishonor upon the family. His daughter Clara, on the other hand, is pious, obedient, and thoroughly virtuous. When Clara's childhood sweetheart goes away to study and fails to write to her, she believes herself deserted and accepts the attentions of an unscrupulous suitor named Leonhard, who has designs on her small dowry. In order to assure himself of her, Leonhard requires her to choose between him and her childhood sweetheart, who has just returned as town secretary; and he insists that she guarantee her choice by giving herself to him. Believing she has lost the man she loves because he is now her social superior, and fearing ridicule if she loses both suitors, she submits to Leonhard's demands. As soon as she has done so, Leonhard discovers that Master Anton has given away his life savings, including Clara's dowry, to help a former benefactor. When Carl is falsely accused of stealing some jewelry, Leonhard uses the scandal as an excuse to break off the engagement, even though he knows that Clara is pregnant. By the time Carl is proved innocent, Leonhard has succeeded in getting the mayor's daughter in trouble too.

Suspecting Clara's predicament, Master Anton makes her swear over her dead mother's body that she will never bring dishonor upon him; and thus he practically exacts a promise of suicide. When the distraught girl finally jumps into a well to save her father's honor, his greatest regret is that an eye-witness testifies that her death was intentional. The secretary seems to speak for Hebbel when he denounces the bigoted father in the last scene. Returning mortally wounded from a duel in which he has killed Leonhard, he reproaches the father for having driven his daughter to her death and declares him unworthy of her sacrifice. He also blames himself for having been so concerned with demanding satisfaction from Leonhard that he did not remain with Clara to prevent her from taking her fatal and easily foreseen step.

Master Anton's exaggerated sense of honor causes the tragedy in more ways than one. When the court bailiff arrests and humiliates Carl without valid evidence and thus triggers the catastrophe, he does so to repay Master Anton for having once insulted him by refusing to drink with him and by saying he should wait for his kinsman, the skinner. Master Anton's exaggerated sense of honor is emphasized throughout the play. Perhaps he is so punctilious because he almost had to grow up without honor: he would never have become a master craftsman if his benefactor had not taken him on as an apprentice without demanding the customary tuition. People constantly refer to him as *ehrlich*, in the sense of honest and respectable. It appears, however, that he is not only righteous, but also self-righteous; for he often refers to his own virtue and honesty. On the other hand, he is obsessed by fear of winning *Schande*, by which he clearly means public disrespect. Because he fears disgrace so greatly, he is sure that his son will come to no good; and he immediately believes in his guilt without waiting for proof.

Whereas Master Anton's obsession with honor causes his son to rebel, it has positive influence on his daughter, who is honest in every way and frankly confesses her condition when the secretary proposes to her. She admits that she gave herself to Leonhard partly to avoid other people's scorn and the accusation of false pride; but it is likely that she was really thinking of the embarrassment it would bring her father. She is not vain and would probably bear her shame if her father had not threatened to kill himself if ever she should bring shame upon him. His fear of shame first makes her resolve to marry Leonhard, even after he boasts of many dishonorable deeds, such as making love to the mayor's hunchbacked daughter just before the selection of a new town cashier and getting the rival candidate, the parson's nephew, drunk on the day of the examination. Anton, whose inflexibility has caused the tragedy, is unreconstructed to the very end. All he can say is, "I don't understand the world any more."[1]

As we have seen, all propertied and substantial people, be they noblemen, burghers, or peasants, despised the unpropertied and vagrant classes; and therefore the worst fate that could befall them was to sink into the status of those they scorned. A touching description of such loss of caste is found in *A Village Romeo and Juliet*, a short story published in 1856 by the Swiss poet Gottfried Keller. As its title suggests, this story relates the tragic fate of two young people whose love is thwarted by their parents' hostility. In this case the parents are proud and class-conscious Swiss peasants, contemptuous of all people less fortunate than themselves. When the story opens, the fathers, Manz and Marti, are still friends, who are tacitly united in misappropriating an ownerless strip of land lying between their fields. They well know that the disputed strip of land rightfully belongs to a homeless and therefore "dishonorable" character called the "black fiddler", who is obviously the grandson of the last owner. Nevertheless, like their fellow townsmen, who do not wish to recognize the vagrant's right of domicile, they refuse to ackowledge his claim as long as he can produce no birth certificate.

After Manz and Marti have plowed deeply into the ownerless field,

---

[1] "Ich verstehe die Welt nicht mehr" (*Maria Magdalene*, III, 11).

misappropriating a narrow strip each year for many years, the remainder is auctioned by the local authorities; and Manz wins it at a high price after having to outbid Marti. Because of their previous encroachment, the boundary is no longer definite and soon becomes a bone of contention between the two guilty men. The ensuing litigation benefits only the lawyers and speculators; and the two peasants spend all their time, energy, and money in their bitter fight, which keeps them in town more than on their farms. Spurred on by righteous indignation and secret sense of guilt, they gradually deteriorate not only economically, but also socially and morally. His land mortgaged and his mortgage foreclosed, Manz leaves his farm to run a tavern in town. In his new profession he is as unsuccessful as in his old, until he at last begins to cater to thieves and to receive stolen property. Marti remains on his farm until completely impoverished and degenerate, at which time a blow on his head sends him to the public insane asylum.

When the story opens, Manz's son Sali and Marti's daughter Vrenchen are little children playing together on the unplowed land between their fathers' holdings. When their fathers become enemies, the children part and scarcely see each other, each believing the other more fortunate than himself. At last, when they are twenty and seventeen, they meet again one day while their fathers are having a disgraceful fight. The next day they meet again and discover and confess their love. Marti finds them together in a grain field; and Sali, in defending Vrenchen, strikes him on the head with a rock and deprives him of his reason.

Although knowing their love is hopeless, the lovers come together again as soon as Vrenchen has returned from taking her father to the asylum. They plan to have one last day together, one day to dance and forget their misery. Sali sells his watch to buy Vrenchen a pair of shoes; and the next morning they set out to dine and dance like respectable people. Feeling out of place among prosperous and respectable people, they go to a rural dance resort where the black fiddler is playing for the poor and homeless. The fiddler tries to persuade them to join his gypsy band; but they decline, since they know that they could never rise out this despised group and that their love could never survive in it. Instead, they spend the night on a hay barge and then, at dawn, they quietly slip into the deep water.

In the opening lines of the story, in fact even in his choice of a title, Keller says that his plot is the eternally recurring theme of unfortunate young lovers whose love is thwarted by the hostility of their parents. To be sure, this theme is present; but the parents' enmity is actually only an indirect cause, only one factor contributing to their misfortune; for their parents no longer have any authority over them when the tragedy occurs. As Walter Silz has so ably demonstrated, they die because they cannot overcome their own sense of class honor.[1] Having been born to respectable people and nurtured in contempt for social outcasts, they know they can never be happy without the recognition and approval of their rightful peers. Thus the true theme is not that of *Romeo and Juliet*, but rather that of *Tristan and Isolde*. Tristan and Isolde do not leave the Love Grotto because they must, but because they know that their love cannot survive without the honor and social recognition found only at court. Likewise, Sali and Vrenchen know their love will die if they try to live together with the dishonorable fiddler and his homeless band. As Walter Silz states, they "could never have escaped their tragedy, because they could never have escaped from themselves." [2]

Gottfried Keller was neither a medievalist nor an antiquarian; yet his story presents values and attitudes in perfect accord with those of the Middle Ages. These similarities can be explained by the cultural conservatism of the nineteenth-century Swiss peasants, whose hearts and minds Keller so well understood. Manz and Marti were as proud of their status as ever Father Helmbrecht was; and they were as contemptuous of their social inferiors as any ancient Germanic freeman. Having land, horses, and servants, they represent the substantial backbone of the community. The former social and political status of Marti's family is indicated by the halberd standing in his garden; for it symbolizes both military service and political function. After Marti's social and economic decline, the halberd serves only to support a bean stalk; and it is symbolic that Vrenchen hangs the key on the rusty weapon when she takes her final leave of her dilapidated home.

As substantial citizens, Manz and Marti feel neither compassion nor responsibility for the black fiddler, who, being illegitimate and homeless, can obtain only the most despised work such as mending pots, burning charcoal, and boiling tar. Because his friends, being vagrants, have no honor, they are not legally qualified to testify that he is the rightful heir to the disputed land. When the land is sold and the money is held in trust for the lawful owner, Manz and Marti rationalize by saying that the fiddler, as a vagrant, would only drink the money if it were given to him, whereas he really wants it in order to emigrate. Like their Germanic forebears, they consider poverty a sure sign of shiftlessness and lack of virtue. This is suggested in their use of the opprobrious terms *Lump* and *Hudelvolk*, both of which literally mean people in rags but have

---

[1] Walter Silz, *Realism and Reality*, Chapel Hill, 1954, pp. 79-93.
[2] *op. cit.*, p. 93.

acquired a secondary meaning of ragamuffin or scamp, just as the English word *shabby* has acquired the meaning of despicable.

Whereas the ultimate cause of Manz's and Marti's downfall is their guilt in robbing the black fiddler, the immediate cause is their pride or point of honor. Once the boundary dispute has begun, neither can make any concession through fear that people will think it an acknowledgement of inferiority; for no one takes advantage of another person unless he consideres him a contemptible and defenseless fool.[1] Because they feel their honor impugned, they need even more money to keep up appearances, and therefore they risk their money in lotteries and thus decline even more. When Sali leaves home for the last time, Manz gives him a gulden to spend in some tavern so that people will think them prosperous.

Although Sali and Vrenchen are basically kind and considerate, they have inherited their parents' social prejudices. Even after they have lost, through no fault of their own, the land and status to which they were born, they cannot resign themselves to accepting a lower status. Despite the inevitability of this fate, they try to deny it and they spend their last day together pretending that they are still respectable people. Before leaving her squalid house, from which she has been evicted, Vrenchen reveals her social ambitions by telling a neighbor that she is going to the city to marry Sali, who has become a rich man and will make her into a grand lady. All day the young lovers play make-believe and try to dine and dance like respectable young people. However, although they are neat, clean, well mannered, and respectable, they feel out of place among prosperous and respectable people and prefer to go to the Garden of Paradise, where the day-laborers, vagrants, and other poor and homeless folk assemble.[2] In other words, they join the very people so scorned by their parents and their remote ancestors.

Like most nineteenth-century German writers, Keller does not seem to realize that inner and outer honor are two distinct concepts; for he uses the one word *Ehre* to mean both, often in juxtaposition. Of Sali he says, "The feeling that he can be happy in the bourgeois world only in an entirely honorable (*ehrlich*) and scrupulous (*gewissenfrei*) marriage was just as alive in him as in Vrenchen; and in both lost beings it was the last flame of honor (*Ehre*), which had glowed in earlier times in their houses and which their self-assured fathers had blown out and destroyed by an apparently insignificant blunder when they, thinking to enhance this honor by increasing

---

[1] *Romeo und Julia*, p. 102.
[2] Sali and Vrenchen are frequently referred to as *ehrbar*, *ehrlich*, and *ehrsam*. The people at the Garden of Paradise are *das ärmere Volk, Taglöhner, fahrendes Gesinde* (*op. cit.*, p. 170); *Hudelvölkchen* (173); *Heimatlosen* (179). In other words, they are the very people disfranchised by the *Mirror of the Saxons*.

their property, misappropriated the possessions of a dead man, quite without danger as they supposed."[1] Here *Ehre* is used for both a virtuous sentiment and a social status that can be enhanced by an increase of property. Although Keller uses the word *ehrlich* here and on at least one other occasion in a moral sense,[2] he generally uses it and *ehrbar* objectively.[3]

Keller employs the words *Schande* and *Ehre* with both objective and subjective meaning, often in close proximity. An example is offered in his short story, *Clothes Make the Man*, a farce about a poor tailor who is mistaken for a count and does not have the moral strength to expose himself. Because of the uncertainty of his position, the involuntary impostor begins to regret his false role and has sleepless nights. Keller then moralizes that he was to be censured because his sleep was robbed more by his fear of the disgrace (*Schande*) of being revealed as a poor tailor than by his *ehrlich* conscience;[4] and here we see that *Schande* is used objectively but that *ehrlich* is used subjectively. Later, the heroine's father says that a wealthy man with an irreproachable name is ready to defend her honor by marrying her. The word *Ehre* excites her, and she cries out that it is precisely *die Ehre* that commands her not to marry him, since she can not bear him, but commands her to remain true to the poor stranger to whom she has given her word.[5] Here we have the same linguistic ambivalence previously noted in *Minna von Barnhelm*: the word *Ehre* is used twice in close proximity, once to mean reputation and once to mean obedience to absolute moral law.

---

[1] "Das Gefühl, in der bürgerlichen Welt nur in einer ganz ehrlichen und gewissenfreien Ehe glücklich sein zu können, war in ihm ebenso lebendig wie in Vrenchen, und in beiden verlassenen Wesen war es die letzte Flamme der Ehre, die in früheren Zeiten in ihren Häusern geglüht hatte und welche die sich sicher fühlenden Väter durch einen unscheinbaren Missgriff ausgeblasen und zerstört hatten, als sie, eben diese Ehre zu äufnen während durch Vermehrung ihres Eigentums, so gedankenlos sich das Gut eines Verschollenen aneigneten, ganz gefahrlos, wie sie meinten" (op. cit., p. 176).
[2] "Was kümmern uns die Leute!... Niemand hilft uns und ich bin ehrlich und fürchte niemand!" (*op. cit.*, p. 150).
[3] in his *Grüner Heinrich*, Keller says that at his confirmation he did not care whether or not he had a frock like the "ehrbaren Bürgerskindern" (*Gesammelte Werke*, Stuttgart & Berlin, 1904, I, p. 349).
[4] "und es ist mit Tadel hervorzuheben, dass es eben so viel die Furcht vor der Schande, als armer Schneider entdeckt zu werden und dazustehen, als das ehrliche Gewissen war, was ihm den Schlaf raubte" (*Kleider machen Leute*, p. 34).
[5] "Aber das Wort Ehre brachte nun doch die Tochter in grössere Aufregung. Sie rief, gerade die Ehre sei es, welche ihr gebiete, den Herren Böhni nicht zu heiraten, weil sie ihn nicht leiden könne, dagegen dem armen Fremden getreu zu bleiben, welchem sie ihr Wort gegeben habe und den sie auch leiden könne!" (*op. cit.*, p. 65).

CHAPTER TWELVE

RIDICULE OF TRADITIONAL HONOR

We have as many kinds of honor as social classes.
SUDERMANN, *Die Ehre*, II, 11

Perhaps the most popular German drama concerning honor was Hermann Sudermann's *Die Ehre* of 1889, which was first written as a tragedy but later acquired a happy ending. When the play opens, Robert Heinecke has just returned from the East Indies to visit his family, who live in quarters provided them by a wealthy manufacturer named Mühlingk in the rear of his own mansion. Many years earlier Robert's father had been injured at a festival celebrating the manufacturer's new rank of Commercial Counselor; and Mühlingk, in a public display of generosity, had promised to pension the worker and educate his son. After an apprenticeship in Hamburg, Robert had been sent to the Mühlingk factorage in the Indies, where he performed his duties with grateful diligence for nine years. During his long association with gentlemen, Robert acquired ideas of honor and human dignity quite foreign to his parents, as he discovered soon after returning home.

Because of their humble origins and financial insecurity, his parents are more concerned with material gain than with spiritual values; and Robert soon realizes that he can no longer communicate with them. He is shocked by their subservience and their willingness to accept any charity, even leftovers brought by the servant from the "front-house". Whereas he can pardon them their ignorance and ungrammatical speech, he resents the stuffed furniture and other gifts from their benefactors in the front-house. He has been sending an allowance to enable his dear sister Alma to study accounting; yet he finds that she is studying voice in the city, where she often spends the night with her older sister Auguste. Robert quickly sees that his little sister has become worldly and frivolous and is leading a life incompatible with his sense of honor.

Count von Trask, Robert's best friend in the Indies, arrives and tries to persuade him to leave with him; but Robert replies he must remain behind and protect his sister's honor. It is not long before he realizes the terrible truth that Alma has become the mistress of

Mühlingk's wastrel son Kurt and that his own sister Auguste has acted as paid procuress while their parents connived at the whole affair. As soon as he has gathered enough evidence, Robert goes to Kurt to demand satisfaction, by which he means either marriage or a duel. Meanwhile he has to protect his fallen sister from her hypocritical father, who now wants to curse her to prove himself a man of honor, and from her mother, who wants to punish her by treating her as a servant. Alma, who feigns penitence, declares she is ready to reform herself on the next day... but not today, because she still wants to go to the masked ball tonight...

Realizing his sister is hopelessly corrupted, Robert leaves the room and does not hear Mühlingk come to give satisfaction, in the form of a check for fifty-thousand marks, half to be a dowry for Alma and the rest to go to the parents. The family is so overjoyed by the sum that Mühlingk retracts and offers forty thousand, which they accept just as readily. When Robert rejoins the family, he finds them happily reconciled with their wayward daughter and drinking toasts to the Mühlingks. He is appalled to learn that they have accepted the payment for their daughter's honor; whereas one is not to blame if his honor is taken from him, he is to blame if he willingly sells it. In spite of Robert's eloquent lecture on honor and his promise to support them the rest of their lives, his greedy and shameless parents refuse to return the check, and thus they give further evidence that he and they speak two different languages.

When Robert goes to the front-house to settle business accounts, Trask goes along to restrain him from violence, having seen him take a revolver. While Robert is in the office, Trask tries to prevent him from meeting Kurt, even to the extent of distracting Kurt by attempting to involve him in a duel. In showing his ledgers, Robert is able to prove that he alone saved the Mühlingk investments; and then he returns a check for forty thousand marks to vindicate his family's honor. At this point a tragedy almost occurs; Kurt suggests that perhaps Robert has stolen the money from the Mühlingk accounts, and Robert attacks him, revolver in hand, and almost kills him, as he actually did until the plot was changed during rehearsals. Peace is restored. Mühlingk's virtuous daughter Lenore, Robert's childhood friend, declares her love for him, and Trask announces that Robert will be his associate and heir. Robert and Lenore look forward to building a new home, a new duty, and a new honor abroad.

Modern critics wonder why Sudermann's play was so sensationally successful, since neither its form nor its content was original. In general it employed traditional dramatic techniques, with a fair dose of realism, which was then the vogue. Even the attitudes toward honor were not particularly revolutionary; most of them had been expressed by Schopenhauer, to say nothing of ancient writers. Even Count von Trask, with his ideas on the relativity of honor, was not a new creation, having been based on Prosper Courament, the eccentric traveler in Victorien Sardou's *Les Pattes de Mouche* of 1860, which was popular on German stages under the title *Der letzte Brief*.

At first glance this play seems to be one of social protest, like Schiller's *Love and Intrigue*. In it too we find poor people oppressed by the rich, and in the next to last scene Robert lectures against the wealthy classes who seduce the sisters and daughters of the poor and then compensate them for their disgrace with money earned for them by the poor. Actually, this is not the chief argument, in fact it almost runs counter to the main argument, namely, that honor is a relative thing.

Count Trask, the *deus ex machina* of the play, was once a carefree young cavalry officer who gambled away in one evening a fortune he did not own. When he was dismissed from his regiment, his friends brought him a loaded and cocked pistol to help him end his shame, as any man of honor was expected to do. Upon feeling the barrel against his temple, he realized the stupidity of the custom and went abroad to earn money to repay his debts. By the time the play begins, he has learned that true honor is not public esteem but faithful performance of duty, as Cicero could have told him two millennia earlier.

Because of his financial power and inner resources, Trask can ignore other people's opinions and even ridicule their outmoded concepts of honor, particularly in regard to duels, which he questions as much as Lenore does. In answering Lothar Brandt, a young reserve officer who champions the prevailing military-aristocratic concept of honor, Trask claims that there is no honor. "What we generally call honor," he says "is nothing more than the shadow that we cast when the sun of public esteem shines on us. But the worst of it all is that we have as many different kinds of honor as social groups and strata..." [1]

---

[1] "Was wir gemeinhin Ehre nennen, das ist wohl nichts weiter, als der Schatten, den wir werfen, wenn die Sonne der öffentlichen Achtung uns bescheint. – Aber das Schlimmste bei allem ist, dass wir so viel verschiedene Sorten von 'Ehre' besitzen als gesellschaftliche Kreise und Schichten" (*Die Ehre*, II, 11). When von Trask says that honor is a shadow, he is echoing both Cicero and Seneca. Cf. "Gloria virtutem tamquam umbra sequitur" (Cicero, *Tusculan Disputations*, I, 45, 110); "Gloria umbra virtutis est" (Seneca, *Epistle to Lucilius*, 79, 13); and "Yf as the shadow followeth the body so prayse and reverence followeth him, then he ys called honorable" (*Ashley, Of Honour*, p. 34). The relativistic view on honor was censured in the German parliament in 1896 by Deputy Lenzmann: "Ich kann nicht zugeben, dass der Offiziersstand eine besondere Ehre habe, der Begriff Ehre ist ein absoluter,

When Lothar objects sharply that there is only one honor, just as there is only one sun or one God, Trask illustrates his argument with an experience he once had in Central Asia, where he inadvertently impugned the honor of his noble host by refusing to sleep with his wife. He then goes on to argue that honor, as it is generally understood, is a luxury permitted only to the privileged few and not readily accorded to even the most virtuous "rear-house" dweller, by which he is of course referring to his friend Robert.[1]

Trask's next illustration is even more to the point, and more of a warning. He tells of a mestizo who, returning to his South American home after many years in Spain, finds his sister involved with a young gentleman. Because he has imbibed the honor code of the hidalgos, he is unable to realize that such a liaison is the normal relationship between Spanish aristocrats and their mixed-breed inferiors; and he therefore demands satisfaction. Satisfaction being refused him, he shoots the aristocrat and is executed, maintaining to the end that he has defended his honor. Robert, who arrives in time to hear the story, asserts that the mestizo was right and that he would have done the same thing himself. Fortunately he does not yet know that Kurt has seduced Alma. When Lothar then asks Trask what men of honor should put in honor's place after he has removed it from the world, Trask suggests that duty would be a good substitute.[2]

Later, when Robert goes to the Mühlingk house to demand satisfaction for his lost honor, Trask tries to convince him that he cannot have lost his honor, since no one in the world can take away another man's honor. He says, "What you call your honor, this mixture of shame or tact or integrity and pride, that which you have acquired through a life of good breeding and strict sense of duty can't be taken from you by any rascally deed any more than the goodness of your heart or your power of judgment. Either it is a piece of you, or it is nothing... You have nothing in common with that kind of honor that can be destroyed by the carelessly thrown

---

keiner Steigerung fähiger, die Ehre des Arbeiters, Handwerkers, Kaufmannes, Juristen ist dieselbe wie die des Offiziers." (cited from *Lipperheide*, p. 134).

[1] "sie ist ein Luxusgefühl, das in demselben Masse an Wert verliert, in dem der Pöbel wagt, es sich anzueignen" – "Es ist doch jedem erlaubt, ein Mann von Ehre zu sein?" – "Im Gegenteil. Dann könnte ja der erstbeste arme Teufel aus dem Hinterhause kommen und die Kavaliersehre für sich beanspruchen" (*Die Ehre*, II, 11).

[2] (*Die Ehre*, IV, 2). A few years later Otto von Leixner repeated this thought, as: "Deine echte innere Ehre ist unverletzbar. Will einer dich in ihr beleidigen so kannst du ruhig lächeln. Befleckt werden kann nur die äussere, bürgerliche Ehre" (cited from *Lipperheide*, p. 134).

glove of just any fashionable rowdy. That's only good as a mirror for fops, a toy for idlers, and a perfume for reprobates."[1]

Trask then defends Robert's family, saying that he should not expect them to understand or feel all the sentiments and values he has acquired during nine years of association with gentlemen. Whereas the honor of the front-house can perhaps be paid for in blood, the honor of the rear-house is better restored with a small capital. Even Robert's sister is actually better off in her marriage market with a dowry than she would be with her virginity.[2] Having lost his "honor" a full quarter of a century earlier, Trask is able to theorize objectively on the subject; and he clearly sees that inner integrity is of more value than public esteem. As a result he uses the word *Ehre* only in a moral sense, except when purposely parodying the champions of the other code. Robert, who is just as moral and righteous as he, is confused on the point, just as Major von Tellheim had been. Consequently he uses *Ehre* almost exclusively in its objective sense, for example, when he tells Trask that it would be better for Lenore to remember him as the slayer of her brother than as a man without honor or when he asks Trask if a word of honor is not valid between two men without honor.[3] Fortunately Trask is able to clarify his thinking, just as Minna did for Tellheim; and Robert can renounce revenge and thus be worthy of Lenore, who has also been estranged from her family by her more advanced ideas on honor.

Whereas Sudermann devotes his argument chiefly to combatting outmoded views about duels and vicarious sexual dishonor, he also attacks the validity of "debts of honor". As we have seen, Tacitus mentioned the Teutons' strange obsession with paying gambling debts, even to the extent of sacrificing wives, children, and personal liberty. What Tacitus termed *fides*, later generations called the "debt of honor", as if honor did not require one to pay any other debts. Perhaps gambling debts remained in honor's bailiwick merely because they were not guaranteed by law or contract. Made

---

[1] "Deine Ehre hat niemand angetastet... Weil niemand auf der Welt dazu im stande ist.... Das, was du deine Ehre nennst, dieses Gemisch aus – Scham, aus – Taktgefühl, aus – Rechtlichkeit und Stolz, das, was du dir durch ein Leben voll guter Gesittung und strenger Pflichttreue anerzogen hast, kann dir durch eine Bubentat ebensowenig genommen werden, wie etwa deine Herzensgüte oder deine Urteilskraft. Entweder sie ist ein Stück von dir selbst, oder sie ist gar nicht... Mit jener Sorte von Ehre, die schon der lässig gewordene Handschuh irgend eines fashionablen Rowdys zu zerschmettern vermag, hast du nichts gemein... die ist gerade gut als Spiegel für die Laffen, als Spielzeug für die Müssigänger und als Parfüm für die Anrüchigen" (*Die Ehre*, IV, 2).
[2] *Die Ehre*, IV, 2.
[3] "Besser, als dass sie an einen Ehrlosen denkt!" (*Die Ehre*, IV, 2); "Soll ein Ehrenwort zwischen uns Ehrlosen keine Geltung haben?" (IV, 3).

sociably and often spurred on by pride and alcohol, they were seldom reinforced by written pledges; and therefore only the danger of losing status could make a man honor his promises or take his life in default thereof. Sudermann shows that it was morally better for Trask to refuse to take his life, in spite of his default, and thus be able to pay back his debts.

When Lothar Brandt asks von Trask what he would put in the place of honor, von Trask says he would put duty. The late nineteenth century had another surrogate for individual personal honor, namely national honor. When the Stoic view had finally undermined individual pride and superiority as virtuous goals, people could still strive for these goals by associating themselves with a larger entity such as their nation; because this un-Christian ambition then became confused with performance of duty. This peculiar reasoning can be seen in the present day sense of sportmanship. It is considered bad taste today for an athlete to boast of his own ability or to bet on his own victory; yet he is still permitted to boast about his team and to bet on its success. Whereas most Englishmen can engage in sports for the love of the game, most Germans, like other Europeans and Americans, usually play through a will to superiority. This generalization is indicated in America by the fact that the games imported from England, such as golf and tennis, are more gentlemanly than home-grown sports like baseball and football. It would be in poor taste to boo the putter or throw beer bottles at the server, nor would it be in order to hold a victory rally before a golf or tennis tournament. Whereas Germans do not go to such excesses as Americans, they often show injured pride when defeated. In comparison with their British counterparts, German individuals and teams often give an excuse for losing.

The virtues and vices of team-spirit reach their peak in nationalism. Naturally the Germans had little nationalism as long as they had no true nation; yet some thirteenth-century poets like Walther expressed pride in lands of the German tongue, and men like Celtis and Hutten revived such sentiments in the period of humanism and Reformation.[1] National pride in Germany was usually defensive: poets merely seemed to deny that they were ashamed of their country. Because Italian and French poets praised their fatherlands, the German poets felt compelled to do so too. The Holy Roman Empire was too intangible to love, and the territorial divisions were even less lovable, it being difficult to feel great ardor for a myriad of haphazardly scattered pieces of real estate fortuitously joined by the wars and marriages of some successful but not necessarily

---

[1] The best expression of Walther's patriotism is in his song beginning, "I have seen many lands" (Walther, 56,30 - 57,14). For Conrad Celtis as a patriot, see L. W. Spitz, *Conrad Celtis*, Cambridge, 1957, pp. 93-105.

admirable dynasty. At best one could feel a devotion to his feudal lord.

Long before they had a real nation of their own, the Germans yearned for a sense of national pride and honor, which they were quick to admire in other more fortunate lands. Schiller expressed this ideal in his *Maid of Orleans* with the words, "Unworthy is the nation that does not gladly risk its all for its honor."[1] This sentiment, which he expressed in 1799, was probably inspired by the patriotism then evident in the new French republic. During the wars of liberation against Napoleon a spate of patriotic songs and poems appeared in Germany and contributed greatly to the liberation and eventual unification of the country. Perhaps Germany's best known song of patriotism, or at least of military devotion, was Heinrich Heine's "The Two Grenadiers", which, ironically enough, glorifies two French soldiers.

National honor in Germany was largely borrowed from the French concept of *gloire*, a human delusion that justified any injustice. Aggression and oppression, which are crimes when committed by an individual, become glorious deeds when perpetrated in the name of the fatherland. As an American later expressed this primitive in-group loyalty, "My country - right or wrong." It was poetic justice that France's apotheosis of national glory backfired by spreading to Germany and uniting the various German states in 1870. After 1871, nationalism took on new meaning for the Germans; yet it still meant little to many great thinkers like Nietzsche. On the other hand, it filled a need for those whose Christian-Stoic training inhibited their innate drive for self-aggrandizement and for those petty people who basked in national honor because they could not achieve honor on their own individual merits. National honor, in the primitive sense, became completely dishonorable, in the Christian-Stoic sense, when associated with unscientific racial theories and mystic concepts of blood and soil. During the National Socialist regime there was a conscious attempt to restrict honor to the tribal community, as it had been before the advent of St. Boniface.

In his sarcastic tirade against dueling, Schopenhauer wrote something which very likely bore the germ of *Lieutenant Gustl*, an amusing tale written a half century later by the Viennese writer Arthur Schnitzler. Concerning the "point of honor" the pessimistic philosopher remarked, "How wicked the tyranny of that state within a state and how great the power of that superstition is can be judged by the fact that people have often taken their lives, and thus found a tragi-comic end, out of despair at being unable to restore

---

[1] "Nichtswürdig ist die Nation, die nicht Ihr Alles freudig setzt an ihre Ehre" (*Die Jungfrau von Orléans*, I, 5, vv. 847-848).

their injured chivalrous honor because their offender was socially too high or too low or otherwise unqualified."[1] During the first year of this century, Schnitzler wrote a satire describing the dilemma of such a man of honor, but without a fatal outcome.

This story, an early example of the "stream of consciousness" technique, takes place entirely in the head of Lieutenant Gustl, a conceited and superficial young Austrian officer; for the outside events of the story are revealed only as they are perceived, remembered, or cogitated by the hero. When the story opens, Gustl is waiting impatiently for the end of a choral recital, which he is attending only because a colleague has given him the ticket and because his current girl friend is spending the evening with a wealthier rival. Instead of listening to the music, which he cannot appreciate, he reflects about past and future erotic conquests and about the saber duel he is to have the next day with a doctor by whom he feels insulted. When the performance is at last over, he hurries to get his coat from the cloakroom and thoughtlessly pushes into an older civilian, who is patiently awaiting his turn. An altercation ensues and Gustl speaks rudely to the civilian, who is a master baker. Instead of creating a scene, the baker inconspicuously grasps Gustl's saber hilt and tells him to keep quiet if he does not want his saber shattered and the pieces sent to his regimental commander. Unable to budge the hand of his muscular opponent, Gustl has to submit to the affront until the baker, not wishing to ruin his career, takes a respectful leave as if they had just had a most cordial meeting.

Although the baker has made it quite clear that he intends to keep the insult a secret, Gustl fears he will report it. Leaving the theater in a daze, he wanders for hours while reliving the insult and much of his previous life. He realizes that he will have to resign his commission in disgrace (*mit Schimpf und Schande*) if the colonel ever hears of his humiliation. For a moment he reminds himself that this is nonsense, because no one knows of the affair. Then his nobler nature shows itself and he reflects, "Holy Heavens! It is all the same whether or not anyone else knows it. I know it, and that is the main thing!"[2] And thus he spends the entire night vacillating

---

[1] "Wie arg die Tyrannei jenes Staates im Staat und wie gross die Macht jenes Aberglaubens sei, lässt sich daran ermessen, dass schon öfter Leute, denen die Wiederherstellung ihrer verwundeten ritterlichen Ehre, wegen zu hohen oder zu niedrigen Standes, oder sonst unangemessener Beschaffenheit des Beleidigers unmöglich war, aus Verzweiflung darüber sich selbst das Leben genommen und so ein tragikomisches Ende gefunden haben" (*Schopenhauer*, IV, pp. 427-428).

[2] "Heiliger Himmel, es ist doch ganz egal, ob ein anderer was weiss!... *ich* weiss es doch, und das ist die Hauptsache" (*Leutnant Gustl*, p. 274). Cf. "nihil differt, si nemo videat, cum ipse illos videas" (St. Martin, *Formula*, 4, 53).

between inner shame and fear that people will learn of his dishonor, in which case he will no longer be *satisfaktionsfähig* for the doctor. "Honor lost, everything lost," he says,[1] and therefore he resolves that he must take his life.

Except for a nap on a bench, he spends the whole night walking through the park, his brain fermenting with self-pity, gallows-humor, vanity, self-debasement, and self-justification, with occasional reminiscences of glamorous or sordid love affairs. Because of his frivolous values, the reader is never really convinced that he will take his life. The next morning, when he goes to his favorite restaurant to eat his hangman's meal, he learns that the baker has dropped dead of a heart attack on his way home from the theater, without having breathed a word about the affair. Relieved of all his inner moral qualms, the punctilious young officer eats heartily and makes plans for his afternoon bout with the doctor.

[1] "Ehre verloren, alles verloren" (*Leutnant Gustl*, p. 278).

CONCLUSION

The preceding chapters have investigated ancient Germanic ideas of honor and have shown how they were subsequently modified by Christian and classical teachings. They have shown that, for all practical purposes, the transformation from external to internal honor was completed by the mid eighteenth century and was universally accepted as an ideal before the end of the nineteenth. This study will stop at this point, because a brief reconnaissance into twentieth-century literature has revealed no significant changes or new departures in meaning. Moreover, the mass of evidence to be sifted and the lack of historical perspective would tend to make all judgements both difficult and dubious.

In tracing the gradual development of the old German word *êra* into its modern derivative *Ehre*, this study has shown how the slight change in pronunciation was accompanied by a far more radical change in meaning: a shift from denoting respect, deference, prestige, rank, or superiority to denoting admirable conduct, personal integrity, or innner sense of right and wrong. Honor changed completely in essence; yet it remained constant in function; in both cases it was a spur to virtue, that is to say, an incentive to good and a deterrent from evil. The ancient Teutons admired men who showed courage in battle through a sense of honor, in its original meaning of concern for good reputation. Nineteenth-century Germans also admired men who did good deeds through a sense of honor, but in its altered meaning of disinterested obedience to absolute moral law.

The chief catalyst for this transformation was the Christian faith, which first convinced the Teutons of a divine law transcending the opinions of men. Through promise of reward and threat of punishment, the Church gradually persuaded the converts to practice, or at least to acknowledge, a code of behavior incompatible with their traditional ethos. In presenting their ethic of humility, the missionaries combatted the native idea of honor and damned it as the sin of pride. Being a good of the world, honor was no fitting reward for virtue, but rather an obstacle on the road to salvation. Nevertheless, despite their nominal acceptance of Christianity, medieval laymen tried to reconcile the two conflicting codes. While most clerics damned worldly honor as a snare of the devil, some saw in it a tool for Christian purpose and recognized it as a desirable value, but only in so far as it was won through righteous deeds. The word honor gradually expanded its meaning to include not only the esteem won through good works, but also the disposition leading men to perform them. But even then the clerics taught that such good works and disposition were of value only as long as they aimed at heavenly rewards.

Three basic attitudes toward traditional honor persisted side by side throughout the Middle Ages and down to modern times: retention, rejection, and revaluation. The ancient warrior code of honor, a love of fame and fear of shame, was retained as a vital social force, especially in aristocratic and military circles and was expressed perhaps most blatantly in class pride and point of honor. Wordly honor was generally rejected by clerics and occasionally by secular writers, particularly Catholic ones, as late as Brentano, Droste-Hülshoff, Stifter, Lenau, and Grillparzer. Honor was revalued, in imitation of Cicero and Seneca, first by the clergy and later by the early bourgeoisie, who were excluded from the honor code of the ruling classes. Eventually, as the bourgeoisie became economically and socially dominant, their idea of honor was preached as an ideal for all classes, even for royalty.

During the Age of Enlightenment many intellectuals questioned supernatural reward and punishment for honest and dishonest acts and began to cherish honesty as an absolute good. Thus they reached a stage of moral development similar to that formulated by Cicero and Seneca nearly two millennia earlier. At first glance this would suggest that the many intervening centuries did no more than raise the barbarians to the cultural level of the Romans whom they had submerged; yet this was not the case. The disinterested virtue taught by Cicero and Seneca was an individual matter, possibly more philosophical and theoretical than felt and practiced, and certainly limited to a small number of intellectuals. By the mid nineteenth century, on the other hand, disinterested virtue was the accepted, even if not always practiced, ideal of the German people at large. When presented in Sudermann's play, Cicero's austere concept of honor was comprehensible to the general theater public.

Although the Stoic ideal of inner honor was universally accepted in nineteenth-century Germany, primitive notions of honor still lingered in actual life and appeared often in realistic literature, albeit with moral censure. Writers still described the virtues of the old Germanic shame culture; but they usually presented them as vices and expected the reader to criticize pride of birth, wealth, and power, scorn for weaklings and inferiors, and delight in personal superiority. Once the hallmark of noble and magnanimous hearts, concern for other people's opinions was now condemned as a petty character fault, an indication of retarded moral development. Instead of being "affairs of honor" duels appeared as stupid survivals from a barbaric age, as brutish combats that favored the better shot rather than the better man.

For the sake of brevity, this study has been restricted to honor in German literature, as if German ideas on honor differed essentially from those in neighboring countries. As the excursions into other European literatures have shown, German ideas on honor are actually part of a general European complex, a complex of ideas that can be distinguished more sharply according to professional group or social class than according to nationality. As von Trask states, there are actually as many kinds of honor as there are social strata: in matters of honor and disgrace a German and a French officer would probably understand each other better than either would understand an artist, lawyer, or peasant of his own nationality.

It is safe to say that modern Western ideas on honor are a heritage from pagan Greece and Rome, tempered by Christianity. While all Occidental nations have contributed to these concepts of honor, France was perhaps the main clearing house and usually the chief contributor to their development. This is obvious for the age of chivalry, when French and Provencal culture were models for all genteel European life and literature; and it is also evident for succeeding centuries and especially for the Age of Enlightenment. Perhaps Germany contributed most in helping to internalize honor. German inwardness, including the internalization of honor, was closely related, as both cause and result, to medieval mysticism, humanism, protestantism, pietism, enlightenment, philosophical idealism, and, above all, to popular education and the dissemination of Greek and Roman ideas on the honorable life.

TEXTS ABBREVIATED IN THE NOTES

AND

SCHOLARLY WORKS CONCERNING HONOR (marked *)

ACKERMAN: Johannes von Tepl, *Der Ackerman*, ed. W. Krogmann, Wiesbaden, 1954.
ALEXANDER: *Rudolf von Ems Alexander*, ed. V. Junk, Leipzig, 1928-29.
ALEXIUS: *Das Leben des heiligen Alexius von Konrad von Würzburg*, ed. R. Henczynski, Berlin, 1898.
ARISTOTLE: *Nicomachean Ethics*, trans. F. H. Peters, London, 1893.
The Nicomachean Ethics of Aristotle, trans. D. Ross, Oxford, 1954.
The Rhetoric of Aristotle, trans. L. Cooper, New York, 1932.
ARMER HEINRICH: *Der arme Heinrich von Hartmann von Aue*, ed. H. Paul, Tübingen, 1953.
ARNOLD, AUGUST: *Studien über den hohen Mut*, Leipzig, 1930.
ARTZ, FREDERICK: *The Mind of the Middle Ages*, New York, 1953.
* ASHLEY, ROBERT: *Of Honour*, ed. V. B. Heltzel, San Marino, 1947.
* AUMANN, ERICH: "Tugend und Laster im Althochdeutschen," *Paul und Braunes Beiträge*, 63, 1939, pp. 143-161.
BAETKE, WALTER: *Das Heilige im Germanischen*, Tübingen, 1942.
* BARBER, C. L.: *The Idea of Honour in the English Drama* (1591-1700), Göteborg, 1957.
Barlaam und Josaphat von Rudolf von Ems, ed. F. Pfeiffer, Leipzig, 1843.
* BARROW: *The Works of Dr. Isaac Barrow*, ed. T. S. Hughes, London, 1830, I, pp. 74-101.
BEDE: *Baedae Opera Historica*, ed. J. K. King, Cambridge, Mass., 1954.
BENEDICT, RUTH: *Patterns of Culture, Mentor Books*, New York, 1936.
* BENEKE, OTTO: *Von unehrlichen Leuten*, Hamburg, 1863.
Beowulf, ed. F. Klaeber, Boston, 1936.
Bertold von Regensburg: deutsche Predigten, ed. F. Pfeiffer, Wien, 1862.
* BOPP, WERNER: *Die Geschichte des Wortes "Tugend"*, Dissertation Heidelberg, 1935.
BRAUNE, W.: *Althochdeutsches Lesebuch*, ed. K. Helm, 11th ed., Halle, 1949.
BREASTED, J. H., *The Dawn of Conscience*, New York, 1933.
Brennu-Njálssaga, ed. F. Jónsson, Halle, 1908.
* BROWNE: *The Works of Sir Thomas Browne*, ed. S. Wilkin, London, 1883, Section XLVII.
* BRYSON, F. R.: *The Point of Honor in Sixteenth-Century Italy*, New York, 1935.
BRUT: *Le Roman de Brut de Wace*, ed. Ivor Arnold, Paris, 1940.
BÜCHLEIN: *Der arme Heinrich und die Büchlein von Hartmann von Aue*, ed. M. Haupt, Leipzig, 1881.
* BURCKHARDT, JACOB: "Der moderne Ruhm", in *Die Cultur der Renaissance in Italien*, 3d ed., Leipzig, 1877, I, pp. 171-180.
BUTTKE, H.: *Studien über Armut und Reichtum in der mittelhochdeutschen Dichtung*, Dissertation Bonn, Bonn, 1938.
* CASTRO, A., "Algunas observaciones acerca del concepto del honor en los siglos XVI y XVII" in A. Castro, *Semblanzas y Estudios Españoles*,

Princeton, 1956, pp. 315-382. Previously printed in *Revista de Filología Española*, 3 (1916), pp. 1-50, 357-358.
CHADWICK, NORA K.: *Poetry and Letters in early Christian Gaul*, London, 1955.
Chanson de Roland, La: ed. J. Bédier, Paris, 1922.
CHAUCER: *The Poetical Works of Chaucer*, ed. F. N. Robinson, Cambridge, 1933.
Cherubinischer Wandersmann: Angelus Silesius, *Sämtliche Werke*, ed. H. Held, München, 1949, III.
CHRÉTIEN, EREC: *Kristian von Troyes Erec und Enide*, ed. W. Foerster, Halle, 1909.
CHRÉTIEN, YWAIN: *Chrestien de Troyes Iwain*, ed. T. Reid, Manchester, 1948.
Chronicon Terrae Prussiae, by Peter von Dusburg, ed. M. Toeppen, *Scriptores Rerum Prussicarum* I, Leipzig, 1861, pp. 3 ff.
CITY OF GOD: *Sancti Aurelii Augustini De Civitate Dei Libri I-X*, Turnholti, 1955.
CLARKE, M. L.: *The Roman Mind*, Cambridge, Mass., 1956.
CORTEGIANO: *Il Cortegiano di Baldesar Castiglione*, ed. Bruno Maier, Turin, 1955.
CORY: *Extracts from the Letters and Journals of William Cory*, ed. F. W. Cornish, Oxford, 1897.
* CURTIUS, E. R.: "Das 'ritterliche Tugendsystem'", *Deutsche Vierteljahrsschrift*, 21, 1943, pp. 343 ff. Reprinted in *Europäische Literatur und lateinisches Mittelalter*, Bern, 1948, Exkurs 18, pp. 508-523.
* CYSARZ, HERBERT: "Vom Diesseits und Jenseits der Ehre", *Euphorion*, 42, 1942, II, pp. 73-88.
DE CONSOLATIONE: *Boethius*, ed. H. F. Stuart, Cambridge, Mass., 1953.
De Officiis, ed. Walter Miller, Cambridge, Mass., 1956 (Loeb).
Die Ehre von Hermann Sudermann, Stuttgart und Berlin, 1908.
Die Disciplina Clericalis des Petrus Alfonsi, ed. A. Hilke, Heidelberg, 1911.
DIETRICHS FLUCHT: *Alpharts Tod Dietrichs Flucht Rabenschlacht*, ed. E. Martin, Berlin, 1866 (*Deutsches Heldenbuch*, II).
Diu Klage, ed. K. Bartsch, Leipzig, 1875.
DODDS, E. R.: *The Greeks and the Irrational*, Berkeley, 1951.
* EBERSTEIN, A.: *Über die Ehre und falsche Ehrbegriffe*, Leipzig, 1894.
* ECKSTEIN, J.: *Die Ehre in Philosophie und Recht*, Leipzig, 1889.
* EHRISMANN, G.: "Die Grundlagen des ritterlichen Tugendsystems", *Zeitschrift für deutsches Altertum*, 56, 1919, pp. 137-216.
EMILIA GALOTTI: *Lessings Werke*, ed. J. Petersen, Berlin, n.d., II, pp. 93-163.
* EMMEL, HILDEGARD: *Das Verhältnis von êre und triuwe im Nibelungenlied und bei Hartmann und Wolfram*, Frankfurt, 1936 (*Frankfurter Quellen und Forschungen*, 14).
EMSER, HIERONYMUS: *Eyn deutsche Satyra, Texte des späten Mittelalters*, 3, Berlin, 1956.
ENEIDE: *Heinrichs von Veldeke Eneide*, ed. O. Behaghel, Heilbronn, 1882.
Engelhart von Konrad von Würzburg, ed. M. Haupt, Leipzig, 1890.
ERBFÖRSTER: *Otto Ludwigs gesammelte Schriften*, ed. A. Stern, Leipzig, 1891.
EREC: *Hartmann von Aue Erec Iwein*, ed. H. Naumann and H. Steinger, Leipzig, 1933.
ETHICS: s. Aristotle.
* *Euphorion* 42 (1942), II. Whole issue devoted to articles on honor.
* FARET, NICOLAS: *L'Honneste Homme*, ed. M. Magendie, Paris, 1925.
Freidanks Bescheidenheit, ed. H. Bezzenberger, Halle, 1872.
FRINGS, THEODOR: *Antike und Christentum an der Wiege der deutschen*

Sprache, Berlin, 1949. (*Berichte über die Verhandlungen der sächsischen Akademie der Wissenschaften zu Leipzig*, 97).
GALLIC WAR: *Caesar's Gallic War*, ed. F. W. Kelsey, Boston, 1888.
* GARCIA VALDECASAS, ALFONSO: *El hidalgo y el honor*, Madrid (Revista de Occidente), 1948.
* GEHL, WALTHER: *Ruhm und Ehre bei den Nordgermanen*, Berlin, 1937.
GENESIS: *Die ältere Genesis*, ed. F. Holthausen, Heidelberg, 1914.
GERHARD: *Der gute Gerhard von Rudolf von Ems*, ed. Moritz Haupt, Leipzig, 1840.
GERMANIA: *Cornelii Taciti de Origine et situ Germanorum*, ed. J. G. C. Anderson, Oxford, 1938.
GESTA DANORUM: *Saxonis Grammatici Gesta Danorum*, ed. A. Holder, Strassburg, 1886.
GESTA ROMANORUM: *Die Gesta Romanorum*, ed. W. Dick, Erlangen and Leipzig, 1890. (*Erlanger Beiträge zur englischen Philologie*, VII).
Gregorius von Hartmann von Aue, ed. H. Paul, Tübingen, 1953.
* GRIESE, FRIEDRICH: "Von der bäuerlichen Ehre", *Euphorion*, 42, 1942, II, pp. 22-30.
GRÖNBECH, WILHELM: *Kultur und Religion der Germanen*, Darmstadt, 1954.
GRÜNER: *Briefwechsel und mündlicher Verkehr zwischen Goethe und dem Rathe Grüner*, ed. J. S. Grüner, Leipzig, 1853.
HALLER: *Albrecht von Hallers Gedichte*, ed. L. Hirzel, Frauenfeld, 1882.
HANS SACHS, *Sämmtliche Fastnachtspiele*, ed. E. Goetze, Halle, 1920.
HELBLING: *Seifried Helbling*, ed. J. Seemüller, Halle, 1886.
HELIAND: *Heliand und Genesis*, ed. O. Behaghel, Halle, 1948.
HELMBRECHT: *Meier Helmbrecht von Wernher dem Gartenaere*, ed. F. Panzer, Tübingen, 1953.
HÉRAUCOURT, W.: *Die Wertwelt Chaucers*, Heidelberg, 1939, pp. 63-67.
Herzog Ernst, ed. K. Bartsch, Wien, 1869.
HEUSLER, ANDREAS: *Germanentum*, Heidelberg, n.d.,
HIGHET, GILBERT: *The Classical Tradition*, New York, 1957.
HILDEBRANDSLIED: *Althochdeutsches Lesebuch*, ed. W. Braune, Halle, 1949, XXVIII.
HISTORIA: *The Historia Regum Britanniae of Geoffrey of Monmouth*, ed. A. Griscom, London, 1929.
HUIZINGA, J.: *The Waning of the Middle Ages*, London, 1924.
ILIAD: *The Iliad of Homer*, trans. R. Lattimore, Chicago, 1952.
IWEIN: *Hartmann von Aue Erec Iwein*, ed. H. Naumann and H. Steinger, Leipzig, 1933.
JÓMSVÍKINGS: *The Saga of the Jómsvikings*, trans. L. M. Hollander, Austin, 1955.
* JONES, GEORGE F.: "Lov'd I not honour more", *Comparative Literature*, XI, 1959, pp. 131-143.
* —, "Rüedeger's Dilemma", *Studies in Philology*, forthcoming.
JUDENBUCHE: Annette von Droste-Hülshoff, *Sämtliche Werke*, ed. K. Kemminghausen, München, 1925, III, pp. 5-53.
KABALE UND LIEBE: *Schiller, Werke*, ed. F. Iblher, Leipzig, 1930, I, pp. 258-364.
DER KAMMERSÄNGER: Frank Wedekind, *Gesammelte Werke*, München, 1913, pp. 195-240.
* Karg-Gasterstädt, Elisabeth: "Ehre und Ruhm im Althochdeutschen", *Paul und Braunes Beiträge*, 70, 1948, pp. 308-331.
KASPERL und ANNERL: *Brentanos Werke*, ed. F. Domke, Leipzig and Wien, 1892.
* KATTENBUSCH, F.: *Ehren und Ehre*, Giessen, 1909.

* KETTNER, R. P.: *Der Ehrbegriff in dem altfranzösischen Artusroman*, Leipzig, 1890.
KLAGE: *Konrad von Würzburg Klage der Kunst*, ed. E. Joseph, Strassburg, 1885.
* KLATT, FRITZ: "Über Ehrfurcht und Ehre", *Euphorion*, 42, 1942, pp. 64-73.
Kleider machen Leute: Gottfried Keller Sämtliche Werke, ed. J. Fränkel, München, 1927, VIII, pp. 5-70.
* KLOSE, FRIEDRICH: *Die Bedeutung von honos und honestus*, Dissertation Breslau, Breslau, 1933.
König Rother, ed. T. Frings & J. Kuhnt, Bonn, 1922.
Kronike von Pruzinlant, ed. E. Strehlke, *Scriptores Rerum Prussicarum* I, Leipzig, 1861, pp. 291 ff.
* KUHN, HANS: "Sitte und Sittlichkeit", in *Germanische Altertumskunde*, ed. H. Schneider, München, 1951, pp. 171-221.
Lamprechts Alexander, ed. K. Kinzel, Halle, 1884.
* LANGE-EICHBAUM, WILHELM: *Genie Irrsinn und Ruhm*, München, 1956.
Lanzelet, ed. K. A. Hahn, Frankfurt, 1845.
Laurin und der kleine Rosengarten, ed. G. Holz, Halle, 1897.
LEICHE: *Heinrichs von Meissen Leiche, Sprüche*, ed. L. Ettmüller, Quedlinburg & Leipzig, 1843.
LENAU, NIKOLAUS: *Sämtliche Werke*, ed. E. Castle, Leipzig, 1910.
LEUTNANT GUSTL: *Gesammelte Werke von Arthur Schnitzler*, Berlin, 1918, I, pp. 261-302.
* LÉVÊQUE, ANDRÉ: "'L'honnête homme' et 'L'homme de bien' au xviie siècle", *PMLA*, 72 (Sept., 1957), pp. 620-632.
LEVIATHAN: *Hobbes's Leviathan*, ed. W. G. Pogson Smith, Oxford, 1929.
* LIDA DE MALKIEL, M. R.: *La Idea de la Fama en la Edad Media Castellana*, Mexico, 1952.
LIPPERHEIDE, F. VON: *Sprichwörterbuch*, Berlin, 1907.
* LIST, WOLFRAM, "Preussische Ehre im klassischen Drama", *Euphorion*, 42, 1942, II, pp. 46-64.
* MAGENDIE, MAURICE: *La Politesse mondaine et les theories de l'honnêteté en France au XVIIe siècle, de 1600 a 1660*, Paris, 1926.
MAGIRUS, TOBIAS: *Polymnemon*, Frankfurt, 1661.
MARIA MAGDALENE: Friedrich Hebbel, *Sämtliche Werke*, Berlin, 1904, II, pp. 1-72.
Der Marner, ed. P. Strauch, Strassburg, 1876.
MARTIN: *Martini Episcopi Bracensis*, ed. C. W. Barlowe, New Haven, 1950.
* MAURER, FRIEDRICH: *Leid*, Bern, 1951.
* —, "Das ritterliche Tugendsystem", *Deutsche Vierteljahrsschrift*, 23, 1949, pp. 274-285.
* —, "Tugend und Ehre", *Wirkendes Wort*, 1951-52, Heft 2, pp. 72-80.
* —, "Zum ritterlichen 'Tugendsystem'", *Deutsche Vierteljahrsschrift*, 24, 1950, pp. 526-529.
* Menéndez Pidal, Ramón: "Der Ehrbegriff im spanischen Schrifttum der Blütezeit" (deutsch von Karl Vossler), *Euphorion*, 42, 1942, II, pp. 30-43.
* MEYER, CHRISTIAN: *Die "Ehre" im Lichte vergangener Zeit*, München, 1904.
MICHAEL KOHLHAAS: *Heinrich von Kleists Werke*, ed. Erich Schmidt, Leipzig, n.d., III, pp. 141-248.
MINNA VON BARNHELM: *Lessings Werke*, ed. J. Petersen, Berlin, n.d., II, pp. 13-91.
MINNE REGEL: *Eberhard Cersne*, ed. F. X. Wöber, Wien, 1861.
Des Minnesangs Frühling, ed. C. von Kraus, Zürich, 1950.

MONTAIGNE: *Oeuvres complètes de Michel de Montaigne*, ed. A. Armaingaud, Paris, 1925.
MORALIUM DOGMA: *Das Moralium Dogma Philosophorum des Guillaume de Conches*, ed. John Holmberg, Uppsala, 1929.
Moriz von Craun, ed. U. Pretzel, Tübingen, 1956.
MÜLLENHOFF, KARL: *Altdeutsche Sprachproben*, Berlin, 1864.
NARRENSCHIFF: *Sebastian Brants Narrenschiff*, ed. F. Zarncke, Leipzig, 1854.
* NAUMAN, HANS: "Drengskap-Geist und Ehre im Germanischen", *Euphorion*, 42, 1942, II, pp. 1-11.
* —, "Die Ritter-Ehre der Stauferzeit", *Ibid.*, pp. 12-22.
* —, "Hartmann von Aue und Cicero?", *Deutsche Vierteljahrsschrift*, 23, 1949, pp. 285-287.
Das Nibelungenlied, ed. K. Bartsch - H. de Boor, 12th ed., Leipzig, 1949.
* NORWOOD, LOTTE: *Ére und Scande, eine Untersuchung der Wortbedeutung in vorhöfischer Zeit*, University of Wisconsin dissertation, 1957 (typed).
NOTKER: *Notkers des Deutschen Werke*, ed. E. H. Sehrt and T. Starck, Halle, 1933.
Notker-Wortschatz, ed. E. H. Sehrt and W. Legner, Halle, 1955.
OSWALD: *Der Münchener Oswald*, ed. G. Baesecke, Breslau, 1907.
PANZER, FRIEDRICH: *Das Nibelungenlied*, Stuttgart, 1955.
—, *Studien zum Nibelungenlied*, Frankfurt, 1945.
PARTONOPIER: *Konrads von Würzburg Partonopier und Meliur*, ed. K. Bartsch, Wien, 1871.
PARZIVAL: *Wolfram von Eschenbach von Karl Lachmann*, ed. E. Hartl, Berlin, 1952.
The Poetic Edda, trans. L. M. Hollander, Austin, Texas, 1928.
POLE POPPENSPÄLER: *Theodor Storms sämtliche Werke in acht Bänden*, ed. A. Köster, Leipzig, 1919, IV, pp. 33-90.
* PONGS, HERMANN: "Soldatische Ehre in der Dichtung der Gegenwart", *Euphorion*, 42, 1942, II, pp. 89-129.
* —, "Faust und die Ehre", *Euphorion*, 44, 1944, pp. 78-105.
PRIESTERLEBEN: RICHARD KIENAST, *Der sogenannte Heinrich von Melk*, Heidelberg, 1946.
RAABE, WILHELM: *Die Hämelschen Kinder*, in *Sämtliche Werke*, Berlin, 1913, *Erste Serie*, VI, pp. 171-207.
RECHTSALTERTHÜMER: *Deutsche Rechtsalterthümer von Jacob Grimm*, ed. A. Heusler Darmstadt, 1955.
REDE VOM GLOUVEN: *Des armen Hartmann Rede vom Glouven*, ed. F. v. der Leyen, Breslau, 1897.
REIMCHRONIK: *Michael Beheims Reimchronik*, ed. C. Hofmann, München, 1863.
* REINER, H.: *Die Ehre*, Dortmund, 1956.
REINMAR: *Die Gedichte Reinmars von Zweter*, ed. G. Roethe, Leipzig, 1887.
RENNER: *Der Renner von Hugo von Trimberg*, ed. G. Ehrismann, Tübingen, 1908 ff.
* RIECHERT, IRMGARD: *Studien zur Auffassung von 'ere' bei Konrad von Würzburg und Rudolf von Ems*, Dissertation Freiburg, 1952 (typed).
RING: *Heinrich Wittenwilers Ring*, ed. E. Wiessner, Leipzig, 1931.
RIESMAN, DAVID: *The Lonely Crowd*, New York, 1953.
RITTERMAEREN: *Zwei altdeutsche Rittermaeren*, ed. E. Schroeder, Berlin, 1913.
RITTERSPIEGEL: *Johannes Rothe, der Ritterspiegel*, ed. H. Naumann, Halle, 1936.
ROLANDSLIED: *Das Rolandslied des Pfaffen Konrad*, ed. Fr. Maurer, Leipzig, 1940.

Romeo und Julia auf dem Dorfe: Gottfried Keller, *Sämtliche Werke*, ed. J. Fränkel, Zürich and München, 1927, VII, pp. 83-187.

ROUGEMONT, DENIS DE: *Love in the Western World*, trans. M. Belgion, New York, 1956.

* RUBIÓ Y LLUCH, A.: *El sentimiento del honor en el theatro de Calderón*, Barcelona, 1882.

RUODLIEB: *Waltharius, Ruodlieb, Märchenepen*, ed. K. Langosch, Berlin, 1956.

Sachsenspiegel, ed. K. Eckhardt, Hannover, 1933.

Salman und Morolf, ed. F. Vogt, Halle, 1880.

Salomon et Marcolfus, ed. W. Benary, Heidelberg, 1914.

* SAUER, WILHELM: "Das Wesen der Ehre", *Logos*, IX, 1920-21, pp. 64-82.
* SCHÄFER, DIETRICH, "Honor, citra, cis im mittelalterlichen Latein", *Sitzungsberichte der preuss. Akad.* (phil), 1921, pp. 372-378.
* SCHMID, GERTRUD: *Christlicher Gehalt und germanisches Ethos in der vorhöfischen Geistlichendichtung*, Erlangen, 1937.

SCHNEIDER, HERMAN: *Germanische Altertumskunde*, München, 1951.

* SCHOPENHAUER: *Arthur Schopenhauers sämtliche Werke*, ed. P. Deussen, München, 1913. *Aphorismen zur Lebensweisheit* in Vol. IV, pp. 345-446.
* SCHÜCKING, L. L.: "Heldenstolz und Würde im Angelsächsischen", *Abh. der. phil. hist. Klasse der sächs. Ak. der Wiss.*, XLII, nr. V, Leipzig, 1933, pp. 1-27.
* SCHULZ, HANS: *Studien zum Sinnbezirk von êre im 'Buch der Maccabäer in mitteldeutscher Bearbeitung' und in Nicolaus von Jeroschins 'Kronike von Pruzinlant'*, Dissertation Freiburg, Freiburg/Br., 1957.

SCHWERIN, C. VON: *Germanische Rechtsgeschichte*, Berlin, 1944.

Secreta Secretorum, ed. W. Toischer, *Program des K. K. Staats-Ober-Gymnasiums*, Wiener-Neustadt, 1882.

* SETTEGAST, F.: "Der Ehrbegriff in dem altfranzösischen Rolandslied", *Zeitschrift für romanische Philologie*, IX, 1885, pp. 204-222.
* —, *Die Ehre in den Liedern der Troubadours*, Leipzig, 1887.

SHAKESPEARE: *The Complete Works of Shakespeare*, ed. G. Kittredge, Boston, 1936.

* SIMMEL, GEORG: *Soziologie*, Leipzig, 1908, pp. 532-537.

SIMPLICISSIMUS: H. J. Chr. von Grimmelshausen, *Der abenteuerliche Simplicissimus*, Leipzig, 1908.

SOMBART, WERNER: *Der Bourgeois*, Leipzig, 1913.

STEVENS, C. E.: *Sidonius Appolinaris and his Age*, London, 1933.

STIFTER, ADALBERT: *Gesammelte Werke*, Bielefeld, 1956 (*Bunte Steine* in Vol. 1).

STRICKER: *Kleinere Gedichte von dem Stricker*, ed. K. Hahn, Quedlinburg and Leipzig, 1839.

* STUART, D. C.: "Honor in the Spanish Drama", *The Romanic Review*, 1910, pp. 247-258, 357-366.

SUCHENWIRT: *Peter Suchenwirts Werke aus dem vierzehnten Jahrhundert*, ed. A. Primisser, Wien, 1827.

Summa Contra Gentiles: Sancti Thomae Aquinatis Opere Omnia, New York, 1948, Vol. V.

SUMMA THEOLOGIAE: *S. Thomae de Aquino Summa Theologiae*, Ottawa, 1952.

TALBOT, C. H.: *The Anglo-Saxon Missionaries in Germany*, London, 1954.

TEICHNER: *Die Gedichte Heinrichs des Teichners*, ed. N. Niewöhner, Berlin, 1953.

Des Teufels Netz, ed. K. Barack, Stuttgart, 1863.

Thule: altnordische Dichtung und Prosa, ed. Felix Niedner, Jena, 1923 ff.

TITUREL: *Wolfram von Eschenbach von Karl Lachmann*, ed. E. Hartl, Berlin, 1952, pp. 389 ff.
TOORN, M. C. VAN DEN: *Ethics and Moral in Icelandic Saga Literature*, Assen, 1955.
TRESTON, H. J.: *Poine, a Study in ancient Greek Blood-vengeance*, London, 1923.
TRISTAN: *Gottfried von Strassburg Tristan*, ed. K. Marold, Leipzig, 1912.
TRISTRANT: *Eilhart von Oberge*, ed. F. Lichtenstein, Strassburg, 1877.
TROJANERKRIEG: *Der trojanische Krieg von Konrad von Würzburg*, ed. A. v. Keller, Stuttgart, 1858.
VERBRECHER AUS VERLORENER EHRE: *Schillers Werke, National Ausgabe*, ed. H. H. Borcherdt, Weimar, 1954, XVI, pp. 7-29.
* VOLLMER, VERA: *Die Begriffe der Triuwe und der Staete in der höfischen Minnedichtung*, Dissertation Tübingen, Tübingen, 1914.
VRIES, JAN, DE: *Die geistige Welt der Germanen*, Halle, 1945.
Waltharius, Ruodlieb, Märchenepen, ed. K. Langosch, Berlin, 1956.
WALTHER: *Die Gedichte Walthers von der Vogelweide*, ed. C. v. Kraus, Berlin, 1950.
WELSCHER GAST: *Der wälsche Gast des Thomasin von Zirclaria*, ed. H. Rückert, Quedlinburg and Leipzig, 1852.
WELTCHRONIK: *Rudolfs von Ems Weltchronik*, ed. G. Ehrismann, Berlin, 1915.
Wendenmuth von Hans Wilhelm Kirchhof, ed. H. Österley, Stuttgart, 1869.
* WENTZLAFF-EGGEBERT, F. W.: "Ritterliche Lebenslehre und antike Etik", *Deutsche Vierteljahrsschrift*, 23, 1949, pp. 252-273.
WILLEHALM: *Wolfram von Eschenbach*, ed. A. Leitzmann, Halle, 1950.
WILLEHALM VON ORLENS: *Rudolf von Ems Willehalm von Orlens*, ed. V. Junk, Berlin, 1905.
* WILSON, E. M.: "Othello, A Tragedy of Honour", *The Listener*, 47, no. 1214, June 5, 1952, pp. 926-927.
WINSBEKE: *König Tirol, Winsbeke und Winsbekin*, ed. A. Leitzmann, Halle, 1888.
WOLFDIETRICH, A.: *Ortnit und die Wolfdietriche*, ed. A. Amelung and O. Jänicke, Berlin, 1871 (*Deutsches Heldenbuch*, III).
* WUNDT, MAX: *Die Ehre als Quelle des sittlichen Lebens in Volk und Staat*, Langensalze, 1937.

INDEX

adel 16, 17
Ackermann aus Böhmen, see *Plowman from Bohemia*
adultery 29, 85
Agnes Bernauer 134
Agricola 8, 28
Alberta, Leon Battista 125
Albigensians 98
Alexander (Rudolf of Ems) 31, 66, 67, 73, 74, 83, 92, 111
allodium 18
St *Alexis* (Conrad of Würzburg) 58, 95, 104
ambition 23
St Ambrose 84
Anderson, J. G. C. 13
Andreas Capellanus 71
anagogical method 121
Angelus Silesius, see Scheffler
St Anselm 105
antifeminism 98
aphoristic poets 104
arc 31
Ariovistus 12, 18
Aristotle 11, 12, 32, 83, 91, 92, 105, 112, 141
arm bands 19
arme liute 131
Arminius 8, 27
Arndt, E. M. 159
artisans, honor of 7, 129
Artz, Frederick 81
asceticism 57, 58
Ashley, Robert 1, 79, 140, 183
Attila 22
Auerbach, Bertold 164
St Augustine 44, 45
A Village Romeo and Juliet, 176-180

Bachmann, Albert 4
bailiff (*Gerichtsdiener*) 135
Barber, C. L. 160
Barlaam and Jehosaphat (Rudolf of Ems) 49, 86, 102, 111
baroque literature 138
Barrow, Isaac, 142
bathers 133
Bayard 32
beasts, lack honor 10, 75
beauty brings honor 22, 145
Bede 44, 51
Beethoven 132
Beheim, Michel 131
Bell, C. H. 107
Benedict, Ruth 2
Benedictine Rule 43
Beneke, Otto 129, 134, 135
Beowulf 10, 19, 24, 27, 28, 30, 33, 38, 56
Bernard Silvester 104, 125
Bertold of Regensburg 133
Bescheidenheit, see Freidank
beschämen 164
beschimpfen 164
biderbe 23, 110, 124
bieder 110, 124
Bismark 154
Bitzius, Albert 165
blond hair 22
bloodmoney 36, 39, 130
boasting 95
boese 23, 31, 94
Boethius 45
St Boniface 29, 49, 51, 57
Bopp, Werner 61, 76
Boppe 75
Bossuet 141

Bostock, J. K. 5
bourgeois honor 123
Brant, Sebastian 137
Breasted, J. H. 9
Brennu-Njálssaga 93
Brentano, Clemens 135, 165, 171
Browne, Thomas 155
Brut, see Wace
Büchlein (Hartmann) 73, 119
Bühler, Johannes 82
buoze 39
Busse 39
Burckhardt, Jacob 81
Buttke, Herbert 18

Caesar, Julius 12, 19, 24, 98
Calderón 138
Canaan, curse of 53, 128
The Canterbury Tales, see Chaucer
captivity, shame of 19, 69, 129
Castiglione, Baldesar 81, 102, 126, 141
Castro, Américo 126, 138
Celtis, Conrad 136, 186
Chadwick, Nora 49
Chamisso, Adalbert 165
Chanson de Roland 20, 32, 37, 42, 43, 68, 69
Chapelain, Jean 139
Charlemagne 56
Chartres 48
Chaucer 3, 6, 46, 81, 93, 97, 106, 120, 130
chivalric code of honor 88
Chronicle of Prussia (*Kronike von Pruzinlant*) 112
Chrétien of Troyes 99
Cicero 12, 27, 35, 46, 47, 48, 49, 60, 105, 111, 114, 125, 153, 155, 183
Cimbri, see Teutones
City of God, see St Augustine
Clark, M. L. 12
clothing 43, 64, 65, 163
Clothes make the Man (*Kleider machen Leute*) 180
Clovis 52

Cluny Reform 57, 59
Coleman-Norton, P. R. 12
comitatus 14
compurgations 43
conflict of duties 76
Conrad of (Konrad von) Würzburg 27, 58, 61, 62, 75, 86, 87, 90, 97, 100, 101, 104, 110, 111, 116, 123
conscience 39, 156
Consolation of Philosophy, see Boethius
Corneille 99, 139
Cory, William 122, 156
Coulton, George 130
courage 14, 22, 71, 72, 101
court epics 60
The Courtier, see Castiglione
crimen 48
Criminal through Lost Honor (*Verbrecher aus verlorener Ehre*) 167-169
Crusade epics 56
Curtius, Ernst 114

Dante 60, 81, 112
debt of honor 28, 183, 185
declaration of war 27
dedecus 48
defeat, shame of 67
De Finibus, see Cicero
De Gloria, see Cicero
De Officiis, see Cicero
desidia, see sloth
Devil's Net (*Des Teufels Netz*) 109, 133
didactic poets 104
Die Ehre (Sudermann) 181-186
Dietrich's Flight (*Dietrichs Flucht*) 63
dignatio 14, 15, 17, 36
dignitas 14, 15, 36, 86
Dirne 163
dishonorable people (*unehrliche Leute*) 129, 146, 153, 172, 178, 179
diu Klage 77
Dodds, E. R. 17
dôm 6, 33
Droste-Hülshoff, Annette von 172
dualism 58, 120, 121

duels, see point of honor
Duke (Herzog) Ernst 78, 90, 118
duty 140, 184
duty culture 157

Eberhard Cersne 75
Eckstein, J. 109
Edda, see *Poetic Edda*
edel 17, 71, 106, 149
Ehrfurcht 17
Ehrgeiz 24, 171
Ehrismann, Gustav 5, 114
ehrlich, Ehrlichkeit 124, 152, 159, 176, 178
Eike of Repgau 128
Eilhart of Oberge 72, 82, 96, 115
Einhard 46
Emilia Galloti (Lessing) 161-162
Emmel, Hildegard 112
Eneide, see Henry of Veldeke
Engelhart (Conrad of Würzburg) 61, 62, 116
êra 4, 5
êre 4 ff.
Erec (Hartmann) 61, 62, 67, 68, 79, 80, 83, 85, 89, 92, 95, 99, 100, 101, 112, 115, 120, 121
Ethelred the Unready 3
executioners 135, 172
expedience, see *utile*

Fallada, Hans, 158
Faret, Nicolas 141
Farmer (Meier) Helmbrecht 49, 94, 105, 107, 108, 122, 135
fealty, see *triuwe*
feminine honor, see women
Fetial Code 27
feuds 35, 36
feudum 17
Fichte, J. G. 154
fides 24, 28
flitings 35
Fontane, Theodor 149, 157
fortitudo 23, 41

Francis I 69
Frauendienst 95
Frederick of Sunnenberg 106
Frederick the Great 153
Freidank 73, 94, 104, 105, 107, 108, 117, 119, 123
freude, fröude, 23, 93
Freiligrath, Ferdinand 165
Frings, Theodor 5
frivolity in religion 121
fröude, see *freude*
furor teutonicus 55

Gallic War, see Caesar
Gehl, Walther 80
gemach 73
genâde 93
generosus 31
Genesis A (Anglo-Saxon) 25, 26, 41, 54
Genesis (Old Saxon) 25, 41
gentle law (Stifter) 166
Geoffrey of Monmouth 99, 120
Gesta Danorum, see Saxo
Gesta Romanorum 36, 39
gîticheit, see miserliness
gloire 187
gloriae cupiditas 45
God as warlike king 55
God as source of honor 117, 141, 142
Godfrey of Winchester 46
Goethe 2, 6, 20, 67, 102, 103, 123, 136, 162
goliards 121
good birth, see nobility
Good Gerhard (Rudolf) 61, 69, 91
gotes huld, see *huld*
Gottesurteil, see trial by combat
Gottfried of Strassburg 5, 60, 62, 65, 72, 73, 74, 76, 81, 86, 90, 92, 96, 103, 107, 119, 136, 178
greetings, see salutations
Gregorius (Hartmann) 19, 53, 62, 68, 70, 73, 92, 93, 97, 104, 110, 115
Gregory the Great 49
Grillparzer, Franz 143, 165

Grimmelshausen 145-148, 160
Grönbech, Wilhelm 21
Gryphius, Andreas 138, 144, 160
Guevara 145
Guillen de Castro 139
guilt culture 38, 173
guot umbe êre nemen 78, 131
guot und êre 114

Haller, Albrecht von 143
hangman, see executioner
Hardenberg, Friedrich von 113
Hartmann of Aue 5, 19, 27, 53, 60, 61, 62, 66, 67, 68, 69, 70, 72, 73, 74, 75, 76, 79, 80, 82, 83, 85, 89, 90, 92, 93, 95, 97, 99, 100, 101, 104, 110, 111, 115, 116, 118, 119, 120, 121, 132
Hauptmann, Gerhard 134, 165
Hebbel, Friedrich 134, 135, 174
heil 50, 55, 117, 119
Heine, Heinrich 187
Helbling 73, 105, 131, 134
Heinrich, see Henry
Heliand 25, 26, 33, 39, 41, 42, 43, 56
Helmbrecht, see *Farmer Helmbrecht*
Henry of (Heinrich von) Meissen 85, 109
Henry of Morungen 66
Henry of Veldeke 19, 60
herdsmen 128, 173
Herrendienst 60
herzeleit, herzen kumber, herzesêr 89
Herzog Ernst, see *Duke Ernst*
Heusler, Andreas 34
Hildebrand, Lay of (*Hildebrandslied*) 15, 19, 22, 31, 35, 37
Hildegard of Bingen 61
hoard 19
Hobbes, Thomas 1, 18, 63, 66, 67, 158
hôher muot 23, 72, 102
Hohn, hôn 32, 35
Hohnreden 35
hold 30, 31, 78
honestas 47
honestum 5, 46, 47, 49, 114, 125

honestus 8, 47, 48, 71, 146
honnête homme 141, 149
honos 5, 8, 15
horn of Gallehus 7
hospitality 31, 79
hövisch, hövischeit 71, 93
Hrabanus Maurus 16
Hrothsvith, Roswitha 25
hudelvolk 178
Hugdietrich 90
Hugo of Trimberg 71, 106, 123, 146
Huizinga, Jan 82, 127
huld 30, 31, 51, 55, 91, 114
Humboldt, Wilhelm 8
humility 49, 92
Huss, Karl 135
Hutten, Ulrich von 186
iactantia 45

Ibsen 100
Iceland 7
Iliad 8
Immermann, Karl 165
immortality of fame 33, 34, 84, 140, 144
indignatio 36
infamis 48
iniquus 48
insults 34, 35, 36, 85
invidious nature of honor 20
inwardness 144, 149
Iwein (Hartmann) 19, 60, 66, 67, 68, 69, 70, 72, 73, 74, 75, 76, 82, 85, 90, 92, 93, 95, 99, 110, 115
Of Honour, see Ashley

St Jerome 98
The Jews' Beechtree (*Die Judenbuche*) 172-174
John of Salisbury 120
Johnson, Samuel 59
Joinville 109
Jómsvikings Saga 34, 74, 98
Jones, George F. 4, 100, 123, 125, 133
Juvenal 105

203

Kant 154, 157
Karg-Gasterstädt, E. 4, 5
Kasperl and Annerl 135, 170-172
Keller, Gottfried 165, 176, 180
Kindermörderin 162
kinship 14, 21, 41, 69, 70, 130
Kirchhof, Hans 127
Kleist, Heinrich von 135, 153, 154, 169
Klose, Friedrich 5, 8, 19
Kluge, Friedrich 4
König Rother 19
kränken 66
Kuhn, Hans 6, 19, 34
Kwakiutl Indians 2

labor, dignity of 107, 109, 146
Lamprechts Alexander 67
Lanzelet, see Ulrich of Zazikhoven
largess 18, 30, 44, 77, 91, 124, 148
laster 32
lästern 32
Latin concepts 7, 33, 104
laughter 32
Laurin 74
law 40
Lehmann, Paul 121
Leiche (Conrad) 87, 90, 100
leid 72
Lenau, Nikolaus 143
leprosy 116
Lessing, G. E. 149, 157, 161
L'honneste homme (Faret) 141
Lieutenant Gustl 187-189
Lillo, George 160
linen weavers 134, 147
lop 86
Lope de Vega 138
loss of honor 167
Louis the Pious 56
Louis, Lay of (Ludwigslied) 52
Love and Intrigue (Kabale und Liebe) 163-164
Lovelace, Richard 100
Ludwig, Otto 131
Lump 178

Luther, Martin 6, 136, 155

Magirus, Tobias 147
Maistre, Joseph de 130
Makkabäer, die 57, 112
Maria Magdalene (Hebbel) 135, 174-176
Marius 8
Marner, der 84
St Martin 32, 43, 45, 49, 52, 54, 86, 92, 105, 155, 188
mastersingers 95
Maurer, Friedrich 5, 6, 8, 33, 46, 80, 111, 114
Meier Helmbrecht, see *Farmer Helmbrecht*
Meistergesang, Meistersänger, see mastersingers
memento mori 57
Meyer, Christian 17
MHG, Middle High German, see preface
Michael Kohlhaas (Kleist) 135, 169-170
millers 133
milte, see largess
Milton 1
ministeriales 71
Minna von Barnhelm (Lessing) 149-154
Minnesang, Minnesänger 60, 94, 95, 137
minstrels 123, 131
Mirror of the Saxons (Sachsenspiegel) 22, 29, 116, 130, 131, 132
misalliance 30
miserliness 31, 118
moderation 92, 93
Molière 137
Montaigne 68, 126, 142, 158
Moralium Dogma 46, 48, 49, 105
moralists 104
Moritz of Craun 31, 67, 73, 78, 83
Müllenhoff, Karl 2
Muspilli 41, 55

names 16, 18, 19, 23, 24, 25
namhaft 129
Narrenschiff, see Brant
national honor 53, 186
nefas 15
neiding 23, 27
NHG, New High German, see preface
Nibelungs, Lay of (*Nibelungenlied*) 21, 22, 26, 27, 36, 37, 59, 60, 63, 64, 65, 66, 67, 68, 69, 73, 75, 76, 77, 78, 79, 82, 83, 87, 88, 91, 93, 94, 99, 102, 106, 117, 118, 119, 131 132
Nietzsche 50
nobilis 106
nobility of birth 13, 16, 60, 141, 147
nobility of conduct 105, 147
Norwood, Lotte 112
Notker 5
Novalis, see Hardenberg

Odericus Vitalis 28
oaths 77, 111, 164
OHG, Old High German, see preface
omniscience of God 39
Opitz, Martin 132, 160
opprobrium 48
St Oswald 74
Otfried 52, 53
Ovid 1, 98

pactum 52
Panzer, Friedrich 76
Partonopier (Conrad) 75, 86, 97, 100, 111
Parzival (Wolfram) 61, 62, 63, 65, 67, 68, 69, 70, 77, 84, 85, 89, 91, 93, 94, 95, 96, 101, 114, 117, 118, 120, 139
Peter of Dusburg 56
Peter of Staufenberg 63, 83, 96
Petrus Alphonsus 105
Philip van Artevelde 127
philotimia 24
Pied Piper 130
Plato 10, 98, 104
Plowman from Bohemia (*Ackermann aus Böhmen*) 68, 103, 136
Poetic Edda, 16, 30, 34, 64
point of honor 34, 140, 147, 178, 187
Poor Henry (*Armer Heinrich*) 60, 61, 110, 115, 116
Possevino, Giovanni Battista 140
potlach 31
poverty, shame of 61, 62, 63
power 17, 18, 19, 65
preudhome 109
Previté-Orton 81
Priesterleben 44
priests' children 130
prîs 86
Protestant ethic (Max Weber) 125
Prudentius 53
Puknat, Siegfried 113

Raabe, Wilhelm 129, 130
Racine 27
Randall, J. H. 155
rank 15, 70
Reformation 144
recht, reht 40, 124, 169
rehtelôs 72
Reimchronik, see Beheim
Reinmar of Zweter 75, 84, 117
relativity of honor 183
Renaissance 81
Renner, see Hugo of Trimberg
renown 24
reputation 160
revenge 35, 36, 85
reward and punishment 19, 38, 44, 55, 136
Richardson, Samuel 161
ridicule 32, 95
Riechert, Irmgard 110, 111
Riesman, David 31
Rig, Lay of 16, 22
Ring, see Wittenwiler
Ritterspiegel (Rothe) 123
riuwe 39
Robinson, F. N. 81
Rolandslied 54, 57, 73

205

Ronsard 129
Röntgen 158
Rougemont, Denis de 98
Rudolf of Ems 31, 61, 66, 67, 69, 73, 74, 75, 77, 83, 86, 91, 92, 102, 110, 111, 115, 123
Ruodlieb 26, 59

Sachs, Hans 127
Sachsenspiegel, see *Mirror of the Saxons*
sacramentum 14, 25
saelec 72
Salman and Morolf 78
Saloman et Marcolfus 80
salutations 94
sans reproche 80
Sardou, Victorien 183
satisfaktionsfähig 37, 189
Saxo Grammaticus 18, 19, 22, 28, 29, 30, 36, 47, 98, 99, 101, 133
scham 32, 84, 119
schande 48, 49, 108, 118, 119, 162.
Scheffler Johann 144
Schiller 71, 76, 160, 163, 164, 165, 167, 187
schimpf 32
Schnitzler, Arthur 187
Schopenhauer, Arthur 29, 34, 183, 187
schult 39
Schulz, Hans 36, 112
Schwerin, C. von 2, 21, 23, 29
scripture 11, 38, 40, 42, 43, 44, 45, 47, 49, 54, 57, 61, 64, 71, 84, 98, 103, 104, 115, 119, 125, 154, 155, 172
Secreta Secretorum 74
Seneca 13, 46, 85, 125, 138, 156, 183
sensus 121
sentencia 121
Settegast, F. 21, 81
Shakespeare 1, 15, 34, 37, 85, 100, 119, 126, 139, 143, 145, 157, 163, 167
shame 31
shame culture 10, 13, 95, 173
Ship of Fools (*Narrenschiff*), see Brant

Sidonius 50
Silz, Walter 178
Simonides 10, 75
Simplicissimus (Grimmelshausen) 145
sirventes 60
skinners 134, 135, 170
Sklavenmoral 50
sloth 14, 49
Sombart, Werner 62, 125
Spanish drama 138
Spenser, Edmund 68, 120, 141
Spervogel 18, 117, 123
sports 186
Spruchdichter 104, 107, 137
Stanhope, George 1
Stifter, Adalbert 165, 166
Stevens, C. E. 50
Stoics 5, 9, 11, 12, 41, 109, 139
Storm, Theodor 118, 130, 135
Stricker 63, 118, 123
Stuart, D. C. 138
Suchenwirt 109
Sudermann, Hermann 181
summum bonum 114
sumptuary laws 124
sünde 49, 118
superbia 72
swach 23, 108
swachen 66
swacher gruoz 94
Swiss mercenaries 27

Tacitus 8, 13, 14, 15, 17, 25, 28, 35, 36, 69, 98, 131
tadel 32
talents, parable of 125
tanners 134
Tasso 142
Teichner, Henry 59, 82, 90, 110, 119
Tennyson, Alfred 100
Teutones and Cimbri 8, 12, 27, 33
St Thomas Aquinas 62, 71, 82, 84, 86
Thomasin of Zirclaere 67, 73, 79, 91, 95, 104, 105, 106, 116, 120
timê 10

Titurel (Wolfram) 82, 83, 101
tiur 66
trêve de Dieu 25, 42
trial by combat 19
Tristan, see Gottfried
Tristrant, see Eilhart
triuwe 25, 26, 41, 52, 73, 74, 75, 76, 124
triuwelôs 74
Trojan War (*Trojanerkrieg*, Conrad) 27, 97, 101, 111
trôst 93
tugent 23, 108
tühtic 23, 124
turpitude 32

Ulrich of Zatzikhoven 67, 69, 77, 78, 83, 84, 90, 102
unbescholten 80, 152
unverschämt 80, 153
utile v.s. *honestum* 48, 114

vagrants 130, 176, 178
varendiu diet 131
Varro 115
Vegetius 134
vengeance, see revenge
verecundia 84
Vergil 15
Vermögen 20
verschamt 80
vicarious revenge 36, 88
victory, honor of 24, 67, 95
Vidal, Peire 131
A Village Romeo and Juliet (*Romeo und Julia auf dem Dorfe*, Keller) 176-180
virtus 14
vitium 47, 48
Vogel, Jacob 144
Volksepos 63
Vollmer, Vera 3
voluntary poverty 64
vridu 21, 25, 35, 37, 41, 42, 43, 74, 88
vriunde 41
vriundlôs 21
Vries, Jan de 2, 25, 51

vrum 23, 66, 108

Wace 102
wacker 23, 124
Waddell, Helen 121
Wagner, H. L. 163
Waltharius 28, 36, 37, 45, 59, 95, 99
Walther von der Vogelweide 5, 60, 66, 69, 72, 78, 80, 84, 88, 90, 94, 95, 103, 111, 113, 114, 117, 118, 119, 121, 122, 132, 144, 186
wealth 14, 17, 124
weavers 134
Weber, Max 125
Wedekind, Frank 158
Welscher Gast, see Thomasin
Weltansicht (Humboldt) 8
Weltfrömmigkeit 124
Wenceslaus, Emperor 133
wench 163
werdekeit 15, 66, 86
Wends 129
Wessobrunn Prayer 56
White, Beatrice 136
Widsith 7
Wiessner, Edmund 105, 131
Willehalm (Wolfram) 61, 71, 72, 74, 79, 83, 89, 90, 101, 102, 118
William of Conches 104
William of Orleans (*Wilhelm von Orlens*, Rudolf) 61, 63, 66, 72, 74, 75, 77, 83, 91, 115, 116
Willibald 51
Winsbeke 93, 95, 106, 114, 120
Winsbekin 82
wirde 15, 66, 86
Wittenwiler, Henry 6, 19, 27, 48, 69, 70, 75, 89, 97, 98, 106, 107, 118, 119, 121, 125, 127, 128, 133
Wolfdietrich 64
Wolfram of Eschenbach 5, 32, 60, 61, 62, 63, 65, 67, 68, 69, 70, 71, 72, 74, 77, 79, 82, 83, 84, 85, 86, 89, 90, 91, 93, 94, 96, 101, 102, 114, 117, 118, 120, 132, 139

women 14, 20, 25, 29, 33, 88, 95, 96, 97, 126, 161, 174
Wordsworth, William 1
World Chronicle (*Weltchronik*, Conrad) 97
wrekka 22

wretch 19, 22, 31
Würdenträger 57
Xenophon 10, 125, 145
Ziemann, Adolf 4
zuht 77, 108